Theories of Democracy

Theories of Democracy: a critical introduction is a comprehensive and accessible introduction to the main theories of democracy, covering the historical development of the many different forms and the problems faced by each.

Frank Cunningham begins with the development of democracy from ancient Greece to the present day, examining the views of prominent figures such as Aristotle, John Stuart Mill, Rousseau, Alexis de Tocqueville, and Schumpeter. He explains the main objections to democracy, including the challenges of majority tyranny, irrational decision-making procedures and ineffectual government. Cunningham distinguishes between several competing theories of democracy: liberal democracy, classic pluralism, catallaxy, participatory democracy, deliberative democracy, and radical pluralism. A detailed case study uses the example of globalization to show how the various democratic theories are concretely applied, and notes the strengths and weaknesses of the different theories in coping with the problem that globalization poses for democratic structures. *Theories of Democracy* contains three helpful discussion sections that concentrate on the recurrent themes of liberal democracy and capitalism, democracy and representation, and the value of democracy.

Clearly written and focusing on contemporary debate, *Theories of Democracy* provides an accessible introduction for the student or general reader and also makes an original contribution to contemporary political philosophy.

Frank Cunningham is a lecturer in the philosophy department at the University of Toronto. He is the author of *Democratic Theory and Socialism* (1987) and *The Real World of Democracy* (1994).

Routledge Contemporary Political Philosophy

Edited by David Archard, University of St Andrews
and Ronald Beiner, University of Toronto

Routledge Contemporary Political Philosophy is an exciting new series for students of philosophy and political theory. Designed for those who have already completed an introductory philosophy or politics course, each book in the series introduces and critically assesses a major topic in political philosophy. Long-standing topics are refreshed and more recent ones made accessible for those coming to often complex issues and arguments for the first time. After introducing the topic in question, each book clearly explains the central problems involved in understanding the arguments for and against competing theories. Relevant contemporary examples are used throughout to illuminate the problems and theories concerned, making the series essential reading not only for philosophy and politics students but those in related disciplines such as sociology and law. Each book in the series is written by an experienced author and teacher with special knowledge of the topic, providing a valuable resource for both students and teachers alike.

Forthcoming titles:

Multiculturalism
Ayelet Shachar

Equality
Melissa Williams

Public Reason and Deliberation
Simone Chambers

Theories of Democracy

A critical introduction

Frank Cunningham

Routledge
Taylor & Francis Group

LONDON AND NEW YORK

First published 2002
by Routledge
2 Park Square, Milton Park, Abingdon, Oxon OX14 4RN

Simultaneously published in the USA and Canada
by Routledge
270 Madison Ave, New York, NY 10016

Reprinted 2005, 2006

Transferred to Digital Printing 2008

Routledge is an imprint of the Taylor & Francis Group, an informa business

© 2002 Frank Cunningham

Typeset in Goudy and Gill Sans by
Florence Production Limited, Stoodleigh, Devon

Printed and bound in Great Britain by
TJI Digital, Padstow, Cornwall

British Library Cataloguing in Publication Data
A catalogue record for this book is available from the British Library

Library of Congress Cataloging in Publication Data

Cunningham, Frank, 1940–
    Theories of democracy: a critical introduction / Frank Cunningham.
        p. cm.– (Routledge contemporary political philosophy)
    Includes bibliographical references and index.
    1. Democracy. I. Title. II. Series.
    JC423 .C794 2001
    321.8–dc21   2001034998

ISBN 10: 0-415-22878-6 (hbk)
ISBN 10: 0-415-22879-4 (pbk)

ISBN 13: 978-0-415-22878-7 (hbk)
ISBN 10: 978-0-415-22879-4 (pbk)

Contents

Figures

Acknowledgements

This book was commissioned by David Archard and Ronald Beiner on behalf of Routledge to be an introduction to democratic theory addressed to an educated readership. The plan of the book is outlined at the beginning of Chapter 1. In its preparation I was aided by Professors Archard and Beiner themselves and by Nader Hashemi and the editoral staff of Routledge. I am also grateful to Derek Allen, H.D. Forbes, Joseph Heath, Lynda Lange, Chantal Mouffe, Richard Sandbrook, and Melissa Williams for valuable feedback on draft chapters. Though the book is by no means a publication of lectures, I have greatly profited from the stimulating and insightful contributions of my philosophy and political science students in a course on democratic theory at the University of Toronto over the past several years. My wife, Maryka Omatsu, generously endured me through another writing project, which, yet again, proved to be easier to undertake in anticipation than in fact.

Toronto
August 2001

Chapter 1

Introduction

This book aims to provide a map through a selection of contemporary democratic theories. As with an actual map, readers already familiar with the terrain will find it lacking in important detail, and as is known by students of cartography there are alternative and quite different strategies for organizing a map. Still, the book should give readers with little prior background in democratic theory one overall picture of the lay of the land. Or rather, it covers some land, as the map is not a global one, but is confined to democratic theories in Western Europe and North America and, even more narrowly, to theorists whose work is written in English or that have found their way into widespread publication in this language. The reason is not belief that no other important democratic theorizing is to be found, but simply because the book is prepared by an Anglo-North American, drawing upon the democratic-theoretical work of his own intellectual environment.

Just as a map indicates routes to a variety of destinations while remaining mute about which of them one should take or what to do on arrival, so this book will be more descriptive than prescriptive. At the same time, it would be naive of me or of readers to suppose that the discussions that follow are not influenced by my political values and democratic-theoretical proclivities. Partly to make these opinions transparent, Chapter 8 ('Democratic Pragmatism') will outline the perspective in terms of which I strive to make sense of democracy and democratic theories. It is adopted from the political theory explicated by John Dewey in his *The Public and Its Problems* (1927). While I shall not attempt to persuade readers of views I favour, there is one respect in which Deweyan pragmatism structures the approach of the rest of the book.

Central to this orientation is the conviction that practical and theoretical undertakings in politics (as elsewhere) are mainly efforts in problem solving. Accordingly, Chapter 2 will list some main problems said to beset democracy: that it involves majority tyranny, that it makes for ineffective government, that it is beset by irrational decision-making procedures, and other challenges. Subsequent chapters will then summarize the main tenets of current theories of democracy – liberal democratic, participatory, deliberative, and so on – looking for resources within them to address one or more of the problems. This forms the basis of the book's organization, which, however, is deviated from in three ways.

At the end of the book it will be indicated how the democratic theories abstractly discussed in it are concretely applied by taking up one of many possible examples, namely globalization. A second deviation concerns the treatment of themes independently of specific theories. Most studies of democratic theory are organized around such themes: freedom and equality, rights, collective decision-making, legitimacy, justice and democracy, and so on. These and related themes will be touched on within treatments of relevant theories, but three will be addressed in a more concentrated way in 'discussions' appended to appropriate chapters. These are: the relation of liberal democracy to capitalism (Chapter 3); conceptions of democratic representation (Chapter 5); and the value of democracy (Chapter 8).

While the theories surveyed have mainly been expounded from the mid-twentieth century, all of them draw on the work of historical antecedents, for instance, Jean-Jacques Rousseau, James Madison, Immanuel Kant, and John Stuart Mill. Key features of their ideas will be summarized where appropriate, and, in a third deviation, this chapter will conclude by outlining the thought of three such theorists, namely Aristotle, Alexis de Tocqueville, and Joseph Schumpeter, to whom nearly all current theorists make frequent reference. First, some complexities about how to conceive of the ultimate subject matter of this book – democracy – should be flagged.

Conceptualizing democracy

Not long after military suppression in 1989 of the demonstration for democracy by Chinese students in Beijing's Tiennanmen Square, I had an occasion to talk with a participant. He told me that although he had risked his life in Beijing and some of his friends had lost theirs in the democratic cause, neither he nor they could claim to know just what democracy is. In expressing this uncertainty, the student differed from contemporary democratic theorists who, like their predecessors, either advance definitions of 'democracy' with confidence or write of the preconditions, value, or problems of democracy in a way that assumes their readers understand the meaning of the term. Interrogation of the presupposed meanings or a survey of the definitions quickly reveals, however, that taken collectively the theorists are in a similar situation to that of the Chinese student, since their conceptions of democracy diverge (Naess et al. 1956).

The confidence of theorists is easy enough to understand. For the most part academics, they are employed to answer questions not to ask them, and they learn early in their careers the professional risks of tentativeness. More instructive is the divergence of conceptions of democracy. At its root, I speculate this results from the fact that almost all current democratic theorists are writing within and with respect to societies that consider themselves democratic; hence, their theories of democracy are directly or indirectly implicated in actual democratic politics. This means that democracy, like 'justice' or 'freedom,' is what some call a 'contested' concept embedded within rival theories (Connolly 1993b, who takes the term from Gallie 1955–6). In a book that surveys contemporary theories of democracy this creates the by no means unique but nonetheless challenging situation for author and reader alike that there is lack of consensus over what the theories surveyed are about.

EXERCISE

This point can be illustrated by reporting on an experiment conducted in courses on democratic theory where students are asked to write down an example – historical or current, fictional or real – of the most democratic and of the most undemocratic situation, institution, or practice they can think of. Readers of this book may wish to participate in this experiment before continuing; those who do will find the ensuing discussion more meaningful. The exercise has been given to senior students of political science and of philosophy at my university, and in addition to constancy over several years at this locale, I received similar results from students in Japan and in the Netherlands during visiting teaching engagements in these countries.

Surveying responses, I note that they can initially be divided into two categories. The majority of respondents ignored the instruction to give concrete examples and instead offered formal characterizations based on favoured theories. Some samples are:

i.   small, participatory community/totalitarianism;
ii. a state where every citizen plays a role in political decision-making/ a state which does not fulfill this condition;
iii. constitutional guarantees of individual rights/rule of an individual or of mass opinion;
iv. decisions are made by all members of a society, and all are rational and well informed/a tyranny where even those in charge are victims of false consciousness.
v.   a community where the common good is decided by consensus after full debate/a society where rulers decide what counts as the public good.

Readers who followed the suggestion to do this exercise and whose 'examples' are similar to these are no doubt possessed of theoretical aptitude, but can likely profit from trying practically to instantiate their theories. Nonetheless, some tentative lessons about methodologies for theoretical approaches to democracy can be learned from consideration of these responses (fully recognizing that they are drawn from a limited sample). Abstract characterizations of democracy lend themselves to drawing dichotomies such that anything matching the characterization is democratic and anything else is not democratic, while the exercise invites the students to think of democracy as a matter of degree. (To employ James Hyland's terms, conceptions of democracy may be either 'sortal' or 'scalar,' 1995: 49–50.) Many agree with Samuel Huntington (1991: 11–12) that the political world should be classified simply into democratic and nondemocratic categories. The pair of 'examples' labelled *ii* exhibits such dichotomization, as does *iii* (where the intent must charitably be interpreted to specify a necessary condition for democracy, unless it is assumed that democratic rights are among those guaranteed).

Of course, any abstract characterization can be regarded as an ideal type susceptible to degrees of approximation. But this creates an onus to spell out how approximation is ascertained, which is difficult to do without examination of concrete examples. For instance, regarding *iv*, fewer than all people may be rational and informed, or people may be partially informed or partly rational (itself a contested concept), or they may be rational regarding some matters and not others. In the case of *v*, something short of the common good, but better than an unmitigated evil might be agreed upon, and/or there may be only partial consensus, or debate may be less than full. The example of the most undemocratic situation in *v* suggests that the key criterion for ideal-typical democracy is consensus. The most undemocratic characterization of *iv* is indeterminate because it includes two democracy-defeating elements, tyranny and false consciousness. Attempting to give concrete examples forces precision or at least the sharpening of theoretical decisions on such matters.

Another advantage to seeking examples is that abstract characterizations can be instantiated in alternative ways, about which there will be good grounds for disagreement. More radically, someone may challenge an example for not being democratic or undemocratic at all, in which case either finer specifications are needed in the abstraction or the instantiation counts as evidence that democracy should be characterized in some other way. This point may be illustrated by considering the following list of concrete examples, also taken from a class experiment, where the first three of the 'most democratic' sites might be taken as candidates for *i* (small community participation) and the next several examples could be viewed as different ways that citizens might play a role in decision-making:

a. Swiss canton/Hell;
b. an Israeli kibbutz/a fascist state;
c. an election in the US or Canada/the maximum security prison in Newark, New Jersey;
d. a referendum (the most frequently given 'most democratic' example)/ appointment of supreme court judges;

e. decision-making by consensus in aboriginal council meetings/competi-
    tive economic markets;
f. student input to a course curriculum/monopoly power in Mexico by
    one political party;
g. amicable negotiations about the allotment of chores among roommates/
    police crackdown on a (recent) student demonstration;
h. consensus-supported affirmative action campaigns/systemic sexism
    and racism;
i. employment or university admission based only on merit and open to
    all/reverse discrimination policies;
j. a soccer team during play/a high school;
k. an elephant herd/a military school;
l. gambling in a public lottery/rape;
m. a free economic market/a police state.

Striking about this sample is its heterogeneity and the oddness of some of
the examples. One interpretation of these features reflects poorly on the
thinking (or the motivations) of those who proposed them. Readers who
attempted to find examples themselves will likely seek interpretations more
charitable to the students. It is not easy to give prototypical examples of
democracy precisely because the latter is a contested concept. Moreover, the
task can be approached from a variety of optics, which are themselves
combinable in a variety of ways. Thus, the 'most democratic' examples a
through e, in contrast to f and g, suppose democracy to be a formal or quasi-
formal matter. In examples a through g democracy centrally requires or is a
form of collective decision-making. If such decision-making is involved in j
and k, this is only incidental to what is likely thought most important about
them, namely coordinated group action, while in the last two examples independently pursued individual actions suffice for democracy. It will be seen
that developed theories of democracy can be sorted in a similar way.

Another similarity with the formal theories is that while students were
asked to construct examples of general if not universal applicability, there
is clearly a bias in favour of local concerns, which is why examples taken
from university experiences disproportionately figure. This also helps to
explain the apparently bizarre feature of the examples that many of them
seem exaggerated. With all the instances of gross undemocracy in the world
– brutally totalitarian regimes, overt and thoroughgoing paternalism, and
the like – it is strange to adduce suppression of a student demonstration as
the *most undemocratic* thing one can think of, and laudable from a democratic point of view as allowing student input to university curricular decisions
may be, this is hardly the most democratic thing imaginable. But then, this
exercise was put to university students.

Three more features – all of which I found in other such experiments,
both in my university and abroad – bear mention. First, a direct contradiction

should be noted, namely that affirmative action and its pejoratively described analogue, reverse discrimination, are taken by some as democratic and by others as undemocratic, as are competitive markets. In this, the students' diverse reactions map those of democratic theorists, who are also divided on these matters. Among professional theorists, to take note of a second feature, the participatory democrats see democracy as best exercised communally and in small, relatively intimate groups, but such democrats are by no means in a majority or even in a large minority. Students, by contrast, generally, if not unanimously, pick out small group interactions as the most democratic examples.

Finally, in the experiment it is often hard to see how the most and least democratic examples constitute poles of a spectrum except in those cases where they are clearly correlated with states of affairs deemed morally praiseworthy or condemnable. Thus, presumably a lottery is the most democratic because it is a matter of individual choice whether to play, and it is fair since the chances of any one ticket being the winner is equal to that of any other ticket; while rape is an extreme example of force and inequality. In class discussion, it becomes clear that for nearly all students democracy is highly valued, and nondemocratic situations are identified by thinking of negatively evaluated alternatives. As will be seen, not all democratic theorists, and particularly those in earlier centuries, positively evaluate democracy.

Touchstone theorists

Democratic theorists pursue their thought in intellectual vacuums no more than do theorists of any subject, and Aristotle, Tocqueville, and Schumpeter are among the more prominent of traditional thinkers often and appropriately referred to in current writings. This, and the fact that each of these classic predecessors confronts democracy with serious challenges, is one reason for summarizing their essential conclusions about democracy in this introduction. Also, there are additional lessons about the methodology of theorizing about democracy to be learned from seeing how they might approach the exercise put to my students.

Aristotle

Born in Macedonia and living during his intellectual prime in Athens during the fourth century BC, Aristotle headed a large-scale research project that set out to describe and sketch the histories of every currently known political system. This constituted a large number of examples of varied attempts at government, successful and otherwise, both in the city states of that area and the grander efforts of the Macedonian empire of Philip and Alexander and rival empires to the east and south. To these examples, Aristotle brought his considerable talents of nuanced classification and critical evaluation to examine possible, historical, and extant forms of government.

Broadly described, government might be exercised according to him by one person, by a few people, or by many people, and in each case such rule may be exercised properly or improperly. Proper (or 'right') rule is undertaken for the common good while improper rule aims to serve private interests, whether of the one, the few, or the many themselves. By 'common good' Aristotle did not mean the interests that people happen to share, but that which is good for their community, since a good community for him promotes the well-being of all its members by allowing them to exercise their proper potentials and to lead virtuous and successful lives.

This yields an initial classification of six forms of rule: *royalty*, where one person rules in the common interest; *tyranny*, a 'deviation' of royalty, where one person rules in his private interests; *aristocracy* or proper rule by the few; *oligarchy*, which is the deviant form of aristocracy; proper rule of the many, called '*polity*' by Aristotle; and its deviation for which he reserved the term *democracy* (Aristotle 1986 [c.320 BC]: bks gamma and delta). An important wrinkle in this classification is that rule by the many and by the few are not definitive of democracy and oligarchy (or of their ideal analogues) by Aristotle, since he regarded these as essentially rule of the poor and rule of the rich, which in his view are always correlated with the many and the few. Similarly, just as wealth is unequally distributed, so is virtue or nobility in such a way that the majority poor will be less noble than the few rich.

Of these six forms of government, Aristotle argued that the best would be a royalty, where a single, noble ruler performed his proper function, followed by a properly functioning aristocracy. Aristotle allowed, however, that in the world of actual politics, such governments are seldom found, and he lists many ways that when achieved they degenerate into self-serving leadership. With respect to the typical, deviant forms of government, Aristotle reversed the ranking he assigned to ideal politics and considered democracy the 'most tolerable' of the three deviations of proper rule: at least more people profit from a democracy's self-serving rule; some advantages are gained by the collective experiences of many people; and majority discontent is dampened. Thus the often-quoted view of Winston Churchill that democracy is the least bad form of government was in fact much earlier expressed by Aristotle.

Though he makes many references to types of government, it is not easy to extract unambiguous examples from Aristotle's discussion in the *Politics*. This is partly because his empirical attention to detail alerted him to complexities in the messy world of real statecraft; also, writing as he was in prodemocratic Athens, but identified with Alexander the Great (whose teacher he had been), Aristotle was careful about giving unequivocal examples. When certain generals ruled, Sparta exhibited something approaching royalty. More in keeping with the pure idea of royalty was the absolute rule of a king over all matters, much as the head of a household rules over his family (Aristotle: 1285/6 in standardized pagination). Athens, Aristotle suggests, had been a polity from sometime subsequent to the epoch of Solon until the end of the Peloponnesian Wars (431–421 BC) when it became a democracy (1303). Whether he thought Athens an example of the least bad of democracies – namely one where the rule of law is enforced and there is a large middle class which assumes the most active leadership – is unclear.

Tocqueville

There can be no doubt how Tocqueville would respond to the exercise. Democracy as he conceived it was rule by the people, and by the 1830s, when he visited the US (where his initial intent to study its penal system was replaced by a general study of political institutions and mores), Tocqueville found it in what he considered pristine form: 'The people,' he declared, 'reign over the American political world as God reigns over the universe' (Tocqueville 1969 [1835–40]: 60). As to a purely undemocratic society, Tocqueville's view can also be identified, but less straightforwardly.

American democracy is made possible, indeed necessitated, for him by 'equality of condition,' that is, by equality in people's access not just to voting or holding public office but also to economic advantages and culturally, in anti-aristocratic attitudes. Unlike God in relation to the world, the equality Tocqueville's contemporary Americans enjoyed was not created by them out of nothing, but was the product of a long evolution in Europe, beginning with the extension of offices of the clergy beyond noblemen and the encroachment of the power of royal families by lawyers and moneyed tradesmen. To find an entirely undemocratic situation, then, Tocqueville had to look back seven hundred years, when his native France was ruled by a few families in virtue of their inherited landed property (9–10).

Like Aristotle but unlike most of my students, Tocqueville was able to identify a highly democratic situation and to see many advantages and virtues to democracy while remaining critical of it. While for Aristotle democracy was the best option of an available bad lot of forms of government, Tocqueville regarded the 'democratic revolutions' of his time – most notably the French Revolution, which had taken place less than two decades before his birth and which he recalled with the same distaste as nearly everyone who, like Tocqueville himself, was of aristocratic heritage, and the more palatable American Revolution – as the unavoidable outcomes of the history of expanding equality in Europe just referred to.

Tocqueville's famous study, *Democracy in America*, was written, he explained, 'under the impulse of a kind of religious dread inspired by contemplation of this irresistible revolution' (12). The Jacobin aftermath of the French Revolution was the worst example of the culmination of an egalitarian history for Tocqueville, but even the more benign American democracy, where popular sovereignty meant unbridled majority rule, exhibited an oppressive 'tyranny of the majority.' At the same time, Tocqueville found much to admire about American democracy, which he thought gave the country a vitality lacking in the Old World, and he hoped that a Europe doomed to become ever more egalitarian could learn from the American example how best to engender this vitality while avoiding violence and other misfortunes associated with egalitarian revolutions.

Aristotle was prepared to endure democracy only grudgingly and Tocqueville was at best ambivalent about it. Whether this makes their views suspect due to antidemocratic bias or, on the contrary, afforded them an objectivity lacking in democratic partisans is a fine point. However, in different ways each reflects what has come to be called the 'classical' viewpoint on democracy. One pillar of this viewpoint is that democracy involves self-government – of the people in Tocqueville's formulation or of the many in Aristotle's. The other main pillar of classical theory is that democracy promotes or expresses the common good of whatever public is exercising self-government. This will be the case whether the good of the entire polity is in question or one is considering Aristotle's deviant form of popular rule, which promotes the interests of the poor.

In these matters Aristotle and Tocqueville were in accord with those of their contemporaries who were unqualified democratic enthusiasts. For example, in his famous funeral oration during the Peloponnesian War, delivered in the century before Aristotle was writing, Pericles extolled Athenian democracy for exhibiting the civic and personal virtues that Aristotle thought would be best served in a royalty or aristocracy (Thucydides 1972 [c.404 BC]: bk 2, ch. 4). Thomas Jefferson exceeded Tocqueville in praise of vigorous democratic participation in the new American federation, which he saw not only as a socially beneficial exercise of self-government but as a check against what Tocqueville called majority tyranny (for example, 1975 [1816]: ch. 7).

Schumpeter

With the publication in 1942 of his *Capitalism, Socialism and Democracy*, Joseph Schumpeter – earlier a minister of finance in Austria who had retired from politics to teach economics at Harvard – both traditional pillars of democratic theory were starkly criticized in what has come to be called the 'revisionist' or 'realist' challenge to the classical interpretation of democracy. If societies generally called democratic are regarded in terms of how they actually function (hence the realist label) it is obvious, Schumpeter insisted, that they are governed not by the people or by a majority taken as a whole but by elected officials along with nonelected political party and bureaucratic attendants. This is clearly the case on a day-to-day and year-to-year basis, when officials usually (and necessarily to avoid the chaos of perpetual elections or referenda) pursue policies in accord with their own interests or their estimations of what is best done.

As to the public good, Schumpeter maintained that this is nowhere to be found, neither in the motives of those who vote for public officials, each of whom will vote on the basis of private preferences, nor in the outcome of a vote since members of a majority typically have a wide variety of motivations for casting their ballots. The classical view seemed to Schumpeter to mystify the democratic public, whether in the romantic way of Jean-Jacques Rousseau, which, on Schumpeter's interpretation, saw this public as a homogenous entity held together by a shared 'general will' differing from the particular wills of individuals, or in a vain hope, such as that of the utilitarian, John Stuart Mill, that particular preferences will naturally gravitate toward or can be rationally persuaded to converge on common and morally worthwhile ends. Schumpeter's conclusion was that the classical conception should be replaced by one in line with the actual functioning of democracy in the modern world. He thus reduced democracy to a method for selecting public officials and defined this method simply as: 'that institutional arrangement for arriving at political decisions in which individuals acquire the power to decide by means of a competitive struggle for the people's vote' (Schumpeter 1962 [1942]: 269).

Strictly speaking, any political society in which there are free elections is as democratic as any other on this definition, but Schumpeter thought that democracies could still be ranked according to how well they meet the preconditions for the democratic method to 'succeed.' According to him these conditions are: availability of qualified political leaders; assurance that experts and not the public decide matters requiring special knowledge or talents; a well-trained bureaucracy; and a public whose members are tolerant of one another and are prepared to allow politicians a relatively free hand in governing. Despite fear that a form of socialism realizing these conditions could still 'turn out to be more of a sham than capitalist democracy ever was' (302), Schumpeter expressed the view that on balance a social-democratic society held the most promise since it could provide a more skilled bureaucracy than a capitalist-dominated society, and the latter was more prone to foster deep frictions within a population, thus making trust in political leaders and tolerance hard to sustain. Though not an ideal example, Schumpeter praised the Labour government of Ramsay Macdonald, elected in the UK in 1924, for approximating the sort of leadership of which he thought social democracy capable (366–7).

Some lessons

Along with the student exercise, this summary throws into relief some aspects of methodologies for approaching democratic theory. Chief among these is the interpenetration in various and not always transparent ways of: normative questions about the value of democracy; descriptive questions concerning the way societies called democratic actually function or might realistically be anticipated to function; and semantic questions about the meaning of 'democracy.' Different orientations toward democratic theory attach themselves to different approaches depending on which of these three dimensions they focus on or take as their point of entry to the field. This 'triangle' of orientations complicates efforts to compare and evaluate alternative theories of democracy.

Schumpeter purports to begin with the descriptive task and to draw normative and semantic conclusions from his descriptions. As will be seen in later chapters, democratic theorists are divided between those who champion his approach and draw from it even more stark conclusions about what democracy can accomplish and those who challenge his putative descriptions for masking antidemocratic values, which they maintain are the real motivation of Schumpeterian critiques of classical approaches to democracy.

One example of the difficulty of separating descriptive and normative concerns in Schumpeter's account is already evident in the summary above. He ranks better and worse forms of democratic rule according to 'success' without specifying what this is. Mere success in being democratic is not enough to motivate the distinctions he draws (for instance, between governments that allow freedom of manoeuvre for bureaucrats and those that do not), since any government that must periodically compete for the public vote is as democratic as any other such government. In accord with his

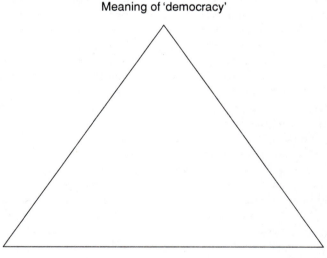

Figure 1

avowed social-democratic political views, Schumpeter may have had in mind success at alleviating class-based inequalities, or, as a close observer of the doomed Weimar Republic (291), he may have thought of success in terms of political stability. Each alternative supposes some normative view about the proper function of government.

For his part, Aristotle explicitly distinguished among the normative, descriptive, and semantic dimensions of political theories of government and built his theory of democracy around the distinctions. Still, despite care in constructing his classifications, it is not always evident which of these three concerns is playing the lead role. One place this may be seen is in Aristotle's acknowledged conflation of rule by the many and by the poor in defining 'democracy.' This is problematic not just because of his assumption that societies will always be divided between the few rich and the many poor (an assumption challenged by Tocqueville's account, which saw a levelling in American society), but also because poverty and virtue are negatively correlated for Aristotle. So when he ranks better and worse forms of democracy it is in terms of the prominence of the middle class, that is of those among the 'many' who are the least poor and most virtuous. Thus, it might be suspected, Aristotle's aristocratic values find their way into his concept of democracy.

Though presented as a sociology-like report of a field trip to the US, Tocqueville's account is overtly motivated by normative concerns. In addition to his conviction that American democracy is one outcome of a worrisome history of growing equality, Tocqueville's passionate tone when he insists that democracy can never elevate manners or nurture 'poetry, renown, and glory' (245) clearly exhibits the aristocratic values he brought to his study. One dimension of Tocqueville's concerns about a tyranny of the majority hinge upon a fear he shared with Aristotle that democracy lends itself to demagoguery. However, both in this critique and in his review of the positive aspects of democracy, Tocqueville often writes as if the will of the majority is the will of the people, so majority vote is an expression of the popular self-government he saw in America. Schumpeter, for whom there is no such thing as popular sovereignty, regarded this as an unwarranted assumption of all the classical theorists (272). Whether he is right or wrong on this matter, the criticism shows that even theorists as astute as Tocqueville left open questions about the meaning of the term 'democracy.'

It should be no surprise that reports of fact, expressions of value, and definitions of terms should be mixed together; nor is there anything necessarily misleading or otherwise amiss about this. Political theory generally, as all inquiry that engages vital issues and perhaps daily language itself, exhibits such interpenetration. Arguably, this is central to the dynamism of any such human undertakings. As will be seen in the ensuing discussions, much democratic theory presupposes the interaction of considerations of fact, value, and meaning and involves debates over which sort of focus should take the lead.

For example, champions of Schumpeter's view prescribe making empirical study of actually existing democracies the leading edge of their theories, while those of Aristotle agree with his starting place, which is to ask about the proper aims of government. At the same time, the interactions in question can create confusions and cross-purpose debate. Students of democratic theories should, accordingly, be alert to these possible distractions.

Another lesson to be learned from the review of these three central theorists is that their efforts are simultaneously time-bound and in a certain sense timeless. The most notorious example of time-boundedness concerns the scope of democratic citizenship. Political participation in Athens, including during the periods Aristotle recognized it as democratic, excluded women, slaves, and from time to time the propertyless. Those remaining were certainly less than a majority (exclusion of women alone ensures this). Similarly, Tocqueville announced that the sovereignty of the people in the US had been adopted 'in every way the imagination could suggest' (60), while later acknowledging that this excluded slaves, servants, paupers, people of modest wealth (in most states), and women. Even Schumpeter's sparse conception of democracy glosses over severe *de jure* and *de facto* voter restrictions and limitation of the ability to compete for the vote with any realistic expectation of success to only some pretenders to political power.

That such exclusions and limitations were commonly accepted in the times of Aristotle, Tocqueville, and Schumpeter does not excuse them from subjecting these things to criticism. Not all of their contemporaries accepted slavery and other persisting restrictions on the power of the franchise, and Aristotle's mentor, Plato, though no democrat, did not see inherent deficiencies to prevent women from being political leaders. In any case one expects critical thinking from political theorists, especially those as good at it in other matters as these three. However, an appeal to common attitudes of their times helps to explain how they could have accepted such exclusions and limitations without apparently feeling the need to justify the acceptance.

What such historical appeal does not do is *justify* the theories advanced by previous theorists. From the fact, for instance, that Aristotle and Tocqueville could at least tacitly sanction slavery and exclusion of women from the franchise, alternative conclusions may be drawn. It might be concluded that the theories are basically sound, but need to be brought up to date by expunging from them racist or sexist exclusions. Alternatively, coexistence of a theory of democracy in the mind of its founder with slavery or sexist exclusion could be taken as evidence that the theory is deeply flawed. Appeal to historical circumstances in which theories of democracy are held will not settle this question, though it can help one to interpret texts, for example, by explaining why authors choose the examples they do, labour certain points and not others, sometimes suffer blind spots, contradict themselves, or lapse into vagueness and ambiguity.

One might thus be helped in reading Aristotle by attending to his precarious situation referred to earlier as a champion of Alexander but living in Athens when its democratic powers of government were severely constrained by Macedonian domination of the region. As a member of the Chamber of Deputies during the short-lived liberal monarchy of Louis-Phillipe, Tocqueville anticipated future democratic upheavals, such as the forthcoming republican revolution of 1848, and his study of American democracy may well have been motivated by the aim of convincing fellow conservatives to bow to the inevitable by employing, in the phrase of Stephen Holmes, 'a democratic cure for a democratic disease' (1993: 23). One commentator sees Schumpeter as a pessimistic conservative arguing for a thin concept of democracy within a social-democratic framework as a sort of rearguard action (Scheuerman 1999a: ch. 7). Another interpretation sees Schumpeter as a sincere social democrat and as such embroiled in the contests in nearly all European countries between social democrats and communists over the values and politics socialists should embrace and the connected question of how to relate to communism in the Soviet Union.

Such historical inquiry will not be undertaken in this book, in part because its author's training is not adequate to such a task, but mainly because there are limits to how far a narrowly historicist account can help to understand or evaluate democratic theories. In what ensues, these theories will be taken at face value as attempts to produce viable accounts of the nature and value of democracy and of the best ways to undertake democratic politics in a variety of circumstances, leaving it to others to identify hidden subtexts or motives. Even so, a certain *theoretical* relativism is unavoidable. This is because democratic theorists undertake their pursuits with theoretical-cum-practical problems – sometimes more grandly called 'problematics' – in mind.

A principal theoretical concern for Aristotle was to figure out how government may enhance, preserve, or at least not inhibit virtuous activity. Tocqueville wished to identify essential strengths and weaknesses in democracy as exhibited in America. Schumpeter set himself the task of bringing conceptions of democracy into line with what he took as the only way that democratic government could realistically function in the modern world. It is by reference to such problems that theories are internally evaluated, namely by ascertaining whether or to what extent they achieve the aims their proponents set out to achieve, but this does not preclude questioning a theory's adequacy with respect to other problems. Chapter 2 reviews main problems for democracy by reference to which both sorts of evaluation of democratic theories can be undertaken.

Problems of democracy

Provisionally thinking of democracy as the exercise of political power where policies and the agents charged with implementing them are directly or indirectly determined by popular voting, leaves open the question of whether this is the best way or even a good way to motivate government. As seen in Chapter 1, Aristotle and Tocqueville had their doubts. In this chapter their misgivings and several others, most of them familiar and some idiosyncratic to professional democratic theorists, will be reviewed as a way of preparing for subsequent surveys of alternative theories of democracy. Both the review and the survey are complicated by the fact that critics have different criteria for evaluating the worth of democracy.

The tyranny of the majority

'What is a majority,' Tocqueville writes, 'if not an individual with opinions, and usually with interests, contrary to another individual, called the minority?' In the most fully realized form of democracy (America for him), this majority is possessed of unbridled power, which occasions the worry that 'if you admit that a man vested with omnipotence can abuse it against his adversaries, why not admit the same concerning a majority?' (1969 [1835–40]: 251). Tocqueville thought that this is exactly what happened in America, and he used the now well-known phrase, 'the tyranny of the majority,' to describe a number of failings. These will be summarized below but under headings other than this one, since most do not exactly correspond to what is commonly complained of as the tyranny of the majority.

A sufficiently radical libertarian, who thinks that almost any infringement of an individual's freedom is objectionable, might consider majority rule necessarily tyrannical, since it produces state-enforced constraints. With a few exceptions (Nozick 1974), such libertarianism is rarely encountered, and when it is, the objection is more pertinent to debates over whether or how democracy can be philosophically justified than to political misgivings over democratic rule. These misgivings usually refer to the possibility of unjustified, oppressive treatment of minorities. When, for example, blacks are in a minority in a society where a majority, white population is racist, members of the black minority will have no resources, or at least no democratic resources on the provisional conception of democracy to which this criticism is pertinent, to prevent the ongoing thwarting of their interests by the majority. Central to the tyranny is that ongoing majority mistreatment or neglect of a minority is unjustified. Except in a strained sense, it is not tyrannical when, for example, the majority endorses laws prohibiting theft, even though the interests of thieves are thereby thwarted. This, however, only exempts a majority from allegations of tyranny in situations of clearly justified suppression of a minority.

It does not exempt the majority regarding most ongoing disagreements about what is justified. Cases in point are debates over the proper functions of government, how scarce resources should be allocated, or moral controversies over matter like capital punishment. Nor does appeal to what is justified apply in more mundane cases of conflicts of (perceived) interests. For example, majority city dwellers may vote that limited resources available for public transit purposes be put into subway and bus systems in large urban centres at the expense of road expansion and repair in sparsely populated rural areas. In these cases the majority is not being tyrannical in the sense of doing something with direct and agreed upon immoral consequences, but it might still be considered tyrannical in the sense of permanently shutting out the possibility of a minority affecting public policy.

Massification of culture and morals

Closer to Tocqueville's main worry is that democracy has undesirable cultural repercussions. The complaint – articulated with vehement eloquence by elitist philosophers such as Friedrich Nietzsche and informally expressed in culturally refined or, depending on one's stand regarding this question, snobbish, social circles – is that both regarding what a majority will vote to fund in the way of cultural facilities and as a result of the fact that a dominant political class will tend to set cultural and moral standards, these standards will become debased in a democracy. The charge – that soft rock will shut out Bach on the radio, Hollywood stars of car chase movies will attract millions of fans and dollars while classical theatre companies go begging, and the like – contains two interrelated but separate elements: that in a democracy the cultural standards of the majority will be the dominant ones and that these standards will be culturally debased.

The second of these charges supposes that the aspiration and the ability for refined cultural development is, like nobility or virtue for Aristotle, a scarce resource and hence to be found only among the few. The term 'hoi polloi' – the people – thus carries a connotation of having simple or even base cultural tastes. Tocqueville thought that America exhibited a general trade off wherein the invigorating satisfaction of political participation gained by the majority and the provision of widespread material contentment such participation was largely used to create was achieved at the expense of 'refining mores, elevating manners, and causing the arts to blossom' (245). Because *hoi polloi* are satisfied with something other than cultural refinement there is no incentive for the majority to endorse educational and government promotion or protection of the arts, and therefore when this majority is politically dominant, these will wither. More insidiously according to Tocqueville and other critics of democracy on this score cultural denigration merges with an informal exercise of the tyranny of the majority wherein by a kind of thought control, people with refined sensitivities will be ignored or socially ostracized. And even more perniciously, those with minority ethical or social/political viewpoints express them at their risk, as Socrates discovered when voicing his unpopular views in democratic Athens condemned him to death.

Ineffective government

In 1975 a nongovernmental, international think tank, 'The Trilateral Commission,' published a report called *The Crisis of Democracy* in which it claimed that democracy in North America, Japan, and Western Europe had lost the ability to pursue common goals due to several 'dysfunctions' caused by democracy itself (Crozier *et al.* 1975). A government is ineffective when it does not or cannot take appropriate measures to achieve the goals of the society it governs. The Trilateral Commission's deepest charge was that democratic societies had become 'anomic,' by which was meant that they had lost the ability to formulate and pursue common goals at all and democratic politics had become mainly 'an arena for the assertion of conflicting interests' (161).

This problem has its source, the authors of the Report claim, in democracy: democratic egalitarianism has delegitimized authority, most prominently in such institutions as 'the family, the church, the school, and the army,' thus simultaneously depriving people of the forums within which a sense of community purpose is bred and undermining respect for leadership in general. Meanwhile, democratic access to government by large numbers of special interest groups has made the aggregation of interests, traditionally carried out by negotiations among mainstream political parties, impossible. Moreover, even were common social goals to be formulated, democracy has impeded government's ability to pursue them by encouraging people to demand too much from the state, thus economically overloading it.

These misgivings mirror two more problems that also occupied Tocqueville, both concerning government leadership. On his view democracy usually produces mediocre leaders – 'slaves to slogans' – for the same reasons that it produces low culture (Tocqueville 1969: 258). Even if good leadership made its way into government, it would be unable to pursue long-range and society-wide projects, due to being at the mercy of a fickle public with diverse interests that changed mandates for government with each election. Tocqueville foreshadowed, though somewhat more reservedly, the Trilateral Commission's appreciation of the potential for political parties to help government withstand the pressures of a multitude of demands upon it, provided that the parties were a few big ones, but he thought there is an unavoidable tendency for the incursion of small parties into government thus making for immobilizing chaos (*ibid.*: 174–88).

Conflicts

While the Commission thought that at least sometimes political parties could negotiate common governmental missions, other critics such as Carl Schmitt (a challenging political theorist and jurist, albeit a member of the National Socialist Party in the Third Reich), saw party-dominated parliaments as no more than debating societies, generally incapable of taking decisive action (Schmitt 1988 [1923]). Schmitt echoed a viewpoint held also by some who do not otherwise share his political views that if democracy can function effectively at all, it requires a relatively harmonious population and that when deep and persisting divisions exist in a society, democracy exacerbates discord, as conflicting parties seek to put government to their particular purposes or, failing this, turn governmental forums into battle grounds. Schmitt further thought that among the ways to forge national unity is to foster hostility to common enemies outside the nation. While by no means endorsing the specific political views of Schmitt, the Trilateral Commission Report shares his assumption that in the absence of an internal source of coherence in a political society, it is likely that its leaders will appeal to or encourage attitudes of ethnic or national chauvinism for unity. This, the authors of the Report believe, is what has been happening within the trilateral countries. Suffering anomic democracy internally, and lacking the unity externally imposed by the communist threat (due to the waning of the Cold War), they see political leaders taking nationalistic stances to garner the unified support of their populations (Crozier *et al.* 1975: 166–7).

These sorts of worries about democracy can be drawn from any of a variety of social theories according to which humans are thought to be naturally prone to mutual fear or hostility. An example is the theory of René Girard, who maintains that any human society is always threatened by the danger of destruction through cycles of revenge-motivated violence. One way this is kept in check is by state-sanctioned legal constraints. Another way (explication of which forms the core of Girard's theory) is to identify scapegoats for ritual sacrifice instead of taking revenge on an offending neighbour. In neither case is democracy an effective means for avoiding hostility. What is more, to the extent that the rule of law is subordinated to democratic pressures or that religious or other traditional supports of ritual are weakened in secular, democratic societies, these bulwarks against violence are denied them (Girard 1979, Wright 1987).

Many people have seen the outbreaks of ethnic violence in Eastern Europe and the former Soviet Union as evidence for one or the other of theories such as Girard's or the Trilateral Commission's. One common journalistic account of these outbreaks is that ethnic or national hostilities had been seething beneath the surface of life in these regions but was kept in check by communist, authoritarian rule. When that rule gave way to democracy, this constraint was removed and the hostilities burst forth (Kaplan 1994). This is the Girard-type approach. An alternative, or complementary, account in keeping with the Commission's approach is that political leaders in the new democracies took advantage of preexisting hostilities and exacerbated or even created them in order to consolidate their positions of political power (Gagnon 1994, and see Hardin 1995: 160–2).

Demagogy and the empty space of democracy

It will be recalled that for Aristotle democracy was tolerable as long as it abides by the rule of law (and is dominated by a middle class). In its un-bridled form, however, rule by the many is similar to a tyrannical monarchy. In both, rule is by decree, not law, and disproportionate power is in the hands of those who can sway either the monarch or ordinary people, in each case masking their political privilege as monarchal or democratic rule; these are, for Aristotle, the court 'flatterers' and the democratic 'demagogues' respectively (1292a). That democracy could function outside the law was later to worry Tocqueville. What concerned Aristotle was that this unchecked power could easily be coopted by individuals playing to and manipulating public opinion.

In an interpretation of Tocqueville's critique, the French democratic theorist, Claude Lefort, finds the seeds of an explanation for how democracy is especially susceptible to demagogy and of why demagogy is especially pernicious. As Tocqueville often notes, the majority in a democracy is like a monarch or a ruling aristocracy. A difference is that whereas the latter are or are comprised of actual, identifiable people, the majority is a shifting mass that is taken to represent the people as a whole. But 'the people' is even more of an abstraction than 'the majority.' Taken literally, in the way that Schumpeter underlined in his critique of the classical democratic notion of popular sovereignty, the people as a whole do not govern, express opinions, take actions, suffer consequences, or any of the other things that persons, such as monarchs, do. In this way the locus of rule in a democracy is void of real people – an 'empty place' as Lefort calls it – represented by those appointed or self-appointed to do so (Lefort 1988: ch. 1).

This makes possible not only demagogy of the sort often aspired to by populist politicians, but also authoritarianism masked as democracy. Drawing on the work of the historian, François Furet, Lefort suggests that the Jacobins exhibited this form of authoritarian rule as did the Bolsheviks. What makes rule of the sort exercised by these bodies so pernicious is that in claiming to represent 'the people' they were able to carry out authoritarian measures in the name of democracy. Democracy, on this criticism, is not just susceptible to such pretense – this is true as well of monarchies, as when occupiers of a throne claim divine ordination – but that it facilitates active complicity within a population even (or especially) when they are imbued with democratic values. The notion of 'the people' is at once contentless and unstable. It is without content, because it is not supposed to be coextensive with any specified individuals, not even the majority at any one time. Thus, elected politicians in a democracy typically announce that 'the people' have spoken in electing them. At the same time, publics, like nature in general, abhor vacuums and are prone to identify the space of democracy with specifiable people. This is one explanation for the excessive attention devoted to the lives of high elected officials in some (if not all) democracies, as they are perceived to embody the popular will. Demagogues are experts at taking cynical advantage of these features of democracy, and populistic authoritarians use them to justify autocratic rule.

Mask of oppressive rule

While Tocqueville and others worry that democracy may be oppressive in itself, some theorists, particularly on the political left, are concerned that it allows for other kinds of oppressions or even facilitates them by providing a sort of cover. In the background of this concern is recognition of the historical cohabitation of democracy with a variety of political exclusions, which, as noted in Chapter 1, have been either ignored or justified within democratic theories of the times. At issue here are no longer (or decreasingly) overt exclusions, but different forms of systemic oppressions, so this will be considered a problem only for those who think that such oppressions persist and are widespread in modern democracies. Because there are not a few theorists of democracy who believe this (including this book's author), resources within alternative approaches to democracy for addressing the problem will be surveyed in each chapter. Those readers who doubt that systemic oppressions, structural domination or subordination, unwarranted political exclusions, or the like are prominent features of modern life will consider this a nonproblem. They may wish to read subsequent discussions of this topic as kibitzers.

Socialist, feminist, and antiracist theorists have typically criticized Schumpeterian revisionism and favoured approaches to democracy involving much more citizen participation than just voting. However, in one respect they have been in accord with a feature of Schumpeter's approach. In the name of empirical realism he insisted that democratic theory should begin by asking the question, 'who actually governs?' and, concluding that elected officials along with their government and political-party bureaucracies are the rulers, he prescribed that democratic theory should concern itself with electoral methods and conditions for effective rule. An analogously empirical orientation has motivated theorists primarily concerned with ongoing and widespread subordination or exclusion of large numbers of people in virtue of features like their class, gender, or 'racial' membership. The question with which they begin is, 'who does not govern?,' and they conclude that government is dominated by middle- and upper-class males of a society's dominant race who promote interests specific to them and to the exclusion of other groups. Grist for the mill of the antioppressive theorists is that the groups with whom they are concerned have been and in some places still are formally excluded from democratic rule.

I do not know of any such theorist who maintains that no matter what form or conduct of democracy is in question, it will always be an exclusionary tool of oppression, and most of their systematic criticisms of democracy have been directed more at liberalism than at democracy *per se*. Still, some of the views typical of antioppressive theorists are pertinent to the general working conception of democracy addressed in this chapter. Since these theorists think that informal exclusions continue in current electoral systems and is constant across a wide range of different styles of government, they do not share Schumpeter's enthusiasm for the benefits of electoral politics and are primarily concerned instead to expose the ways these systems perpetuate group subordinations.

Lenin argued against Karl Kautsky that before discussing democracy one must first put the question, 'democracy *for which class?*,' and maintained that the parliamentary democracies of his times served exclusively capitalist interests (Lenin 1965 [1918]: 248–9). More recently, similar viewpoints have been expressed by feminist and antiracist theorists, for example Carole Pateman and Charles Mills, who argue that modern political societies can be seen – in some respects literally – as based on, respectively, a sexual and a racial contract on the part of men and of dominant races to exclude women and racial minorities (or even majorities) from effective participation or representation in democratic forums (Pateman 1988, Mills 1997). These and other such criticisms contrast the public realm of formal government and election of officials who conduct it with private realms such as the workplace, the family, and the media to argue that disparities of wealth, power, access to appropriate knowledge and skills, perpetuation of prejudicial attitudes, and the like in the latter realm ensure exclusion of effective representation of people from subordinated groups in the public realm. The result is that even after legal exclusions are removed (relatively recently when one thinks of women's suffrage or slavery in North America), discrimination in everyday life perpetuates political discrimination now masquerading as universally accessible democracy.

Democracy as irrational

Many antidemocrats in ancient times and aristocrats at the time of the French and American Revolutions (not, however, including Aristotle or Tocqueville) considered democracy irrational in the sense of being rule by ignorant masses of people, incapable of knowing their interests or constraining their emotional impulses and running amok. Contemporary democratic theorists have in mind irrationality in a different sense. Rational choice theorists take as their point of departure the preference rankings of individuals, and, abstracting from the content of the preferences and setting aside efforts to prescribe what people's preferences morally *ought* to be, these theorists ask instead what conditions must be fulfilled for people thus motivated to be rational.

Two general categories of irrationality are identified: when people adopt measures that they can reasonably be expected to know will fail to achieve their preferred goals and when an individual's preference rankings are incoherent. An example in the first category would be an employee whose top priority is to make extra money quickly and who could do this by working overtime but chooses instead to take an unpaid holiday. An example of irrationality in the second category would be an employee who simultaneously preferred a change in job position to working overtime on current duties, working overtime to taking a holiday, and taking the holiday to changing positions. This person would have an intransitive preference ranking and therefore would not be able to make a decision if confronted with a choice among these three options.

Examination of the conditions for rationality along these lines becomes interesting from the point of view of democracy when collective decisions are appropriate to confront situations where people's preferences affect one another and may conflict. This is the domain of social or collective choice theories, and it is from within them that challenges to the rationality of democracy arise (Hardin 1993, and see Hardin 1982 for a general introduction to collective action theory). One such challenge questions whether it is ever rational for individuals to make use of democratic means to further their interests. The reason for doubt is that democratic decision-making is a public good the benefits of which (for instance, keeping politicians honest or preventing autocracy) accrue both to those who take the time and effort to engage in democratic politics and those who do not make this effort; hence it is in the interests of any one individual to profit from this good without exerting the effort (even to take the time to vote). In the case of nearly all public goods, on this perspective, the rational individual will see it as an advantage to be a free-rider (Downs 1957: ch. 14).

Another critique regards the majority as if it were a single individual and challenges its rationality. The best-known version of this application of collective choice theory to democracy is that of Kenneth Arrow, who reviews the conditions that rational choice theorists apply to individual people and shows that majority vote sometimes violates one or more of these conditions. For example, a voting public or a legislature confronted with the options of raising taxes, borrowing money, or cutting social services might be equally divided into three groups whose rankings of these options creates a cyclical majority, where the favoured option of any one group will be outvoted by a coalition of the remaining two groups. In this case, as in the case of the irrational employee imagined above, the condition for rationality that preference rankings be transitive is violated and no rational decision is possible (Arrow 1951).

Great ingenuity has been exerted by social choice theorists to show that sophisticated voting procedures or legislative rules employed to circumvent this and other 'voter paradoxes' will fall short of one or more conditions for rationality (for instance by Riker 1982: ch. 4). At this level of abstraction it does not matter that voter paradoxes do not always arise or can be handled in an *ad hoc* manner when they do arise, as is often possible (Davis 1974), since what is being questioned is the very existence of a 'majority will' considered as if it were the will of a rational individual. Just as one can challenge the rationality of an individual who might at any time lapse into irrationality, so is it with the majority taken as a single entity.

Conditions for democracy

Subsequent chapters will survey alternative theories about democracy to see how they are either motivated by the aim of meeting one or more of these challenges to democracy or, even if not explicitly so motivated, how they could contribute to meeting them. But first an approach to democracy that might be thought to obviate this exercise and to throw into question the very need for theories about democracy should be noted. The approach is to focus on pregovernmental, social or economic conditions that make well-functioning democracy possible, or in the strongest version ensure it.

Putnam and Schumpeter

A recent effort to focus attention on the conditions for democracy is by Robert Putnam, who compares regions of Italy where democracy has flourished and where it has been ineffective. In his *Making Democracy Work*, Putnam concludes that the difference is due to the presence in some regions but not others of the essential preconditions for democracy, namely: active participation of citizens in public affairs; the interaction of citizens as equals; and mutual trust and respect among citizens. The main thrust of Putnam's thesis is that these conditions exist when and to the extent that people are actively engaged as equals in such local organizations as sports clubs, cooperatives, mutual aid societies, cultural associations, and voluntary unions. The conditions are absent when the main or only forms of non-governmental institutions available to citizens are hierarchical such as the Mafia, the Church, or the main political parties (Putnam 1993: see chs 4 and 6).

Putnam adduces this account explicitly to meet two of the criticisms of democracy: that democratic government is ineffective and that it is irrational. In regions where the institutions to which he refers are strong, government functions well in translating social demands into public policy. In such regions, too, problems like the impulse to be a free-rider that social choice theory raises are overcome as participation in organizations creates 'social capital' or the mutual trust and commitment to common projects necessary for democratically coordinated activity. Putnam does not present his study as an alternative to democratic theory, but as an exercise of it (3); however, it is not hard to imagine an argument that if the availability of certain sorts of organizations in civil society creates values and habits that successfully promote effective democratic government and overcome impediments to collective action based on rational self-interest, then democrats should devote themselves to the practical questions of how to nurture participation in such organizations rather than to the concerns of abstract theory.

That an approach like Putnam's, suggestive as it is for the practically-oriented democrat, cannot altogether displace theories about the nature and value of democracy is evidenced by contrasting it to the conditions for a properly functioning democracy proposed by Schumpeter. It will be recalled that for him democratic government requires, among other things, a relatively passive citizenry that concerns itself with governmental affairs only to vote. Literally interpreted, Schumpeter could accept Putnam's condition interpreted to mean that activity in nongovernmental associations left citizens with no time or energy to attend to the comportment or policies of elected officials, but this is entirely out of keeping with Putnam's intention. For him, inegalitarian, authoritarian associations are better suited to engender political passivity. Meanwhile, some US political theorists who locate themselves in this 'realist' tradition have gone so far as to extol the virtues of political apathy for democracy (for instance, Berelson et al. 1954). The principal reason that considerations of theory cannot be displaced by those of empirical conditions for democracy is that theory is required to indicate what the conditions are supposed to be for.

Putnam approvingly cites Tocqueville's emphasis on the importance of a political culture of engagement and attention to local voluntary political associations conducive to this culture. This is apt because, while not endorsing Tocqueville's misgivings about democracy, Putnam shares the notion that a democracy is at its most robust when there is energetic citizen participation in taking collective action, in its ideal form in local forums like town hall meetings or voluntary associations. Members of the realist school are, however, much closer to Tocqueville's early contemporary, James Madison, whose *Federalist Paper No. 10* (1987 [1788]) is often cited by them.

Protective and developmental democracy

For Madison (to whose views we shall return in Chapter 5), the main virtue of 'republican government' (by which he meant representative government in contrast to 'democracy' which involves direct citizen participation, *ibid.*: 126) is its potential for containing and diffusing the worst effects of conflict among factions (mainly engendered by what Madison, again differing from Tocqueville, saw as inevitable economic inequalities in a society). For this purpose it is best that the factions of a republic be widely diffused across a large jurisdiction and governmental functions be exercised exclusively by representatives who are, moreover, constrained by the checks and balances of a division of powers.

One commentator, Richard Krouse, sees in Madison and Tocqueville 'two competing classical theories of democracy,' on one of which democracy's main function is to protect people from incursion on one anothers' economic and other interests; while on the other democracy provides forums for the exercise and the development of energetic citizen participation in public affairs (Krouse: 1983). Krouse borrows the terms given to these two viewpoints on democracy by C.B. Macpherson, 'protective' and 'developmental,' which, Macpherson was at pains to emphasize, designate quite different conceptions of democracy and its value and for which there are, accordingly, different conditions (Macpherson 1977: chs 2 and 3). Hence, to identify conditions for democracy is already to suppose democratic-theoretical principles.

Alternative conditions

This point is not meant to be confined to Putnam or to Tocqueville and Madison, but will apply to any list of putative conditions for democracy. For instance, Robert Dahl (1989: ch. 18) sees a highly developed economy and modern, European or North American style society as a favouring and almost exceptionless condition for democracy in a way that would exclude the aboriginal societies that other theorists regard as viable, and in some respects, superior forms of democracy (Alfred 1999, Tully 1995). While Schumpeter thought democracy required relative freedom of government from public scrutiny, Michael Margolis makes encouragement of public criticism of government one of the conditions for a viable democracy (1979: 174–5). Joshua Cohen and Joel Rogers list publicly organized debate as a precondition for the form of democracy they favour (1983: 153–7), unlike Schmitt, who, as noted earlier, criticized parliamentarianism largely for spawning what he saw as debilitating and divisive debate. Cohen and Rogers (157–61), think the absence of large economic disparities is required for democracy to function well, a claim explicitly criticized in his discussion of conditions for democracy by Carl Cohen (1971: 118–19) and concurred with by J. Roland Pennock regarding agrarian, but not industrialized societies (1979: 231). Pennock lists nationalism as a condition for democracy in the modern world (246–7), thus disagreeing with the view of Karl Popper who sees nationalism as incompatible with a democratic, 'open society' (1962: 49).

Recommending conditions for securing, protecting, or extending democracy (be they necessary, sufficient, or just facilitating) is, of course, a most important task for democratic theorists who want their views to have practical effect, and alternative prescriptions along these lines will be noted in subsequent discussions in this book. But such prescriptions will always be themselves laden with prior theories about the nature and value of democracy.

Chapter 3

Liberal democracy

As part of his highly publicized, provocative thesis that after the fall of communism in Europe and with it the withering of grand ideological contests, history has ended, Francis Fukuyama maintains that Western liberal democracy has become 'the final form of human government' (1992: xi). Whatever the merits of Fukuyama's 'end of history' theory, his claim about liberal democracy has in its favour that nearly all democracies or aspiring democracies are typically described, both in theoretical circles and in popular discourse as liberal democratic.

As will be seen, not all theorists believe liberal democracy to be either the best or the only feasible form of democracy, but such theorists are in a minority, and positions that even a decade ago were advanced in opposition to liberal democracy are now proposed as versions, deepenings, or realizations of it. For these reasons, this chapter and the next will begin the book's survey of democratic theories with an extended discussion of liberal democracy. In so doing, I shall abstract from efforts to explain the pervasiveness of institutions and practices called liberal democratic to focus on core features of the theory.

J.S. Mill's formulation

In his essays, *On Liberty* and *Considerations on Representative Government*, John Stuart Mill set out what is often considered the first systematic explication and defence of liberal democracy. As a prodemocrat, Mill welcomed the progress in equality about which Tocqueville was anxious; yet in a review of *Democracy in America* he still enthusiastically recommended the work to his fellow Britons, among other reasons because he found Tocqueville's warnings about the tyranny of the majority well taken (Mill 1976 [1835/40]: 213–19). In particular Mill agreed with Tocqueville's claims that majority, mass culture stifles free and informed thought and that an omnipotent majority could oppress a minority. Taken together, Mill's essays may in large part be read as a sustained effort to confront this problem by the straightforward method of combining democracy and liberalism.

In previous eras, Mill observed, tyranny was something experienced by the majority of a nation's people at the hands of a minority so there was no danger of the majority 'tyrannizing over itself.' But with the emergence of large democratic nations (he cites in particular the US) a need was created for the people 'to limit their power over themselves' (Mill 1991b [1859]: 7). The aim of *On Liberty*, then, was to identify the principles in accord with which the people should secure this limitation. Most of the essay is devoted to explication and defence of Mill's claim that 'the only purpose for which power can be rightfully exercised over any member of a civilized community, against his will, is to prevent harm to others. His own good . . . is not a sufficient warrant.' (14). In form, this injunction prescribes against government paternalism as well as against overt tyranny and in favour of what is often now called the 'pluralist' mandate that citizens ought as far as possible to be able to pursue what they see as their own goods and in their own ways (17).

In giving his principle content, Mill listed the most important liberties to protect, namely the freedoms of conscience, thought and feeling, holding and expressing opinions, pursuing one's life plans, and combining with others for any (nonmalicious) purpose. Because these civil liberties typically and directly affect only those who enjoy them, people should be exempt from the interference, paternalistic or otherwise, by others and especially by the state, including the democratic state (16–17). Mill devoted little space to working out the details of how the liberties are to be safeguarded, but it is clear that in general he thought there should be areas of citizens' lives free of state regulation and legal limits on what even a democratically mandated government can legislate. That is, he favoured preservation of a distinction between private and public realms and the rule of law. Regarding democracy, direct citizen participation in the affairs of government is, in Mill's view, to be encouraged primarily for its functions of engendering confidence in people about their ability to govern themselves and of developing intellectual talents and communal, moral values. However, since direct participation is impossible in a large society, Mill thought that 'the ideal type of a perfect government must be a representative democracy' (Mill 1991a [1861]: 256).

Varieties of liberal-democratic theory

With the exception of one of these provisions, almost no theorist prepared to accept the liberal-democratic label would wish to make substantive changes in Mill's characterization of democracy and liberalism, though there is obviously room for many differences over how best to preserve civil liberties or structure representative democracy. For instance, regarding representation some theorists favour parliamentary and others presidential systems of government, some (including Mill) proportional representation, others first past the post representation, some a free hand for elected officials, others provision for inter-election accountability such as recall. These and other such differences are clearly very important at the level of ongoing liberal-democratic practice, but their connection to general theory is no more than indirect. Similarly, debates over how to interpret civil liberties – for instance, whether or not advertizing is a form of expression to be protected as freedom of speech or whether restrictions on campaign financing are a violation of civil rights – reflect differences over the application of liberal-democratic principles rather than differences over the principles themselves.

Participation

In most controversies of political theory the line between principled differences and variations in application, interpretation, or emphasis is blurred. One exception is in Mill's enthusiasm for participation. This is the element of his characterization of liberal democracy in the list above that is not shared by all liberal-democratic theorists (for instance Giovanni Sartori or William Riker). In fact, some *critics* of liberal democracy from the direction of participatory democracy see in Mill's participationism a (for them welcomed) deviation from liberal-democratic theory (Pateman 1970: 28–34). If Mill held that democracy should only be by direct participation or that representative democracy is not only necessary, but a necessary *evil*, these critics would be right. However, Mill thought that representative democracy had some positive features of its own (such as making it easier to ensure that government decisions would be made by educated people) and that, when feasible, it should be combined with direct participation. Because a measure of participatory democracy, albeit limited, is allowed to be possible and desirable by theorists even more closely identified with liberal democracy than Schumpeter, such as Robert Dahl (1970a: 102–3, 1989: 338–9), a case can be made to consider this an area of disagreement *within* liberal-democratic theory, rather than as a dividing line between it and alternatives.

Equality

Other differences concern equality. Mill is often and in important respects justly classified an egalitarian. He was among the few males of his time forcefully to advocate extension of the franchise to women (Mill 1971 [1869]), and his views on the distribution of wealth put him toward the socialistic end of a spectrum of stances on the question of how far liberal democrats should insist on politics favouring social and economic equality. Ronald Dworkin (1983) may also be located somewhere in the egalitarian 'camp,' as, according to most interpreters, may John Rawls, and Dahl has moved in this direction over the course of his career (contrast Dahl, 1956 and 1985). Robert Nozick (who does not classify himself a liberal *democrat*) insists that liberal principles dictate anti-egalitarianism (1974). The late Isaiah Berlin, while not explicitly anti-egalitarian, was sceptical about sanctioning more than formal, political equality in the name of liberal democracy (1969 [1958]).

For Mill 'the pure idea of democracy' is 'government of the whole people by the whole people, equally represented,' which requires proportional representation so a minority is not denied government representatives (1991a [1861]: 302–3). However, this egalitarianism does not carry over to the vote, where Mill's view differs with most other liberal-democratic theorists. On the mainstream view, political equality is a central value and is interpreted as equality in the polling booth. Mill did not agree: 'I do not look upon equal voting as among the things that are good in themselves,' he announced, and he went on to explain that by granting the educated and the uneducated equal votes, a democracy harmfully declared 'ignorance to be entitled to as much political power as knowledge' (ibid.: 340).

The relation between democracy and liberalism

Sartori identifies liberalism primarily with the protection of individual freedoms and democracy with equality, which, in agreement with Tocqueville, he thinks includes not just political equality but grows out of and promotes a measure of social and economic equality as well. In the nineteenth century the liberal element prevailed over the democratic, while in the twentieth 'the pendulum has swung and today it is the democratic component that prevails over the liberal.' Thinking that this swing has been too great (Sartori was writing this in the 1980s), he maintained that now 'we confront two futures: a democracy within liberalism, and a democracy without liberalism'. (1987: 386–7). Sartori's focus here is not the content of the component parts of liberal democracy, but the relation between its liberal and democratic dimensions. He expresses the view shared by all liberal-democratic theorists that the former ought to contain the power of democratically elected governments over individuals by putting constraints on state actions and by limiting the scope of permissible state action.

For some liberal-democratic theorists, Sartori included, this relation of containment is the only important one between liberal principles and democratic practice, but others see an interactive relation between liberalism and democracy. This is clearly the case with 'political liberties' such as the right to vote, run for office, or form political parties, which makes ongoing democracy more secure. In addition, Mill describes one way that democracy strengthens civil liberties as well as political ones. This is by conferring legitimacy on liberal laws, which a populace is more likely to respect if they have been popularly mandated (as in a democratically endorsed constitution) than if imposed (1991a [1861]: 329). At the same time, liberalism strengthens democracy. By restricting the domain of proper government activity to the public realm, bureaucracy is kept in check, which not only protects people from its interference with their freedoms, but also enables the citizenry at large to develop skills important for self-government (1991b [1859]: 121–8).

In his arguments for protection of civil liberties such as freedom of speech, Mill expresses another interactive viewpoint, echoed by some more recent theorists. On the assumptions that citizens empowered to govern themselves would prefer to do so from the vantage point of knowledge and that restrictions on the freedom of speech impede this by stifling vigorous debate and the exploration of unconventional ideas, this liberal freedom should be protected for the sake of an ongoing and vibrant democracy (Mill 1991b [1859]: 24, Oppenheim 1971). A similar point is made by theorists who insist that because people who are in the majority on one occasion or with respect to one issue may be in the minority at other times or regarding other issues, or because their preferences may change, democracy requires the preservation of means whereby people can regroup and educate themselves and others – as one theorist puts it, democracy requires that majorities be 'anonymous' (May 1952) – and preservation of the liberties especially of expression and of association are clearly among such means. Or again, while many liberal-democratic theorists value the rule of law for its function of containing democracy, some prescribe that such things as judicial review be made subservient to democracy. For instance, according to John Hart Ely this should be limited just to ensuring procedural fairness in dispute resolution and prohibiting individuals and minorities from being denied access to democratic participation (Ely 1980: 87).

The role of philosophical underpinnings

The differences among liberal-democratic theorists so far listed are mainly advanced and defended without reference to rival philosophical positions. Some additional differences, however, are strongly influenced if not strictly entailed by philosophical or general social-theoretical opinions. These will be taken up after a digression on political philosophy and liberal-democratic theory in general.

In the background of Mill's political theories are philosophical views he is famous for holding, in particular utilitarianism, according to which political institutions or policies, like the actions of an individual, are to be valued according to their propensity to promote overall social utility (usually interpreted as 'welfare,' or in Mill's terminology, 'happiness'). He also championed theories in the philosophy of the social sciences of causal determinism and what is sometimes called 'methodological individualism,' that is, the recommendation to take individuals as the basic explanatory units of society in

terms of which references to social groups like classes or nations can in principle be reduced (Mill 1973 [1843]: chs 6 and 9). Indeed, critics of liberal
democracy sometimes identify it with individualist reductionism in social
philosophy (Unger 1976: 81–2). However, it is not evident that commitment to basic philosophical principles is an unavoidable part of someone's
broad understanding of liberal democracy or commitment to it.

Alternatives to utilitarianism for justifying liberal democracy include:
those appealing directly to *individual rights* taken as something like moral
primitives – John Locke is a forerunner of some versions of such a view, and
Dworkin's deployment of rights theory in an egalitarian manner is a current example (Locke 1963 [1690], Dworkin 1977); theories such as those
of Will Kymlicka that draw on the Kantian principle that individuals, as
autonomous agents, deserve *equal respect* (Kant 1998 [1785], 1965 [1797],
Kymlicka 1989: ch. 2); *contractarian* approaches such as in Rawls' *A Theory
of Justice* (1971), which seek to justify liberal-democratic principles in hypothetical agreements among rational and self-interested individuals; and
various *combinations* of these, such as Rawls' later deployment of Kantian
contractarianism (1996: Lec. 3).

Still, some variations in the characterization of liberal democracy can be
partly explained by reference to the philosophical positions of the theorists
involved who, themselves, often explicitly correlate democratic-political
views with philosophical ones. A challenging task in the history of ideas is
to interrogate such claims of correlation by questioning whether adherence
to philosophical positions motivates stances regarding democratic politics or
determination to justify political positions motivates theorists to invent or
seize upon philosophical positions for this purpose. Examples of theorists
who, in different ways, take on aspects of this task are Quentin Skinner
(1978) and Russell Hanson (1985).

In the interests of getting on with a more elementary survey of democratic theories, historical undertakings supporting one or the other of these
alternatives will not be addressed in this book. Still, I cannot resist registering a suspicion that democratic theorists are rarely if ever driven by
abstract philosophy to major political stances they would rather not take.
Conversely, when theorists presuppose or are actively committed to important politically relevant matters, they will find a way to make their
political-philosophical positions accommodate them. An example is offered
in recent work by philosophical students of racism who have shown how
such things as racial exclusion and colonialism were justified by Locke, Kant,
and Mill alike, notwithstanding the differences among their philosophical
theories (Eze 1997, Mills 1997, Goldberg 1993). Putting aside the sceptical
observations in this digression, four areas of theoretical controversy where
philosophical and political considerations overlap will now be added to those
reviewed above.

Flexibility and prioritization

Mill's version of utilitarianism where general rules of conduct are justified by the overall expectations of the utility of actions conforming to them (called 'rule' as opposed to 'act' utilitarianism) is well suited to making *presumptive* political prescriptions, from which deviations are possible depending upon specific circumstances. For example, freedom of association may be curtailed when it can be shown that it would so dramatically harm others that an exception should be made to a general rule favouring this freedom, but the burden of proof resides with one who would limit this freedom. Also, when there are conflicts among civil liberties or between one of them and requirements for maintaining democratic structures, Mill's approach invites one to make local judgments about trade-offs rather than appealing to a generally applicable prioritization. A theorist in the 'basic rights' tradition may have some room for flexibility and prioritization among rights, but when rights conflict with the demands of democracy such a theorist will be prone to insist that the rights are, to employ Dworkin's term, overriding 'trumps' (1977: ch. 4). Similarly, contracts more easily admit of renegotiation than of flexibility in interpretation, and Kant's prescription for respect of individual autonomy was supposed to be 'categorical,' thus admitting of no exceptions.

Notwithstanding such dispositions to rigidity, liberal-democratic theorists of all philosophical persuasions, like their analogues in actual political arenas, have proven adept at finding ways to introduce flexibility into their prescriptions regarding specific issues, and some room for manoeuvre is to be found within the non-utilitarian positions. Kant provided for a distinction between 'perfect' and 'imperfect' duties, where the latter are not subject to categorical employment but may be waived when circumstances do not permit carrying them out. Most basic rights theorists recognize that rights claims may conflict and that rights do not admit of strict hierarchical ordering, so sometimes *ad hoc* decisions must be made. Philosophical contractarians have in mind not actual, explicit contracts, but hypothetical contracts about what rational people would agree to. In addition to prompting disagreements depending on what is thought rational, this allows for alternative interpretations of what a hypothetical contract mandates in real political circumstances. Moreover, contemporary political philosophers, like their classic predecessors, provide themselves with additional flexibility by limiting the appropriate subjects of rights or democratic entitlement to just certain types of individuals, for instance to citizens or to adults. It was mainly by denial of full personhood that classic theorists were able to withhold rights and entitlements from women, aboriginal peoples, or slaves.

Developmentalism and protectivism

Mill is sometimes classified as a developmental as opposed to a protective democrat, as these positions were described in Chapter 2, because he believed that nearly all people have the moral and intellectual potentials for mutually enriching cooperative behaviour and that democracy can help to develop these potentials (Macpherson 1977: ch. 3, Held 1996: 115–18). Protective democrats in the tradition of Madison, on the other hand, think that inevitable disparities in people's abilities combined with the equally unavoidable centrality of self-interest in human behaviour will ensure economic inequalities and, in turn, prompt factional conflict over perpetual scarcity of resources.

Developmental and protective democrats can agree on the importance of combining the constitutional protection of civil liberties with representative democracy, but their divergent theories of human nature shape alternative focuses and institutional prescriptions. Thus, while Mill favoured combining representative and participatory democracy, Schumpeterian theorists are wary of citizen participation which they pessimistically think is no more capable of educating masses of people to effective government than anything else. Mill believed that formal and informal education could increasingly bring people to cooperative values, but Madison and those who followed him saw no prospect for overcoming factional conflict and competition within populations and hence prescribed, for example, systems of checks and balances and divisions of powers between state and federal government to contain it.

The encumbered self

Will Kymlicka has forcefully argued that, despite charges of social-scientific individualism, liberal democrats need not assume that people's preferences (or aspirations or values) are formed by them independently of social forces or of their group identifications (1990: 207–16). The question of whether or how individuals' aspirations are formed is different from the question about whether and how to protect their efforts to act on such aspirations (however these came to be). A main argument of Kymlicka's is that it is precisely because people's values are socially informed by their group memberships that liberal democrats should support multicultural group rights, since these memberships provide a 'context of choice' essential for autonomous action (1995).

One theorist cites these viewpoints of Kymlicka as evidence that he is a nonindividualist communitarian whose credentials as a liberal can therefore be questioned (Hardin 1995: 208). The term 'individualism,' like 'freedom,' 'equality,' and 'democracy,' is one of those contested terms of political theory that admits of several interpretations (Lukes 1973). If it is taken to refer to the doctrine that reference to group membership is inappropriate in assigning rights to individuals then Kymlicka does, indeed, count as a nonindividualist. This topic will be taken up later in the chapter. If, however, to be an individualist is to think that people's values and beliefs are somehow shaped only by themselves, independently of the social contexts of their birth, rearing, and lives, then not only would Kymlicka cease to be an individualist but so would such famous individualists as Locke or Mill.

There remains, however, a specifically political sense of individualism central to liberal democracy, namely that whatever the causal origins of people's preferences, social arrangements at least as far as government can affect them, should respect the freedom of individuals to act on their preferences rather than being obliged to forgo this ability or to adjust their preferences to socially determined goals. Taken in this sense the claim that liberalism is 'atomistic' (levelled, for instance by Levine 1993: ch. 7) is on target. Like all political-theoretical controversies, focused debate is often impeded by the rhetorical use of terms like 'individualism' (or 'collectivism,' 'atomism,' 'freedom,' and so on) to announce or label stands and evoke positive or negative feelings for or against them. Assuming, however, that it is possible to set such usages aside with respect to the conception of individualism specific to liberal democracy, two theoretical debates remain. One debate is over whether societies *ought* to accommodate themselves to existing preferences of individuals. This debate will be taken up in later chapters, especially those treating civic republican, participatory, and deliberative theories. Another debate, which will not be pursued further, is over whether indifference or agnosticism about fundamental theses of social ontology or philosophical anthropology can, after all, be sustained. Perhaps the consistent liberal-democratic theorist must be an existentialist, or, alternatively, a deterministic individualist of the Hobbesist variety. If some such connection could be proven and if in addition the position to which the liberal democrat is committed were decisively defeated, then, depending on how vital to liberal democracy the position in question is, this would constitute grounds for its rejection. Despite the attraction of strategies like this to political philosophers, success of arguments at such fundamental levels are rarely if ever acknowledged by anyone but their proponents.

Freedom and autonomy

Short of these debates there are differences within liberal-democratic theory where alternative conceptions of personhood and of how robust an individual's freedom can be are reflected in political viewpoints about what measure or kind of freedom should be permitted or encouraged. Citing Kant and Rawls, Kymlicka insists that for the liberal democrat, we 'can always step back from any particular project and question whether we want to continue pursuing it' (1990: 207). By contrast, those in the lineage of Hobbes see freedom as the ability simply to act on present preferences, so people may still be free even if their aspirations are fixed or determined outside their own control.

Modest political prescriptions that come from these 'determinist' and 'autonomist' camps (to pick some rough labels) are, respectively that the state ought as far as possible to enable people to act on their preferences or that it ought to preserve the ability of people to revise their goals. Thus put, the two prescriptions are compatible in principle, since the autonomist's freedom can be described as the freedom to act on a preference to be able revise one's values. But those in the autonomy camp are wont to advance the more ambitious prescription that the liberal state ought actively to promote autonomy. This will likely generate policy recommendations, for instance, favouring public education about alternative life options and training in critical thinking to assist people in examining and revising their goals. These are less likely to be advanced by the determinists, who will gravitate toward 'protective-democratic' policies 'as described above' p. 25). That such a correlation is a tendency rather than a necessity is indicated by the fact that Mill was both a determinist and a developmental democrat.

Also, there is considerable variability among autonomists over how often or easily the ability to act autonomously is exercised, and while, again, there need not be perfect correlations, such viewpoints will no doubt affect and be affected by relevant political values. Hence, to defend himself against fellow advocates of group rights who fear that his viewpoint might undermine group cohesion, Kymlicka is at pains to indicate that defection by a person from his or her group-determined values is relatively rare (1995: 85). Meanwhile, Russell Hardin, who is sceptical about the centrality or strength of group identifications to one's preferences, sees such advocates as foes of liberal democracy (Hardin: 1995).

Positive and negative liberty

Berlin argued that the 'autonomist' conception of freedom should be shunned as a dangerous precursor to totalitarianism, and he recommended in its place a 'negative' conception according to which political liberty (or freedom, terms used interchangeably by him) is nothing but the absence of impediments deliberately placed by some people in the way of other people's efforts to pursue their chosen goals (1969 [1958]: 122). To this he contrasted the 'positive' notion of 'self-mastery' motivated by a desire of people to conceive of and act on their own goals (131). Attractive as the conception of positive liberty is, due to its connotation of the free individual as a 'doer' and as 'self-determining,' Berlin thinks that to integrate it with political theory and practice is to take a first step down an unavoidable slope through paternalistic authoritarianism to totalitarianism.

One element in this progression is a division of the 'self' into that which dominates and as something within people that needs to be 'brought to heel' or into a higher self, identified with one's true autonomy or reason, and a lower, irrational, self which stands in the way of autonomous freedom (132). This opens the door to authoritarian control paternalistically justified in the name of acting in people's higher selves and hence of their true freedom. The progression takes a decidedly totalitarian turn when it is further maintained that the 'ends of all rational beings must of necessity fit into a single, harmonious pattern, which some men may be able to discern more clearly than others,' and that when laws enforcing rational behaviour on everyone are in place, conflict will be overcome and people will be 'wholly free' in being 'wholly law-abiding' (154).

On behalf of the liberal-democratic champion of autonomy it might be argued that simply to insist that people have the ability to select and revise the goals they follow and that this ability should be nurtured and protected does not commit one to any conception of a higher and a lower self, much less to a theory about essential harmony among autonomously chosen goals. An alternative reaction to Berlin is expressed by Charles Taylor who, while granting the attractiveness of negative liberty as a 'Maginot line' against authoritarianism, argues that it cannot be supported. Part of his argument works as well against a conception of autonomy.

Taylor faults Berlin's view for allowing no qualitative comparison among negative freedoms, since merely quantitative comparisons lead to ridiculous conclusions such as that people in (the former) communist Albania are more free than are people in England because the impediments to religious and political freedoms in Albania are proportionally fewer in number than are the impediments to things like a free flow of traffic in England, due to there being more traffic lights there (1979: 183). Such examples illustrate that 'freedom requires a background conception of what is significant,' but this equally applies, Taylor notes, to people's purposes, some of which (to engage in political or religious practices) are more important than others (to drive quickly through city streets). To the extent that, due to weakness of the will or the like, a person's fleeting desires or less important purposes may interfere with pursuing more important ones, something like Berlin's notion of positive freedom involving the mastery of a lower self by a higher one must be admitted. What is more, a person may be 'profoundly mistaken about his purposes,' in which case 'he is less capable of freedom in the meaningful sense of the word' (193).

Taylor thinks that there is no defensible alternative to a positive conception of liberty, but this does not at all distress him, since he believes that political theorists *should* integrate conceptions of freedom and policies aimed at achieving it with considerations about what makes human lives worthwhile. In this respect he shares the orientation of another defender of positive liberty against Berlin, (the late) C.B. Macpherson. In addition to challenging Berlin's exclusion of poverty and other structural features of a society from counting as impediments to freedom (since for Berlin they are structural rather than being deliberately intended), Macpherson was primarily concerned to articulate two positive alternatives to Berlin's conception. One of these he calls 'developmental liberty' (1973: 119), which is the ability of an individual 'to use and develop his own capacities under his own conscious control for his own human purposes' (41).

The other sense of positive liberty for Macpherson is 'the democratic concept of liberty as a share in the controlling authority' (109). With this notion, he is taking issue with a nineteenth-century theorist, Benjamin Constant, on whose views Berlin draws. Constant distinguished between 'the liberty of the moderns,' which is focused on individuals' freedom from interference and 'the liberty of the ancients,' which involves collective and direct participation in self-rule. On Constant's view the liberty of the ancients is necessarily a thing of the past, since it requires societies of much smaller scale than in the modern world (1988 [1819]). Macpherson did not agree, and thought that this conception of democracy could and should be 'retrieved' in contemporary democratic theory and practice, just as he thought that the notion of freedom as the development of human potentials could and should be retrieved from traditions stretching from Aristotle to the idealist philosophers and the liberal democrat, John Stuart Mill.

Macpherson and Taylor are prodemocrats and they are also defenders of standard liberal rights, so they certainly do not want their conceptions of positive liberty to give aid and comfort to authoritarians. One way that Macpherson tries to avert this is by insisting that democratic freedom is a prerequisite for developmental freedom: participating in collective decisions is one exercise of developmental freedom, and no political movement to secure social and economic conditions conducive to general developmental freedom could succeed 'unless it is strongly and effectively democratic' (109). A question remains, though, about whether or how their conceptions of positive freedom should count as options within specifically liberal-democratic theory.

As noted earlier, Mill is properly classified a 'developmental' as opposed to a 'protective' democrat, since he thought that a major virtue and aim of democracy is to develop people's potentials, and in this sense Macpherson is justified in seeing his conception of developmentalism as contained in the thought of this prototypical liberal-democratic theorist. However, Mill did not qualify the freedoms that are to be protected by liberal rights or figure in democratic processes with the specification that they be compatible with the development of human potentials, political engagement, or the pursuit of objectively worthwhile goals. He could not do this consistently with his endorsement of pluralism according to which the state is not to specify what sorts of life aims people may try to pursue. At the same time, like any other liberal-democratic theorist, Mill recognizes that it is sometimes necessary to constrain some freedoms, as when confronting the 'paradox of tolerance' (discussed in the next section), and perhaps the norms implicated in a positive-libertarian conception could be appealed to for guidelines. My own view is that this is as far as one can go in the way of fitting conceptions of positive liberty into a liberal-democratic theoretical framework and that they find a more comfortable home in theories of participatory democracy (Chapter 7) or civic republicanism (discussed in Chapter 4).

Limits of tolerance and the public/private boundary

Liberal democrats famously confront a 'paradox of tolerance.' If a liberal state is one that favours tolerance of people's pursuits of alternative goods in alternative ways, then how can it avoid tolerating goals or manners of pursuing them that contradict liberal values themselves? (See Sullivan et al. 1982; the problem is akin to a 'liberal paradox' which results when some people have 'nosy' preferences about how others must comport themselves, Sen 1970, and Barry 1991b: ch. 4.) This problem does not admit of easy solution from within a liberal-democratic framework. To maintain that people should be free as long as their freedom does not restrict that of others would too severely limit the scope of pluralism, due to the pervasiveness of conflicts. For example, if there are not enough positions in a certain workplace for everyone who wants employment there, some people's freedom to hold a job in that workplace will unavoidably limit the same freedom for someone else. To outlaw such situations would be foolish, and it would be small comfort to unsuccessful candidates to argue that at least their freedom to *apply* for a job has not been in conflict with that of the successful candidate.

It is sometimes held that a liberal society should be tolerant of all pursuits that do not undermine liberal tolerance itself. But in addition to being subject to contested interpretation and abuse (for instance, of the sort justified in the name of liberal values during the McCarthy era in the US), this does not easily work to rule out things like religious intolerance that, unlike limitations on freedom of political expression or association, do not always have direct political consequences. It also does not easily rule out practices oppressive to the members of a minority population that is sufficiently isolated that general tolerance in its larger society is not threatened. Arguing that tolerance is inviolate in the private realm but not the public shifts the problem to identifying the boundary between the private and the public domains, or, alternatively, of determining when private-realm behaviour merits exceptional state interference.

These difficulties have sparked lively and protracted debates among liberal-democratic theorists about whether or how tolerance should be limited. An analogous paradox confronts the *democratic* side of liberal-democratic theory, since sometimes democratic procedures can yield democracy-threatening results, as when in 1992 antidemocratic, religious fundamentalists were positioned to win elections in Algeria. Prodemocrats at the time were justly troubled by annulment of the elections by the Algerian government, but they were also troubled by the prospect of electoral victory by the antidemocratic fundamentalists. Electoral successes in Europe from time to time of extreme right-wing political parties pose the same problem.

Generic political prescriptions in response to these problems may be arrayed between two poles, one of which recommends strict state neutrality in the face of alternative values and undertakings guided by particular visions of the good life or the good society, including ones deemed to be illiberal or antidemocratic, while the other pole mandates liberal-democratic state encouragement and enforcement of certain such visions both legally and, as in educational policy, culturally. Few liberal-democratic theorists are prepared to defend positions at these poles; though Berlin represents a viewpoint close to the first polar position and William Galston (1991) and (the late) Jean Hampton (1989) are close to the second pole.

Political-philosophical strategies for motivating a response to the paradox of tolerance may also be sorted according to how 'neutrality-friendly' they are. Thus, unlike Galston and Hampton, Bruce Ackerman (1980) and Charles Larmore (1987) seek defences of the principle of liberal neutrality that are as far as possible void of philosophical commitments to a concept of a good society or life. These authors attempt to defend neutrality by reference to the conditions required for people with different values to carry on fruitful and nondestructive debates about matters like the distribution of political powers. Consistently with this orientation, they hold that disagreements in actual political forums over basic moral values be set aside when they impede attempts to pursue political dialogue, thus differing from Hampton or Galston. Joseph Raz (1986: pt 2) defends liberalism by reference to the nonneutral moral principle of individual autonomy, but derives political prescriptions from it which are more pluralist than those of Hampton or Galston. An analogously 'mixed' strategy is pursued by Amy Gutmann and Dennis Thompson, who attempt to combine 'procedural' neutrality and 'constitutional' commitments by subsuming these within processes of ongoing public deliberation (1996: 92–3).

Rawls' contribution to these debates is in his discussions of the conditions under which a liberal-democratic society can gain the allegiance of people with divergent conceptions of the good life or a good society. He distinguishes 'political' values, such as support for civil liberties, the rule of law, and rights of political participation, from the 'comprehensive' values embodied in such things as religious traditions or philosophical systems of thought. Rawls thinks that there is sufficient overlap among the political values in modern liberal democracies to make realistic his prescription that these values should govern public life without requiring comparable (and unlikely) consensus over comprehensive values which may be safely left to inform thought and action in the private realm (Rawls 1996: lec. 4). Critics of Rawls have maintained that this position is unstable and should be pushed in the direction either of more neutrality (Larmore 1987) or of less neutrality (Hampton 1989).

Another tack is taken by Kymlicka, who, like Raz, thinks that the 'comprehensive' values favouring individual autonomy should guide public policies, but typically by persuasion and education, not legal imposition (Kymlicka 1995: 165–70). By contrast, Jürgen Habermas argues that submission to legal constraints is essential if 'equal weight' is to be given 'to both the private and the public autonomy of the citizen,' but only if the positive laws that define permissible interactions express basic rights that he thinks are founded in the preconditions for free and equal discourse among people who might otherwise have differing moral values (1998: ch. 3.3).

Yet another response is that of the radical pluralists, whose views will be discussed in Chapter 10. Defending what she considers a radicalized form of liberal democracy, Chantal Mouffe (1993: chs 3, 9) regards approaches like those of Rawls, as of Habermas, as efforts to impose some form of philosophical orderliness or closure on political realms that admit of neither. On her view, things like the paradox of tolerance should be viewed as uniquely political problems and hence subject to perpetually ongoing negotiations among political actors motivated by a variety of alterative values, both 'political' and 'comprehensive.' This approach is consonant with the radical pluralists' rejection of philosophical 'foundationalism,' according to which answers to core questions of morality (or of any other domain) can be found by appeal to philosophical first principles. That the connection between pro or antifoundationalism and philosophical or political approaches to such topics as tolerance is not clear cut is indicated by the ambiguous stance of Rawls who is criticized for foundationalism by Mouffe (while also recognizing the ambiguity, 1993: 43) at the same time as he is claimed by Richard Rorty as a fellow antifoundationalist (1990: ch. 17).

Just as in the cases already discussed, it is doubtful that there is a *necessary* connection between a theorist's philosophical views and how he or she comes at the problem of the limits of toleration and analogous puzzles. For instance, agreeing with the value Kymlicka puts on autonomy, but also thinking that his reluctance to prescribe legislation against groups or activities deemed intolerant is well founded, someone could favour neutrality even in matters of education on the grounds that the distinction between force and persuasion in this domain cannot be sustained. A philosophical moral relativist, who thinks that value judgments cannot be justified by any but prudential considerations, might be drawn to a very generous interpretation of the scope of tolerance, since nobody would have objective grounds for prescribing intolerance. But Mill also favoured a generous interpretation for the *objectively* proposed reason that general human happiness is promoted by protection of civil liberties, and a relativist might prescribe *intolerant* policies to escape the chaos of power politics in a world with no objective moral standards, just as Hobbes favoured monarchy to escape the violent chaos of amoral conflict and competition.

The nation state

It is probably fair to say that the majority of champions of liberal democracy as well as most of its critics think of it as mainly or even exclusively a matter of government in modern nation states and as either requiring or being required by a developed capitalist market. That there are *historical* associations among liberal democracy, the nation state, and capitalism there can be no doubt, and on some political-theoretical methodologies this fact illustrates that these three things are unavoidably integrated. This is the viewpoint, for instance, of Fukuyama, who embeds his conception of political and economic arrangements in an historically evolutionary theory according to which capitalism and state-based liberal-democratic government represent the pinnacle of human development.

Regarding capitalism, there is no paucity of prosocialist theorists who, while rejecting the end of history thesis, agree with Fukuyama's view that capitalism and liberal democracy are essentially connected. This is most clearly the case for those Marxists who regard political values and institutions as nothing but superstructural reinforcements of economic forces and relations (for instance, Hoffman 1983, Wood 1981). A less widespread example is the methodology of the participationist, Benjamin Barber, for whom politics is a form of 'epistemology,' such that different political configurations constitute ways that people comport and think of themselves. On his view liberal democracy and capitalism are united in one such epistemological package (Barber 1984: 251–7). Against their views are those of liberal-democratic socialists, such as Norberto Bobbio (1987), who champion socialism in part because they think it better realizes the values of liberal democracy than does capitalism.

Even those who disagree with Bobbio about whether socialism or capitalism can best serve the liberal-democratic aspiration to guarantee access to democratic procedures while protecting civil liberties, ought to grant that *on the face of it* there is a conceptual difference between this goal and the sorts of economic structures or class relations that characterize capitalism and socialism. It is imaginable that a prosocialist political party or coalition would form a government and implement economic policies strongly enough egalitarian and market constraining to count as noncapitalist, while maintaining representative government and protection of civil rights. Gaining electoral support for programmes containing both liberal-democratic and socialistic components was the main quest of the 'Eurocommunists,' a misleading term applied as well to the democratic wings of communist parties in Japan and some countries of South America as well as in Western Europe and most successfully in Italy in the 1980s. Unlike their critics from the orthodox Marxist left, most nonsocialist liberal-democratic critics at the time charged the Eurocommunists not with conceptual confusion, but with insincerity in their adherence to liberal democracy. Of course, the issue is more complex than this, and, especially after the collapse of communism in

Eastern Europe and the Soviet Union, there is a lot more to be said about the relations of capitalism and socialism to liberal democracy. This topic will be pursued in the discussion appended to this chapter.

Fully to interrogate the relation between liberal democracy and the nation state would also be a complex task, largely requiring historical analyses beyond the scope of this book. However, it may be useful to disentangle some of the concepts and controversies involved in this topic. Debates on it are clouded by an often-encountered fusion of the notions of nation and state. It may be that there is a tendency for nations to become states, but since nations are primarily social and cultural entities and states juridical and administrative ones, the two are different, and bi- or multi-national states, such as Canada, Belgium, or Spain, are viable, if not always comfortably so (Taylor 1993, Ware 1996). On this score Mill (1991a [1861]: ch. 16) differed with Lord John E.E.D. Acton (1955 [1862]) about whether liberal democracy functions best within a single nation, which, as Mill thought, provides requisite fellow feeling and commonality of culture, or within a mixed state where, on Acton's view, no dominant nationality can exercise majority tyranny over minority ethnicities.

Mill's single-nation requirement certainly has implications for the *scope* of viable liberal democracy, which may be too severely narrowed by it, and Acton's view is in keeping with the Madisonian approach that sees conflict as best contained when contests involve multiple agents so that popular divides or monolithic majorities are avoided. But in neither case is the debate between them over whether there is an essential connection between liberal democracy and nationhood. A two-step argument in defence of such a connection can be constructed whereby putatively necessary cultural roots of liberalism or democracy are established and then it is argued that such cultures are uniquely nationally located. Something like the first part of this argument may be found in Tocqueville, who cites the egalitarian and communal culture of the American town hall meetings as prerequisites for its democracy, and Seymour Martin Lipset (1994), among others, has noted the way that Protestantism lent itself to liberalism in its origins. However, the second part of the argument is harder to make, since even if liberal democracy (or either of its component parts) first took roots in nations with the requisite cultures, it spread to other parts of the world, including more class divided societies than the early US and to Catholic countries.

A more compelling case can be made regarding the state. Here, Acton and Mill agree with one another and almost all liberal-democratic theorists in assuming that liberal democracy has to do with relations between a state (that is, institutions of law and enforcement as well as formal executive and legislative functions and their bureaucratic accompaniments) and people subject to its authority. Moreover, to be properly democratic, this relation between state and citizen must be in accord with formal democratic procedures. It would be difficult to find liberal-democratic theorists who disagree with Brian Barry's opinion about some workers' riots in eighteenth-century England that 'however efficacious the rioters might be, I would not say that their ability to coerce the government constituted a democratic procedure' (1991a: 26).

The proceduralism Barry's comment is meant to illustrate issues from the related liberal-democratic commitments to pluralism and the rule of law. To maintain neutrality about what values motivate people's efforts to shape public policy the only constraints on what a democratic procedure might yield are liberal ones, which themselves are formal – for instance, to protect freedom of speech is not to dictate what those enjoying this freedom may choose to say. Because the democratic procedures and the liberal freedoms are thus formal, they need to be embodied in laws, which are typically set down and enforced by states. It is in this way that, aside from any historical connections there may be, liberal democracy is theoretically disposed to be centred on people's relations to one another as citizens within states. Similarly, on the democratic side, an emphasis on representative democracy, where the representatives are supposed to be in some way responsible to individual voters, supposes state or state-like enforcement of formal electoral procedures.

Faced with the assignment in Chapter 1 to designate examples of more and less democratic situations, liberal democrats would be tempted to classify unbridled mass action outside of formal procedures as not far behind anti-democratic totalitarianism as examples of the least democratic. To identify the most democratic example, the prototypical liberal democrat would likely look to states with formal procedures to elect representatives and constitutional protections of rights. As to *which* state would be selected, this would depend upon what combination of features of liberal democracy is favoured. Someone sharing Mill's egalitarianism and enthusiasm for proportional representation might nominate the Netherlands, while someone with more libertarian sentiments would favour Regan's US or Thatcher's Britain.

To be sure there are analogues of representative-democratic procedures and civil rights defended by the rule of law in substate settings, such as clubs or neighbourhood associations, and theorists like Thomas Pogge (1989) and Charles Beitz (1979) make strong cases that principles of justice, such as those Rawls defends as essential to liberal democracy, ought to extend beyond states. It is noteworthy, however, that the extension they have in mind still supposes states as the primary liberal-democratic institutions. Pogge and Beitz are urging that the interactions *among* states should be governed by principles of justice, and cosmopolitan theorists such as David Held (1991 a), who argue for a relaxing of state sovereignty so as to promote liberal-democratic institutions in superstate groupings, view resulting structures like the European Union as state-like entities in their own right.

Regarding substate associations, it should be noted that the less formal interactions of people are the more strained it is to think of democratic relations among them as liberal democratic. Indeed, one reason for distinguishing between the public and the private in liberal-democratic theory is to make room for domains within which people may chose to comport themselves in ways not consonant with the liberal constraints or democratic procedures appropriate to a state. Examples are the workplace, the family, and religious organizations. Efforts on the part of liberal democrats to democratize or to liberalize these sites of human interaction challenge the impermeability of boundaries between public and private realms by making them subject to some measure of government control, thus, again, linking liberal democracy to the state. By contrast, prescriptions for internal democratization of informal associations or institutions are usually in the direction of participatory democracy even when advanced by liberal democrats like Mill or Dahl.

Recap

To summarize briefly, virtually all liberal-democratic theorists can agree in their endorsement of representative democracy where representatives are chosen in accord with formal procedures (at some point involving majority voting) combined with state protection of political and civil liberties and a private sphere free of state interference. Pluralism and political individualism provide core points of orientation for these theorists as well as being regarded important values in popular political culture for sustaining liberal democracy. Within this shared core, liberal-democratic theorists may be sorted according to stands on various positions: developmentalist/protectionist; containment of democracy by liberalism/interactive support of liberalism and democracy; 'autonomist'/'determinist;' (perhaps) positive liberty advocacy/ negative liberty advocacy; political liberalism/comprehensive liberalism; foundationalism/antifoundationalism. And they differ in their locations on some spectrums where one may be more or less accommodating to: informal political participation; flexibility in the political interpretation of basic principles; group rights and group character formation; state neutrality regarding concepts of a good society or life; national diversity; and egalitarian economic policies.

A challenging exercise would be to try grouping stands on polar positions and locations along spectrums into coherent and mutually exclusive packages. Such a task would not be straightforward, in part because stands and locations are only correlated approximately, if at all, with philosophical commitments and in part since the explicitly stated views of liberal-democratic *theorists* does not lend itself to easy classification (for instance, Mill and Berlin share similar views on liberal rights, but differ on developmentalism and egalitarianism); so contestable principles about what ought to be placed together in coherent *theories* would have to be appealed to. This task will not be undertaken in this book, which turns instead in Chapter 4 to the resources within liberal-democratic theories for addressing challenges to democracy. As will be seen, the availability and power of such resources differ depending on how liberal democracy is conceived.

DISCUSSION: LIBERAL DEMOCRACY AND CAPITALISM

Arguments that liberal democracy is essentially capitalistic are given both by antiliberal-democratic socialists and antisocialist liberal democrats. As in the case of all the disputes addressed in this book, much depends upon how the subject matters in question are interpreted and evaluated. The approach followed in this discussion treats the relation of liberal democracy to capitalism along with its relation to socialism: if socialism and capitalism are thought of as alternative economic systems and liberal democracy can be shown compatible with socialism, then it is not essentially capitalistic. Ronald Beiner resists such an approach on the grounds that conceiving of socialism in economic terms gets one 'enmeshed in the language of rights and entitlements' definitive in his view of liberalism and thus detracts from what he takes as the desirable potential of socialism as a 'basis for social solidarity' (1992: 144). On Beiner's version of civic republicanism, as on some participatory-democratic viewpoints (see Barber 1984: 253), capitalism, socialism purely economically conceived, and liberal democracy are compatible with one another insofar as they all contribute to an objectionably individualistic and passive political culture.

This topic will be set aside (until the end of the discussion) to review some main issues involved in ascertaining the relation of liberal democracy to capitalism and socialism where the latter are economically defined. The principal justification for this is that most who see liberal democracy as essentially capitalistic have an economic conception in mind, as do those who differ with them. Also, I agree with those who, reacting against a penchant of earlier socialists to build all their valued goals into the conception of socialism, think it better to conceive of socialist arrangements modestly as economic preconditions for things valued on socialist-independent, moral or political grounds.

A capitalist society, roughly defined in economic terms, is one with a predominantly market-driven competitive economy in which individual or corporate private owners of major means of production, distribution, and the like are presumptively (though obviously not completely) free of state interference to dispose of their holdings or of profits derived from them as they please. One conception of socialism is, then, as an alternative to capitalism where the presumption that guides political and economic policy is to achieve substantial social equality and to promote cooperation. Socialists in the mainstream Marxist tradition wish to reserve the appellation 'social democracy' for such an arrangement and often further distinguish between classic social democracy, which they see as employing egalitarian rhetoric to cover policies compatible with ongoing capitalism, and 'left social democracy,' where the egalitarian presumption is sincere and policies actually challenge capitalism.

Meanwhile, increasing numbers of socialists prefer to call themselves social democrats to distinguish themselves from that aspect of the Marxist tradition where 'socialism' designated dictatorship on the part of a vanguard party supposed to represent true working-class interests as a preparation for the 'higher' phase of classless communism. Debates over the adequacy of the 'dictatorship of the proletariat' conception as a political ideal and over whether it led inexorably first to Stalinism and then to the demise of communist governments occupied generations of socialist theorists (Cunningham 1994: ch. 4, 1995), but it is clear that vanguardist socialism would have little in common with liberal-democratic emphasis on representative government and formal government, and neither would the stateless communism for which it was a preparation, since communism was to be thoroughly participatory. If, however, one has socialism or (left) social democracy in the egalitarian sense in mind, the question of whether liberal-democratic political institutions and values are compatible with it, and hence not essentially capitalistic is not obviously closed, as reference to the electoral attempts to secure a version of socialism embodying core liberal-democratic values (see p. 42) was meant to illustrate.

In order for such a scenario to be at all realistic, mobilization of widespread opposition to a capitalist economy would have to take place and debate over economic systems would have to be a central part of public deliberation and electoral politics, but many socialist theorists think that liberal democracy impedes these things. Marx criticized liberal thought for regarding people in narrowly individualistic and formally juridic terms and for placing the class conflicts in civil society outside of public accountability (Marx 1975a and b [1843]). Socialists both in and out of Marxist traditions all criticize liberal democracy for according most people and in particular wage labourers and the unemployed only formal rights and for allowing those with money and other forms of economic clout to manipulate electoral politics.

Whether these criticisms are decisive depends on how liberal democracy is regarded. To anticipate themes to be developed in Chapter 4, one might imagine a spectrum stretching from a 'thin' view of liberal democracy (formally procedural, exclusively individual-rights oriented, placing narrow limits on the public realm) and a 'thick' view (granting political provision of resources effectively to exercise rights, admitting group rights, sanctioning a flexible and wider view of the public realm). Since thick liberal democracy is more conducive to radical political organization than the thin variety, the compatibility question in part turns on whether this is a genuine form of liberal democracy. This issue will be pursued in Chapter 4 when responses of liberal-democratic theorists to the charge that liberal democracy masks a variety of oppressive social structures will be surveyed.

David Beetham (1999: ch. 2, and 1993) notes that to be consistent, liberal-democratic socialism would have to be attained by democratic elections, but raises a doubt shared by many about whether capitalists would permit this to happen. There is clearly something to this view, dramatically illustrated in 1973 when a socialist government elected in liberal-democratic Chile was militarily overthrown with the well-documented support of large capitalist enterprises and US government agencies. Less dramatically, recent years have seen several examples of social-democratic governments reneging on egalitarian electoral promises sometimes in the face of threats of capital flight or international monetary punishment. That these efforts involve decidedly illiberal and antidemocratic elements does not challenge the essential connection of liberal democracy and capitalism thesis, because, as Beetham notes, the claim is only that capitalism is necessary for liberal democracy, not that it guarantees it, so illiberal and anti-democratic capitalist societies are possible (Italian, German, Spanish, and Portuguese Fascist governments were examples, as have been a large number of military dictatorships in other parts of the world). Its force for the case that liberal democracy must be capitalistic is that capitalism and some, perhaps 'thin,' form of liberal democracy *can* coexist and that this is the only option for liberal democrats, since they cannot tolerate dictatorial socialism, and capitalism will not permit democratic socialism.

This argument that liberal democracy has only capitalism to be compatible with, is supported by standard criticisms that even if socialists are motivated by liberal democratic-friendly values, a socialist economy has an unavoidably antidemocratic dynamic built into it. One such critique aims to show that state measures to enforce equality constitute the first step on an inexorable 'road to serfdom,' as Fredrick Hayek put it in his book of this title (1944). Egalitarian and market-constraining policies beyond what can be tolerated in a capitalist, profit-driven economy but which are essential for socialism to realize its aims require central planning and coordination on a scale that will concentrate excessive power in the hands of politicians and bureaucrats at the top of state institutions and that will oblige individuals to accommodate their preferences to the exigencies of plans and the political planning process. This charge clearly has some force, but as an empirical claim it requires supplementary argumentation to prove that economic planning will *always* lead to these consequences. Amassing inductive evidence is apt, but in assessing such evidence the fact would have to be taken into account that no effort to pursue economic planning on a large scale has yet enjoyed the opportunity to try this free of powerful and persisting capitalist efforts (often involving quite illiberal and undemocratic means) to prevent success.

Central to theses about the historical association of liberal democracy and capitalism is that liberal democracy affords political justification and protection for capitalist markets against both residual feudalism and working-class threats (Macpherson 1977: ch. 2). Such an historical association undoubtedly shows that liberal democracy at least *permits* extensive freedom of markets. But the additional claim that markets ought to be more extensive and unfettered than any variety of socialism could sanction is defended in different ways. One defence appeals, again, to the bureaucratic dangers of plannification. According to Milton Friedman, there are 'only two ways of coordinating the economic activities of millions . . . central direction involving the use of coercion – the technique of the army and of the modern totalitarian state [or] voluntary cooperation of individuals – the technique of the market place' (1962: 130). Friedman cannot mean that these are entirely mutually exclusive consistently with his acknowledgment (10) that capitalism is only a necessary, and not a sufficient condition for political freedom or, indeed, with his own practice as a professional economist, in which capacity he acted as an advisor for the military dictatorship in Chile (Peter Dworkin 1981).

An often-expressed reaction to Friedman's argument is the observation (though not exactly on target regarding the compatibility debate) that markets can also be suppressive of the freedoms essential to most or at least very many liberal democrats. A more apt response for present purposes is that liberal-democratic governments regularly sanction constraints on markets, sometimes in the interest of public goods, sometimes to assist the coordination of capitalist activities impeded by unregulated competition, and sometimes by allowing monopolization to suppress free markets. Another appropriate reaction is that there is room, indeed large room according the advocates of workers' self-managed socialism, for markets within a socialist economy. Books by Howard (2000), Schweickart (1996), Ollman (1998), and Bardhan and Roemer (1993) may serve as introductions to a large literature.

Some of the disputes over these matters concern the characterization of markets. For instance, John Roemer distinguishes between a neoclassical concept of the market as a structure where 'entrepreneurs capitalize their talents' and a modern concept where markets are complex networks within which 'profits are distributed to many owners,' arguing that on the latter conception there is no reason in principle why managers of firms could not distribute profits to publicly diffused owners (Roemer 1994: 5–6). Most of the debates, like the one about bureaucratization in general and about impediments to achieving socialism by liberal-democratic means, are primarily empirical. However, there are some more theoretical or philosophical arguments to support the conclusion that market freedoms in excess of what socialism can allow are essential to liberal democracy or at least compatible with it.

An argument from *human nature* is that socialism requires more in the way of cooperative behaviour than can be expected from human beings, who are genetically self-interested or even attracted to competition, whereas a capitalist market depends upon these traits, and liberal democracy can accommodate conflict. An argument from *morality* reverses the claim of the early cooperativist theorist, Pierre-Joseph Proudhon, that 'property is theft' (1994 [1863–4]) to maintain that socialist infringement on private property constitutes illegitimate interference of people's ability to dispose of what belongs to them.

Socialism, as Nozick puts it, 'would have to forbid capitalist acts between consenting adults' (1974: 163). In support of his conclusion that this is morally unsupportable, Nozick and other libertarian theorists appeal to a Lockean principle of *self-ownership*, to generate a third argument. On this view, people are the private owners of their own capacities and talents who therefore have the right to dispose of these talents and the fruits of their exercise as they wish including to rent out their labour power for wages (Nozick 1974: 172, 262). Capitalists thus acquire the right to use these powers to serve their own purposes.

To review the many controversies over human nature, the extent of property rights, or whether people own themselves or to attempt adjudicating among them would be a very large task. Rather than embarking on it, this section will conclude by outlining main alternative positions on these topics insofar as they relate to the question of the compatibility of liberal democracy and socialism and hence to that of whether it is essentially capitalistic. Cases for or against compatibility cannot be made simply by endorsing one or the other of opposing positions regarding human nature, property rights, or self-ownership, because any one such conclusion must be accompanied with defence of a similarly contested view about what constitutes liberal democracy and/or socialism.

Thus, while it would be odd for a prosocialist to argue for unrestricted property rights in the manner of Nozick, it does not follow that his position supports liberal democracy. Nozick, himself, sees the position as liberal but not democratic (268–71) and many, if not most, liberal democrats recoil from the consequences of a view that leaves no room for state provision of any public goods save for the enforcement of contracts. Perhaps, as some on the neoliberal right maintain, the consistent liberal democrat *ought* to be a minimum-state libertarian, but unless such an extreme position can be established, then rather than proving incompatibility between liberal democracy and socialism the moral argument for unlimited property rights puts them in the same boat.

As in the case of unlimited property rights, not all advocates of liberal democracy hold that people are essentially self-interested or competitive or that they are the exclusive owners of their capacities. Mill is an example regarding human nature, which he saw as comprising a mixture of self- and other-regarding motivations (1969 [1874, posthumous]: 394–5). Rawls and Dworkin hold that people's natural talents are arbitrarily distributed (the product of 'a natural lottery') so it is not unjust for distributive policies to compensate for natural deficiencies of talent (Rawls 1971: 72–4, 103–4, Dworkin 1981: 311–12). This is out of keeping with the self-ownership thesis, or at least with any version of it strong enough to support the incompatibility position now being addressed.

Debates over this position are further complicated by the fact that some socialists, such as Roemer (1988: 168), share with some egalitarian liberal democrats (Kymlicka 1990: 120–2) the view that self-ownership does not have the capitalist-supporting consequences of Nozick's Lockean conception. The socialist philosopher, G.A. Cohen (1995: ch. 5), claims that even Marx assumed this position. However, Cohen also argues that Marx was mistaken and that justification of socialist, egalitarian distribution requires abandoning the self-ownership claim. For the same reason he believes that Rawls and Dworkin ought to be classified as social democrats and not liberal democrats.

Those who think that good arguments are to be found on both sides of the compatibility of socialism and liberal democracy controversy (and hence of that over whether liberal democracy is essentially capitalistic) may be attracted to the approach of Macpherson, who, probably more systematically than any other critic of capitalism, addressed himself to the relation between it and liberal democracy. On his view liberal democracy has, from the eighteenth and nineteenth centuries, embodied a complex and uneasy union of two conceptions of freedom, as the 'freedom of the stronger to do down the weaker by following market rules,' and as the 'effective freedom of all to use and develop their capacities' (1977: 1) or positive liberty (see pp. 36–9). This union is uneasy because the two conceptions are incompatible in practice, as is seen when liberalism is wedded to democracy and yields the alternative, protective and developmental orientations described earlier (p. 25).

Models of democracy that incorporate the market-friendly sense of freedom fit capitalism much better than models incorporating a developmental sense; socialism on Macpherson's analysis is incompatible with liberal democracy in the protective sense but not with developmental democracy, provided the latter is interpreted along the lines of his version of positive liberty. Macpherson's approach thus suggests yet another orientation toward capitalism and liberal democracy, namely that the latter is *both* essentially tied to capitalism *and* not restricted to capitalism, depending upon which aspects of liberalism or of its marriage with democracy is in question. This orientation supposes that developmental democracy on something like Macpherson's interpretation is in fact compatible with liberal democracy. My own view is that this in turn depends upon whether positive liberty can be interpreted flexibly enough to be compatible with pluralism.

If (as I now think, Cunningham 2001) this is possible then there may well be sufficient affinities between an ideal of democratic socialism and the values and policy options of 'thick' liberal democracy that the notion of a liberal-democratic socialism is *coherent*. Whether in addition it is *desirable* from the point of view of theorists otherwise sympathetic to both democracy and socialism such as Beiner or Barber will depend upon whether a developmental interpretation of liberal-democratic socialism provides a basis for social solidarity or citizen participation. Later discussions of civic republicanism (in Chapter 4) and participatory democracy (Chapter 7) may help to focus thought for those who wish to pursue this topic.

Chapter 4

Liberal democracy and the problems

This chapter will address theoretical provisions (or the lack thereof) within liberal-democratic thought for confronting the problems described in Chapter 2. Estimating the success or failure of societies considered liberal-democratic in actual practice will not be attempted. This is not the result of an anti-empirical bias – on the contrary, readers are urged to compare theory to practice wherever the approaches surveyed have putative application – but because this exercise is undertaken just as a way of explicating democratic theories. What is more, when a liberal-democratic policy or institution fails in practice with respect to some problem, the question is left open as to whether this is because of deficiencies in its guiding theory or because the policy or institution does not live up to it.

Massification of culture

Consideration of the massification of culture problem alleged by Tocqueville and others to beset democracy illustrates one area about which liberal-democratic theory is largely, though not entirely, mute. Public funding for the arts in North America is low relative to several countries of Europe. On the Tocquevillean perspective this might be interpreted to mean that the majority with its debased tastes is more effectively denied control over government policy regarding the arts in Europe than in North America, or, alternatively, that debasement includes indifference to there being any arts funding at all. But it would be most difficult to trace such a putative effect to practice in accord with liberal-democratic theory.

It may be that Tocqueville's elitist attitude toward popular tastes is wrong. One alternative is a populist one according to which high culture grows out of and is sustained by popular-level culture. Another possibility is that there is no natural correlation between class and culture, but that how and in what ways people of any class are cultured depends upon such things as historically inherited traditions, educational access and content, and the entertainment media. On these alternatives it might be argued that under the cover of liberal protections, moneyed entertainment industries have been able to shut out vibrant popular culture or to shape popular culture in a debased direction. While purely theoretical considerations cannot settle such questions, some theories, for instance about human nature or the political-economy of cultural industries, will at least point one in the direction of a favoured hypothesis. Liberal-democratic theory by itself, however, does not do this.

The tyranny of the majority

One dimension of Tocqueville's cultural concern *is* addressed by liberal-democratic theory. This is his worry that in a democracy people with cultural proclivities, not to mention political beliefs, out of accord with the majority will be marginalized or otherwise mistreated by a majority with alternative political views and (according to him debased) cultural tastes. Liberal constraints cannot guarantee that such individuals will escape informal ostra-cizing, but in theory they should at least inhibit overt discrimination. This is the *forte* of liberal-democratic theory with respect to the problems often said to beset democracy, namely the protection of minority rights advocated by Mill and all his successors against what they feared as majority tyranny. Indeed, the commentator on US democracy, Louis Hartz, thought that his country carried such protection to unnecessary extremes. Writing in the 1950s he complained that 'what must be accounted one of the tamest, mildest and most unimaginative majorities in modern history has been bound down by a set of restrictions that betray fanatical terror' (Hartz 1955: 129). Hartz's observation, whether overstated or not, highlights the centrality of the problem of the tyranny of the majority for liberal-democratic theory, which certainly does not lack resources for its confrontation.

While there are disagreements among democratic theorists about how severe the problem of majority tyranny is, none sanctions permanent exclusion of people as a result simply of their being in a minority. However, some regard the way that liberal-democratic theory and practice protect minority rights as unfortunate. The two key elements of this protection and of the related commitment to pluralism are to give pride of place to individual rights and to ensure state neutrality with respect to alternative visions of a good life or a good society. Theorists who place themselves in the tradition of civic republicanism consider these linchpins of liberal democracy destructive of a shared public morality by reference to which people see themselves as members of a civic community.

The civic republican challenge

According to Michael Sandel, a leading proponent of civic republicanism, one outcome of the political culture and practice of liberal individualism and neutrality is that the sense of community itself is threatened as 'from family to neighborhood to nation, the moral fabric of community is unrav-eling around us' (1996: 3). Another result is that when concerns about what is morally good are relegated entirely to private realms, people lose the ability collectively to govern themselves, which for Sandel requires 'deliberating with fellow citizens about the common good and helping to shape the destiny of the political community' (*ibid*.: 5).

Civic republicanism is a challenge especially to the liberal dimension of liberal democracy, though some who champion civic republicanism also crit-icize democracy for reasons similar to Tocqueville's that it counteracts what they see as its undesirably levelling features. Thus one of the forerunners of current civic-republican theory, Hannah Arendt, criticized liberal-democratic institutions for impeding the formation of an 'aristocratic elite' (1977 [1963]: 275–6, and see Jeffrey Isaac's defence of her democratic cre-dentials, 1998: ch. 5). Civic republicans who present themselves as fully prodemocratic do not articulate a unique democratic theory, but typically endorse some version of participatory or, more recently, deliberative democ-racy (for example, David Miller 2000).

Critique of autonomy

In Sandel's critique of what he calls 'liberal proceduralism,' he targets Rawls' principle that in conflicts between pursuing goals based on a conception of what is good in comprehensive, moral theory and protecting individual rights, the latter should take precedence. Sandel's point is not to endorse the reverse position, but to challenge what he sees as two related and faulty principles that support such prioritization. One of these is the normative view that the most important thing about individuals to protect and promote is their autonomy, or the ability to evaluate alternative life plans and other such important goals and to decide for themselves which to pursue.

As noted in Chapter 3, liberal-democratic theorists who focus on auton-omy differentiate it from the bare ability to act on one's preferences. But for Sandel these views are both deficient in comparison to what he sees as the more important conception of freedom as 'the capacity to share in self-government' (1996: 302 and *passim*). Jeremy Waldron observes that this distinction mirrors the one described in Chapter 3 between 'the liberty of the moderns,' which is focused on the freedom from interference and 'the liberty of the ancients,' which involves collective and direct participation in self-rule drawn by Benjamin Constant (Waldron 1998, Constant 1988 [1819]), and he notes that for Constant the liberty of the ancients is impos-sible in large-scale societies. Sandel grants that this might be so when 'societies' on a transnational scale are in question, but that it should be possible to retrieve in smaller social units, provided they are such that economic and political forces within them can be brought under public control (1998: 326, 1996: 334–9).

The unencumbered self and communitarianism

Also essential to self-government, however, is that people wish to pursue it and are possessed of the requisite civic virtues, importantly including what John Adams described as 'a positive passion for the public good' (quoted by Sandel 1996: 126). To see how such virtues can be nurtured, Sandel believes that a second underpinning of liberal proceduralism needs to be abandoned, namely its picture of the individual as an 'unencumbered self' (1996: 12, and see his 1982: ch. 1). In this connection he thinks that the notion of the individual as nothing but a centre of autonomy is a myth. Sandel thus concurs with his fellow defender of 'communitarianism,' Alasdair MacIntyre, that nobody is simply a pure individual, but that 'we all approach our own circumstances as bearers of a particular social identity,' for instance as someone's son or daughter, a citizen of some country, a member of some profession, and so on (MacIntyre 1981: 204–5). It is within the communities comprised of such relations that people define themselves and that values and loyalties are formed. Civic virtues must draw upon the same sources and in particular on the identifications and loyalties bred of participation in various arenas of self-government.

Procedural liberalism for Sandel presupposes that 'universal identities must always take precedence over particular ones,' an extreme version of which he finds expressed in Montesquieu's view that a virtuous man would 'come to the aid of the most distant stranger as quickly as to his own friend' and that if 'men were perfectly virtuous, they wouldn't have friends' (quoted in Sandel 1996: 342). On Sandel's view such a position is not only unrealistic, but pernicious. A world without friends would be 'difficult to recognize as a human world' and it would deny people one of the particular locuses where 'we learn to love humanity' (342–3).

Sandel's most widely-read exposition of civic republicanism is in a book entitled *Democracy's Discontent* (1996) where he explains the theory in the course of describing how, in his view, the US has largely lost a civically virtuous ethos and lacks bonds among citizens forged by commitment to shared conceptions of public goods. This book prompted sometimes strong reactions from leading North American political theorists, many of which are usefully collected with a response by Sandel (Allen and Regan: 1998). One criticism is that his communitarianism commits him to sanctioning exclusions based on such things as patriarchal family traditions (Shanley 1998). Sandel's response is to maintain that reform of exclusionary values within families can only be achieved by engaging in public discourse about the good life against which desirable and undesirable sides of family life can be identified, and that, unlike civic republicanism, liberal proceduralism does not allow for such engagement in the public realm (1998: 333).

Ronald Beiner concurs that at the core of the republican ideal is that citizens sense themselves as inhabiting 'a shared world of political concerns that affect them in common' and that these concerns should be addressed in a 'community of discourse' (1992: 33–5), but he wishes to distinguish this from communitarianism. On his view communitarian grounding of values within existing traditions and pluralistic liberalism's reluctance to defend moral visions deny *both* of them independent, external standards by which 'the good life for individuals or for communities' can be specified (*ibid.*, and see his call to develop a republican conception of citizenship that is neither individualistic nor communitarian, 1995b: 12–16).

In addition to Kymlicka's criticism referred to in Chapter 3 that communitarians raise a false issue in their claim that liberal-democratic theory ignores or denies the social determination of people's identities and values, he also challenges Sandel's way of framing Rawls' prioritization of the right over the good. Kymlicka reiterates the liberal-democratic principle that the state 'should protect the capacity of individuals to judge for themselves the worth of different conceptions of the good life,' justifying public policy by reference to this principle rather than to 'some ranking of the intrinsic worth of particular conceptions of the good' (1998: 133). But, contrary to Sandel, he argues that this does not mean liberals are unable to promote some goods and help to develop some virtues, namely those goods and virtues required to sustain the ability of people to act autonomously. He thus defends a distinction made by Rawls between 'classical republicanism' and 'civic humanism,' where the former, according to Rawls, is the promotion of virtues essential to maintaining a liberal society, while civic humanism prescribes policies on the basis of some vision of the good independent of autonomy (*ibid.*: 136–8, Rawls 1996: 205–6).

Aristotelian and Ciceronian civic republicanism

According to some, this use of 'civic republicanism' by Rawls is justified. While Sandel looks mainly to Aristotle and Tocqueville in explicating his view, others look to Cicero and Machiavelli. Philip Pettit is one such theorist who, while agreeing in the main with Sandel's criticisms of contemporary political culture in the US, finds his identification of freedom with self-government not only tenuous but unworkable in a large and complex society and also insufficiently attuned to the problem of the tyranny of the majority (Pettit 1998: 45–7). Instead Pettit recommends thinking of freedom in a 'Ciceronian' way as 'the absence of mastery or domination by any other' (*ibid.*: 49 and see his 1997: ch. 2). This conception is weaker than participation in self-government but it is stronger than a liberal conception of freedom simply as non-interference, since it renders unfree someone who acquiesces in being dominated. (Whether it is also stronger than freedom as autonomy depends upon whether a person could be considered autonomous in, having surveyed various life options, chooses one of subordination, for instance, to a religious order or in the military.)

Quentin Skinner draws upon Machiavelli to defend a similar version of civic republicanism. Machiavelli's overriding project, on Skinner's reading, was to find ways to protect the freedom of a body politic (or 'state'), where this means the ability of its citizens to pursue their common goods, especially to avoid domination. In addition to threats to this freedom from external states, it is jeopardized from within by powerful and ambitious people. For a state to be sufficiently strong to ward off foreign attacks and to be vigilant in thwarting the ambitious self-seekers within, its population must be 'imbued with such a powerful sense of civic virtue that they can neither be bribed or coerced' into allowing the common good of the state to be undermined (Skinner 1992: 219, and see his 1985). Skinner agrees with Machiavelli that what most people want and what political theory should help to secure is 'to be left alone to live as free individuals, pursuing their own ends as far as possible without insecurity or interference,' but to do this they must, in an apparently paradoxical way, place civic virtue or service in the interest of the common good above their desire to 'enjoy a maximum of their own individual liberty' (220–1). Pettit draws a complementary conclusion regarding state neutrality when he recommends replacing the liberal notion of 'no-value neutralism' with 'shared-value neutralism' where what is shared is the desire of all to avoid domination, and this requires collective action inspired by civic virtue (1998: 55).

Sandel recognizes this version of civic republicanism, which he calls 'instrumental' (also 'modest' and 'tame') because the civic virtues are considered means for protecting individual freedom as opposed to the version he draws from the Aristotelian heritage where engaged political activity is regarded as an 'intrinsic' part of freedom (1996: 26). He therefore rejects an attempt of Pettit to reinterpret the Aristotelian version in Ciceronian or Machiavellian terms on the grounds that unless citizens 'have reason to believe that sharing in government is intrinsically important' they will not be willing 'to sacrifice individual interests for the common good' (1998: 325).

Testing civic republicanism

Returning to Kymlicka's claim that liberal proceduralism can also prescribe civic goods provided they serve individual autonomy, it should be clear why Sandel wishes to avoid the interpretation of civic republicanism by Pettit and Skinner, as it is susceptible to being folded into liberalism in the way Kymlicka suggests. Kymlicka recognizes that there is a theoretical difference between the sort of liberalism he defends and Sandel's view, but marshals an argument that at the level of actual political practice the two are allies with virtually indistinguishable policy prescriptions (1998), or at least that they may be indistinguishable in this regard depending on what specific policies one endorses and in fact are indistinguishable in the case of his own 'left-wing liberal egalitarianism' (129) and Sandel's comparably egalitarian political opinions.

To drive home this point Kymlicka challenges Sandel to identify a single example where his civic-republican view 'endorses the promotion of particular virtues or identities even when it conflicts with liberal egalitarian justice' (140). Sandel obliges by maintaining that the civic republican ought 'to discourage practices that glorify consumerism' on the ground that they 'promote privatized, materialistic habits, enervate civic virtue, and induce a selfish disregard for the public good' (1998: 329). This example is of a life vision – to shop until one drops – which for the procedural liberal must be allowed on a menu of options among which individuals may freely choose, but which the civic republican is justified in trying to remove from the menu. This interchange suggests two ways of testing both the compatibility of liberal democracy with civic republicanism and their relative merits.

Assuming that civic republicanism entails removal of consumerism from an individual's options while liberal democracy sanctions leaving it on the menu, the first test appeals to one's intuitions. Somebody who thinks there is nothing wrong with consumerism, even if it breeds materialism, selfishness, and so on (perhaps more neutrally described) or someone for whom this is not appealing, but who intuitively finds denying people this option by means of state policy or even concerted informal pressure less appealing will have one sort of reason to prefer liberal democracy to civic republicanism. Another, more theoretical test is to assume a liberal democrat who agrees that consumerism with the effects Sandel describes is so undermining of individual autonomy that it merits campaigns such as in public education to remove it as an option people are likely to entertain. This would be an instance of what Kymlicka calls promoting 'a vital and indispensable' but still 'secondary' role for one habit of civic virtue (1998: 135), and on this issue, at least, it would bring civic republican and liberal-democratic prescriptions into phase. The test is to ask whether a culture of virtuous non-consumerism could be achieved if success in this venture is seen in an instrumental role and not as a principal value in itself.

A third way of drawing a difference between these two perspectives does not depend on the consumerist or any other example, since it is easy to state in general theoretical terms. The distinction is suggested by a claim of Beiner's that far from abjuring visions of the good, liberalism instantiates one such vision, namely 'that choice in itself is the highest good' (1992: 25). Perhaps with some fancy philosophical footwork it could be successfully argued that this is not a putatively general moral principle, but it does look like one. So the question to ask is whether procedural liberals are, indeed, committed to it. A possible liberal alternative is the principle that all people equally deserve respect, but unless this respect is exhibited by as far as possible protecting everyone's ability to choose, the principle would not obviously support core liberal tenets about the priority of the right and state neutrality. In any case, if Beiner is right about this liberal 'highest good,' a clear line of difference between the liberal proceduralist and the civic republican is drawn, though trying to find out how the issue might be decided (or, indeed, whether it can be decided) leads one into some murky waters of philosophical ethics.

Ineffective government

A quite different 'problem of democracy' is the purely instrumental challenge that it yields ineffective government. The several dimensions of this charge can be roughly divided into four components. The two main concerns of Tocqueville were that political leaders in a democracy will be incompetent (or act as if they were in order to appeal to a mass electorate) and that because of turnovers of leaders and changes in policies, long-range plans cannot be pursued by democratic governments. Mill's solution to these problems was to weight the franchise toward the educated classes to ensure that thoughtful choices of leaders and policies would be made while simultaneously encouraging participatory democracy among the people at large thus giving them practical education in intelligent self-government.

Neither part of Mill's solution is sufficiently widespread among liberal-democratic theorists to count as central to the theory. Rather, they should be classified with alternative or supplementary measures such as lengthening terms of office and staggering elections to legislative bodies, insulating the judiciary from popular selection or recall, and providing for a well-trained and durable civil service. Such measures are not required by liberal-democratic theory, but they are invited by its focus on representative government. Also, by putting liberal rights beyond direct democratic control, a population is acclimatized to the idea that not everything pertaining to their governance should be a matter of regular democratic decision.

The Trilateral Commission's main worry was that democratic societies had lost the ability to act with single purpose. One reason for this, it speculated, was that a democratic egalitarian ethos had undermined respect for authority generally, especially in places where this respect is nurtured: the family, church, school, and military. This might be seen as a conservative version of the civic republican challenge, and some of the considerations surveyed above would apply in trying to decide whether or how liberal democrats can meet it. What differentiates the Commission's charge from that of Sandel (or of Pettit or Skinner) is its attack on equality. This charge will be especially familiar to readers in the US, where the term 'liberal' has taken on a connotation of egalitarianism, pejoratively interpreted in the broad spectrum of the political right as pernicious and unwarranted welfarism and lack of respect for tradition.

Because liberal-democratic theorists may be arrayed along a spectrum from more to less egalitarian, they will react to such complaints differently. Liberal democrats who share Mill's egalitarian sentiments regard this sort of charge as unfounded and derived from essentially antidemocratic motives. Thus, many see an imperative within Rawls' theory of justice for a large measure of substantive equality (Daniels 1975, Gutmann 1980: ch. 5). More liber-tarian theorists (for whom equality is best restricted to formal political and civil rights and who might accordingly be more sympathetic to the Com-mission's concern) have another, clear line of response to this criticism, which is to appeal to the distinction between the public and the private and argue that at least regarding the family and religious institutions a liberal democracy should allow traditional values to reign. Of course, this does not end the debate, since, as seen earlier, the location of the boundary between the public and the private is itself a problematic matter among liberal democratic theorists, but it indicates one reaction to this dimension of the charge against democracy.

The other basis of the Trilateral Commission's claim that democracy is ineffective is that it is mired in conflict among a multitude of special interest groups. Different versions of liberal-democratic theory, again, suggest dif-ferent responses to this charge. A response from the side of developmentalism is to claim that shared public values favouring democracy and civil liberties provide a basis for people to resist use of democratic procedures in the pursuit of narrowly self-interested ends. Protectionist liberal democrats in the tradi-tion of Madison and to be discussed in more detail in Chapter 5 see nothing inescapable or wrong with conflict among interest groups. Indeed, they might with justice identify the Trilateral Commission itself as just such a group whose announcement of the demise of democracy is meant to serve the inter-ests of its principles. (The 'private citizens' who founded the Commission in 1973 included the presidents of Exxon, Wells Fargo, Chase Manhattan Bank, the Bank of Paris, Dunlop, Texas Instruments, and several more such institutions.)

In citing as a problem for democracy the weakening of political parties, the Commission suggests that they have the potential to overcome interest group conflict by aggregating interests and negotiating differences along important divides. Not everyone sees such potential. Thus Tocqueville feared that political parties can exacerbate the problem of debilitating con-flict if they multiply and begin to act as arms of narrow interests. Some theorists argue that political parties are indispensable for formulating poli-cies and providing forums for political deliberation (Christiano 1996: ch. 7) while others see parties as antidemocratic institutions that distort demo-cratic representation (Burnheim 1985: 96–105). Liberal-democratic theory per se does not recommend that democratic politics be largely organized around political parties. However, its focus on representative democracy invites political party formation, which, moreover, cannot easily be prohib-ited without violating the freedom of association. How significant this is for the purposes of evaluating liberal-democratic theory will depend on whether political parties are seen as a solution or as part of the problem here under consideration.

Ethno/national conflict

The next problem to be addressed is the allegation that democracy is ill-suited to head off or contain violent conflict. It will be recalled that on one version of this charge ethno/national confrontations like those that have plagued Eastern Europe since the fall of authoritarian communism were made possible by the removal of this very authoritarianism, which kept ethnic violence in check. It will also be recalled from the discussion in Chapter 2 that for René Girard, a tendency toward downward cycles of revenge-motivated violence is an ever-present danger for all human groups. Religions (of the right sort) can impede this tendency, as can fear of the law. In an increasingly secular world, the religious solution is not generally available. Girard is no fan of democracy which, with Tocqueville, he thinks encourages violence prompting envy, thus exacerbating the problem. However, *liberal* democracy might be thought to contain an appropriate resource in the essential place it gives the rule of law.

Francis Fukuyama draws on two additional features of liberal democracy, namely promotion of a culture of tolerance and preservation of the public/private distinction in his prescription for avoiding the violence that he thinks nationalism and other such group-based movements tend toward. He does not advocate the eradication of nationalism, but he thinks it can be rendered harmless if tempered by liberal tolerance. This is accomplished if nationalism is 'pushed off into the realm of private life and culture, rather than being politicized and made the basis of legal rights' (Fukuyama 1994: 26).

An approach that goes further than this is that of Russell Hardin (1995), who is sceptical about how benign nationalism or any other form of group identification can be. Initial group identifications are usually innocuous and, in fact, rational for the social choice theorist Hardin, since they coordinate efforts among otherwise self-interested individuals. But once 'coordinated on groups,' individuals acquire a stake in defending their group against others, including by preemptive strikes, and they are susceptible to manipulation by bellicose group leaders. Hardin's worries about group identification suggest a solution to conflict that appeals to liberal-democratic individualism. One version of such an appeal (not endorsed by Hardin for reasons shortly to be cited) is that group conflicts will be avoided if people internalize universal liberal values of respect for individual freedom or autonomy. Fukuyama expresses this viewpoint in his explanation for the relative absence of warfare between liberal-democratic states that they 'share with one another principles of universal equality and rights, and therefore have no grounds on which to contest each other's legitimacy' (1992: 263).

An obvious difficulty for recommendations that liberal-democratic values be inculcated in a conflict-prone population is to show how this could realistically be accomplished in the face of the very conflictual attitudes that need to be transformed. Applying Girard's theories to his native Ireland, (the late) Frank Wright (1987) argued with examples from some other parts of the world that respect for the law does indeed inhibit the spirals of violence described by Girard *except* those places, such as at the margins of colonial centres or the intersections of conflicting empires, where violent conflict is the most likely due to lack of identification with a common metropolitan centre and commonly respected law. Similarly, benign nationalism or ethnic commitments no doubt are tolerant (as this is what makes them benign) and susceptible to confinement within private realms, but when group identifications are strongly held they are both the least tolerant or amenable to compartmentalization and also the most violence prone.

Group loyalties

Liberal-democratic theorists may be sorted into two broad categories with respect to this problem. Those in one category view it as imperative to combat ethnic and other group identifications, which, within the limited realm of practical action theorists inhabit, means criticizing other theorists whose views are supposed to give aid and comfort to nationalism or ethnic group loyalties. So Hardin devotes nearly a third of his book on ethnic conflict to criticisms of philosophical communitarianism, and many theorists similarly deplore what they see as dangerous particularism in political theories focused on identities. Alternatively, there are theorists who regard such identifications and attitudes as inevitable and seek ways consistent with the perpetuation of strongly held group loyalties to avoid destructive conflict. Some such theorists lament this perpetuation, but seeing it as unavoidable seek ways to head off its potentially violent consequences, either by containment, as in Fukuyama's suggestion, or by devising institutional structures to encourage political compromise and mutual accommodation on the part of national or ethnic group leaders, as Donald Horowitz argues (1985).

Other theorists see nothing essentially pernicious about group loyalties which, as Kymlicka (1995) and Yael Tamir (1993) maintain, are among the things that liberal pluralism ought to accommodate because they are required for individual autonomy or, as more communitarian inclined theorists argue, are partially definitive of people's sense of self and give meaning to their lives. Michael Walzer exemplifies theorists in this latter category. Any solutions to what he laments as the destructive 'new tribalisms' of Eastern Europe and elsewhere must include sympathetic understanding of people's attachment to community traditions and support for efforts of democrats within communities to nurture their traditions' tolerant elements (Walzer 1994: ch. 4). A similar tack is taken by Charles Taylor with respect to national conflicts in Canada, where he believes already existing liberal-democratic values may be found in its Anglo and Franco communities, though expressed and interpreted in different manners; so one way to address conflict between these two communities is to promote mutual recognition of shared values as well as of differences (1993, 1994). Those who find the approaches of Walzer and Taylor appealing must, however, decide whether they may justly be classified as liberal democrats: neither dissents from core liberal and demo-cratic political norms, but each also expresses communitarian and civic republican-like criticisms of mainstream liberal-democratic theory.

Debates between liberal democrats who seek to accommodate group loyal-ties and those who resist any accommodation have dominated much of the theoretical literature about ethnic and national conflict. Their debates are often couched in terms of pro- and anticommunitarian positions, but this is misleading: Kymlicka and Tamir are normative individualists; Horowitz's viewpoint recognizes the strength of ethnic loyalties without endorsing them, and even the more communitarian friendly Walzer and Taylor do not fully endorse philosophical communitarianism. Walzer thinks individuals are more complex than communitarians hold (1994: ch. 5, 1990) and Taylor (1989a) sees virtues and vices in each of individualism and communitarianism.

While Hardin frames his defence of individualism in anticommunitarian terms, he dismisses solutions to ethnic conflict that advocate inculcation in populations of counter-communitarian individualistic values proposed as universal norms. This is because he does not think that self-interested indi-viduals can be motivated by universal values. Though pessimistic that there is any solution to the problem, Hardin opines that widespread 'anomic capi-talism' might encourage pursuit of individual self-interest thus counteracting temptations to make group commitments (1995: 179). Among other prob-lems (Cunningham 1997a) this solution – also suggested by Fukuyama as an alternative to nurturing tolerant nationalism (1994: 26) – runs the risk of meeting one source of conflict by countenancing another, namely unbridled economic competition for scarce resources.

Competition

This, to recall, was the other main charge that democracy is conflict prone. It is unlikely that anomic capitalism, in and of itself, could prevent compe-tition for scarce resources (whether real or artificial) from subverting democ-racy, as the more economically powerful turn democratic procedures and institutions to their advantage or as those who find themselves impeded by democracy ignore democratic constraints (or even kick over the democratic board, as in the Chilean military coup or in Fascist totalitarianism). A pure capitalism, depending upon the invisible hand of a completely free market to create general prosperity, could not avert destructive conflict if it created large inequalities and an ethos of selfish greed before this goal could be reached. Competition requires constraints, of which it seems only two varieties are available: moral and political.

The alternative of promoting universal liberal-democratic values favouring individual freedom or autonomy, equality of access to democratic procedures, pluralism, and tolerance among people engaged in competition for such things as profits or jobs is rejected by Hardin, because he does not think people are capable of being motivated by such values. If, however, they are thus capable, and if a competitive society has undesirable consequences, then it seems that the values can and should be appealed to for the purpose of severely constraining competition. Or, more dramatically, competitive societies should be transformed into cooperative ones in accord with a liberal-democratic socialist alternative.

Those, like Hardin, who think this unrealistic might seek political constraints instead, as urged by Horowitz with respect to ethnically divided societies. Hardin also dismisses this option, at least if the political constraints are to be democratically sustained, since he thinks that things like the Arrow paradoxes (see pp. 22–3) prove democracy an impossibility (1995: 180–1, 1993), but those in a major school of liberal-democratic theory do not share this worry and embrace just such a political alternative. These are the political pluralists, such as Dahl, who, far from seeing conflict as a problem for democracy, believe that democracy properly conceived and conducted is founded on pervasive and unavoidable conflict. Because this school has been so prominent in democratic theory, it merits extended treatment. This will be taken up in Chapter 5.

The empty space of democracy

As observed earlier (see pp. 30–1), liberal-democratic theorists differ regarding their enthusiasm for the democratic dimension of liberal democracy. At a limit of those who are suspicious of democracy is the approach of (the late) William Riker. He describes democracy as 'populism,' which in his view not only requires liberal constraints but stands in opposition to liberalism. On this viewpoint, the danger of what Riker describes as an 'unfettered agent (whether party or president) of the popular will' arises only when populism has overwhelmed liberalism (1982: 251); hence, this is not a problem for liberal democracy but for societies with insufficient liberal constraints on democracy.

Unlike most liberal democrats, Riker does not consider constitutionally protected liberties central to liberalism; rather, he opines that they may only be associated with liberal democracy by historical accident (248). Liberal democracy for him essentially requires only that there are periodic elections so that leaders who act in ways objectionable to enough voters can be turfed out (241–6). Riker too hastily draws his conclusion that regular elections alone solve what is here called the empty space problem, since skilled demagogic officials might be able to persuade a population whose only control over them is the vote that they represent a popular will, but general dissemination of the sparse and merely punitive role of democracy within a political culture would probably forestall such an endeavour. To this end Riker urges general public education in rational choice theory and its treatment of voters' paradoxes and the like in order to make the citizenry 'aware of the emptiness of the populist interpretation of voting' (252).

A difficulty for such an approach is that it purchases protection against demagogy at the price of a Schumpeterian conception of democracy that is too austere for many, probably most, liberal-democratic theorists. For instance, those at the 'thick' side of the liberal-democratic spectrum, such as Mill and Dahl, could not accept Riker's wholesale dismissal of what he calls populism. To the extent that approaches to this problem are implied in their works these would include Mill's efforts to ensure that an electorate is well educated and hence not easily duped and Dahl's insistence that power be dispersed across a wide variety of interest groupings no one of which could therefore claim to be or to represent the people as a whole (hence his description of a properly functioning liberal democracy as a 'polyarchy').

In general, for less austere champions of liberal democracy than Riker, periodic elections would still provide some measure of protection from clearly visible abuses on the part of demagogic officials as would constitutional defences of liberal freedoms and divisions of governmental power, but the problem under consideration would be more pressing, since they allow some version of a notion of popular sovereignty explicitly ruled out in the Schumpeterian accounts and hence open the door to autocratic posturing in its name. One might say that there is a trade-off between the prominence one gives to democracy and risk of demagogic abuse.

A similar trade-off may be seen regarding liberal-democratic viewpoints on the relation between representation and sovereignty. In the UK, political sovereignty is traditionally held to reside in Parliament, whereas in the French and US traditions the people are considered sovereign, and the Assembly or Congress are seen either as agents or as trustees of them. This means that government leaders can more easily present themselves as direct voices of the people in the latter traditions than in the former. Many of those raised in the Commonwealth find it strange that nearly all announcements of positions by politicians in the US are prefaced with some version of the phrase, 'The American people believe that . . .'. At the same time, US citizens are often struck by the extent of parliamentary powers that are neither mandated nor widely questioned by voters in British and similar parliamentary systems.

Irrationality

Riker reviews nearly all the categories of irrationality alleged by social choice theorists to challenge the coherence of democratic decision-making, and he adds to them the susceptibility of a vote to manipulation by agenda setting or strategic voting and the observation that different methods for generating a social decision may yield different results. For instance, a vote by members of the same population among several options can yield different results depending upon whether a series of pair-wise votes is taken or voters assign weights to each of the options, called, respectively, a 'Condorcet' vote and a 'Borda' count, named after the nineteenth-century theorists, the Marquis de Condorcet and Jean-Charles Borda, who anticipated current discussions of such topics. This is because an option could be knocked out of the running in an early vote in a Condorcet series even though it had more points on a Borda count than one that survived the pair-wise voting. Concluding that these considerations render populism 'inconsistent and absurd' Riker argues in favour of jettisoning this dimension of liberal democracy (1982: 238–41).

One category not treated by Riker is abstention from voting by rational free-riding citizens. This might pose a problem for him since the only aspect of democracy he allows (the ability to vote officials out of office) requires that people do in fact vote. But perhaps he could argue that government officials would be kept honest if free-riding resulted in low voter turnout, or even if *nobody* voted, as long as officials feared that just one, irrational non free-rider might show up at a voting booth. Since what is voted for, or more accurately on this viewpoint against, are government officials, not policies, the problem of majorities selecting policies that represent nonmajority viewpoints does not arise. Cyclical majorities are likewise unproblematic for him as long as there is any mechanism for breaking a tie when election of governments is involved.

Some critics of liberal democracy, such as Andrew Levine, also appeal to the paradoxes of collective choice theory to illustrate what they see as essential shortcomings in it. The thrust of such arguments is that liberal democracy is especially vulnerable because its democratic dimension is exclusively concerned to aggregate individual preferences (Levine 1981: ch. 5). In one sense this characterization is accurate. As pluralists, liberal democrats must insist that political policies be formulated in response to people's preferences (even if it is granted that these may sometimes diverge from their interests, wishes, or values), and these preferences are expressed in voting, which is taken in liberal-democratic theory to be central to democracy. However, the characterization is misleading if it is taken to mean that the purpose of democracy for all proponents of liberal democracy is to use vote counting to discover a collective preference. Riker's claim to escape the voters' paradoxes is based on his argument that the aim of liberal-democratic politics is to 'permit people to get rid of rulers' rather than to amalgamate individual values or choices (241–4).

A similar argument is given by Thomas Christiano, but he has a much more robust conception of liberal democracy and its purposes than does Riker. On his view social choice theorists pose grave problems for utilitarian ethical theorists (or at least for those utilitarians who resist ranking individual utilities by reference to standards independent of the individuals' own preference orderings), since their aim is precisely to find a way of aggregating preferences to determine a social policy with the greatest overall utility. However, the goal of the democrat, according to Christiano, is not to maximize social utility, but equally to distribute the ability to participate in collective decision-making about public affairs. A democratic procedure is deficient on this score when it gives some participants an unjust advantage over others in making these decisions, as, for example, control of an agenda, but these deficiencies, unlike the voters' paradoxes when seen as obstacles to aggregating preferences, are in principle capable of being remedied, for instance, by affording participants equal voices in approving an agenda (Christiano 1996: 95–7).

With respect to the sorts of purposes liberal democracy is supposed to serve, Riker and Christiano are representative theorists, very few of whom outside the social choice school of thought identify the aggregation of preferences for this role. Though himself a utilitarian, Mill cites the development of individuals' capacities and the expansion of thought beyond narrow self-interest as a prominent goal of democracy (Mill 1991a [1861]: 226, 229). For Rawls, constitutional democracy is a procedure to be valued for leading, though not necessarily or infallibly, to just decisions (1971: 198–9, 221, 356–62). The main purpose of democracy for Dahl as for most classic pluralists is the peaceful regulation of conflict (1970b [1963]: 62). According to David Held the purpose of liberal democracy for Jeremy Bentham and for James Mill was to ensure economic, market freedom (Held 1996: 94–5). Charles Larmore thinks that democracy is the best means for ensuring that the state remains neutral regarding alternative conceptions of the good life (1987: 130). Carl Cohen produces a long list including wise government, loyal and well informed citizens, material well-being, and peaceful resolution of conflicts (1971: ch. 17). Brian Barry adduces two purposes for democracy: to give people special reasons to obey the law and to select leaders in a peaceful and orderly way (1991a: 24, 53).

A generic liberal-democratic strategy for confronting the irrationality charge can, then, be constructed. Granting that free-riding abstention from political participation, failure of majority voting to yield conclusions favoured by members of a majority, incongruence among alternative voting methods, manipulation of a vote, and cyclical majorities constitute ongoing problems for democratic politics, it is denied that they prove democracy irrational except for those who see it as an essential aim of democratic decision-making to reveal social preferences analogous to those of a single individual. A counter argument is that if majority voting is to figure as an indispensable component of whatever is thought to be the proper purpose of democracy, it must be possible for it to reveal a majority will, but the problems and paradoxes present such intractable obstacles to identifying such a will that they must count as more than practical problems to be resolved in an *ad hoc* manner. It is unlikely that this theoretical debate will soon be over.

Mask of oppression

Like all the important terms in political theory, 'oppression,' 'domination,' 'subordination,' or 'exclusion' admit of alternative definitions, even among kindred theorists (Jaggar 1988: 5–6, 353, Young 1990: 38, ch. 2, Frye 1983), and they are not always synonymous. In this book I shall take sanctioning or masking of oppression as the key problem, because of its structural or systematic nature and because exclusions or subordinations are objectionable when they are oppressive. 'Oppression' is used here and in subsequent chapters to describe the situation of people who unjustifiably endure disadvantages just in virtue of characteristics they share with others in a group identified by gender, class, assigned race, ethnicity, age, sexual orientation, or state of physical ableness, to list prominently discussed categories.

When oppression involves being politically subordinated to the will of members of other groups or excluded from effective participation in political activity, democracy is directly impeded. Or more precisely, whether democracy is impeded depends on one's conception of it. On a Schumpeterian interpretation only withholding the right to vote from someone by virtue of membership in a subordinated group would technically be democracy-impeding. However, with the exception of those liberal-democratic theorists who are the most wary of its democratic dimension, pro-liberal democrats see such things as racial or sexist discrimination that excludes people from forums for pubic debate and discussion or from forming potentially effective political organizations as not just wrong but as undemocratic.

Because oppressive situations are perpetuated in workplaces, schools, and other parts of civil society, many social theorists and activists endorse affirmative action programmes and campaigns for equality of economic opportunity or cultural and educational efforts to attack discriminatory values and nurture mutual respect and tolerance as integral to consistent liberal-democratic politics. Examples are Susan Moller Okin (1989) regarding gender inequality, Anthony Appiah (1994) regarding racism and Norberto Bobbio (1987: ch. 3) regarding class. For these theorists, professed liberal democrats who sanction continuing oppression or subordination are either hypocritical or inconsistent. But others see liberal democracy as essentially supportive of some category of oppression, independently of the attitudes of liberal democrats themselves.

Oppressive disadvantages are structural or systemic, that is, they derive neither from bad luck nor from the deliberate efforts of some to thwart the aspirations or debase the well-being of others but from features of the society in which people are oppressively constrained. The reasons for this are familiar: when, for example, primary household or child care responsibilities fall mainly to women, it will be difficult for them to acquire the skills or take the time to pursue other life occupations; one result is that professions will not be structured to accommodate women, for instance, by failure to provide adequate maternity leave; men and women themselves will internalize and, as parents or through the media and education, pass on stereotypes according to which women are only suited to certain occupations; and a downward spiral keeps women in a subordinate place.

A major charge by theorists addressing the causes and responses to oppression is that efforts to arrest or reverse systemic discrimination are blocked in a liberal democracy by its formality and by its restriction of democratic politics to a public realm. People may have a formal right to run for public office and to be protected against overt and deliberate discrimination, but part of what makes oppression structural is lack of informal resources necessary for taking effective advantage of these rights. By limiting politics to a public realm of formal rights and procedures, it is further alleged, liberal democrats leave intact private realms such as the hierarchically structured workplace and the patriarchal family where oppressive institutions, habits, and attitudes are born and sustained. Feminist theorists have been especially attuned to this problem; some samples are Alison Jaggar (1988: 143–9), Zillah Eisenstein (1981: ch. 2), and Carole Pateman (1987).

It might, with reason, be said that in limiting democratic politics and liberal rights to the public domain of law and formal procedures, liberal-democratic theory does not thereby *condone* oppressive or otherwise objectionable behaviour in private domains. One line of response to this observation depends on historical theories such as those mentioned but set aside in Chapter 3, according to which preservation of oppressive privilege in the face of popular pressure for egalitarian measures was itself a principal motive for distinguishing between a public, political realm and a private, nonpolitical one. This thesis will also be set aside now in the interests of maintaining a focus on specifically theoretical matters. But it should be observed that such an historical thesis is consistent both with the claim that historical motives are complex, so benign motives may have accompanied self-serving ones, and with the notion that in dialectical fashion, liberal-democratic values and institutions can be turned against oppressive practices, even if the former were originally meant to serve such practices. Something like this orientation lies behind Andrew Levine's book, *Arguing for Socialism*, where he maintains that liberal-democratic embrace even of merely formal and narrowly circumscribed equality of opportunity provides grounds to defend much more substantive, egalitarian policies values and policies (Levine 1984).

More directly challenging to champions of liberal democracy, or at least to those of them who believe there are structured oppressions, is that the foe of oppressive relations in the private realm who also advocates state action to reverse or undo these relations will be subject to criticism on liberal democratic grounds for urging public intervention into private domains thus endangering pluralism. To avoid this problem by attempting to make requisite private-realm changes without relying on state intervention assumes not only that intervention is not needed, but also that the state is not implicated in the perpetuation of oppressive arrangements in the private world. One need not be a conspiracy theorist to see that such implication is unavoidable. Ignoring conspiracy suspicions prompted by the fact that virtually anyone who aspires to office in national and many subnational levels of government must be financially backed by large corporations or millionaires, it strains credibility to think that those in high posts in government, held as they are in virtually all liberal-democratic countries by middle- and upper-class males from a country's dominant ethnicity and 'race,' could be both impartial and sufficiently attuned to discriminations endured by others in addressing the sorts of private-domain contests here under consideration.

This concern joins two related worries based on the claim that in a liberal democracy individual rights, universally considered, override efforts to address group disadvantages. Though sometimes expressed indiscriminately with the view earlier discussed that liberal democracy harbours an asocial or atomistic conception of persons, the force of these objections does not hinge on this social-scientific viewpoint but comprises two, more specifically political objections. One of these focuses on the prominent role liberal democracy accords to rights and, within liberal-democratic rights theories, the priority given to individual over group rights. The other objection alleges that the liberal approach to rights as universal is insensitive to group differences.

The first of these worries applies to collective activities aimed at removing oppressive obstacles common to the members of a group often carried on by means other than the courts or the ballot box. Since illegal strikes or acts of civil disobedience aimed at overcoming structural oppressions are not sanctioned by law-enshrined right, they will be regarded (as in Barry's comment about the riots in England referred to in Chapter 3) outside of democracy. And even a legal strike is subject to challenge on the grounds that the rights of some individuals, namely those who wish to cross the picket line, are violated. The main thrust of antioppression theorists' concern about the universalistic nature of rights as conceived by liberal democrats is that it militates against special treatment such as affirmative action programmes in education or employment requisite for addressing systemic disadvantages (Young 1990: ch. 7).

Yet another defence of the charge that liberal democracy sustains structured oppression or subordination harkens to the exclusions referred to earlier by which at various times women, members of 'racial' groups, aboriginal peoples, or the propertyless were denied full democratic citizenship. While these overt exclusions are now largely things of the past, some shadows of them remain, for instance by the denial of full citizenship in many countries to immigrants or to migrant workers. Moreover, the critic alleges, it should be cause for concern that such exclusions were ever justified by professed democrats. Especially troubling is the sparse attention devoted by democratic theorists to racism. (For some exceptions see Smith 1997 and the contributions to Goldberg 2000.)

A radical argument departs from the observation that exclusion of categories of people was justified by denying personhood or full personhood to those excluded and concludes that this resulted from or was made acceptable by concepts of the democratic citizen in political traditions, prominently liberal democracy, informed by the Enlightenment. On one version of this argument the Enlightenment conception of a full person as a rationally autonomous individual was modelled on the putatively self-sufficient entrepreneur and head of a household, or 'bourgeois man' in contrast to the uncivilized (and hence not fully human) communal and traditional aboriginal inhabitants of lands being colonized around the same time (Goldberg 1993: ch. 2, Allen 1994).

Can, or how might, liberal-democratic theory react to these concerns? In keeping with the neoconservative political culture that had become widespread by the end of the 1990s, many doubt there are significant instances of oppression as defined above (because if people are disadvantaged this is regarded as either their own fault or simply a matter of bad luck in the market places of life). Perhaps there are people who consider themselves liberal democrats and think this way, in which case the challenges now under consideration address nonexistent problems. But even a liberal democrat who recognizes that there are systemically disadvantaged groups of people might argue, as Isaiah Berlin did in his insistence, summarized in Chapter 3, that political liberty be thought of narrowly as no more than the ability of people to pursue their aims without interference by the deliberate interference of other people and that to stray from policies and institutions based on formal procedures and universal individual rights and to allow politics to spill out from a narrowly defined public realm is to take the first, fatal steps toward antidemocratic authoritarianism.

There are, however, liberal-democratic theorists who do not fit into either of these categories and who promote ways to combat structured disadvantages. As earlier noted (and to be more fully discussed in Chapter 5) for some years Dahl has been advocating economic redistribution and group-based schemes for democratic representation as preconditions for genuine polyarchy (1985, 1989: pt 6). Similarly, egalitarian measures going beyond formal equality are advocated by Dworkin (1983), Amy Gutmann, drawing on Rawls, (1980), Andrew Kernohan, who appeals to Mill and other classic liberal democrats, (1998), and several others, all as required for liberal democracy. Okin argues in favour of redrawing lines between the public and the private while agreeing 'with mainstream liberal theorists about the need for a sphere of privacy and . . . with the reasons for that need' (1998: 136). Kymlicka defends group-based rights on liberal-individualistic grounds (1995, 2001). The general strategy common to all these approaches is an appeal to *consistency*: sincere liberal democrats should acknowledge impediments to the realization of values they favour and support appropriate means to removing them. Regarding the Enlightenment, this strategy recommends steadfast support of Enlightenment values while exposing hypocrisy on the part of those who sanction racist and other exclusions while claiming to adhere to them.

It is, of course, possible that some or all of these theorists are mistaken about what liberal-democratic theory, even in its more robust forms, can sanction, as is alleged not just by more austere liberal democrats but also by counter-oppressive theorists who are less sanguine about the extent of liberal-democratic theoretical resources. Melissa Williams, for example, points out that Dahl fails to integrate his recent ideas regarding disadvantaged groups with his basic political theory (1998: 77). Anne Phillips queries whether Okin can achieve the libratory aims she seeks within a liberal theory of justice (1993: 63–4). Chandran Kukathas (1992a,b) likewise claims that Kymlicka's group-friendly deployment of individualism fails to protect and may even subvert efforts to maintain group cohesion on the part of those groups whose traditions do not share the liberal value of autonomy by reference to which Kymlicka supports group rights.

It lies beyond the scope of this work to adjudicate among these positions; though it may be worth marking an orientation in political-theoretical methodology according to which someone concerned to combat group oppressions need not exactly choose between doing this entirely within a liberal-democratic framework or entirely in opposition to it. Anne Phillips, who earlier couched her radical views on democracy in terms hostile to liberal democracy, has more recently relaxed this stance on the grounds that liberal-democratic theory is both sufficiently varied and open to change that its wholesale dismissal by the anti-oppressive theorist or activist is unnecessary (Phillips 1993: ch. 6). A stronger suggestion is made by Williams, who concludes her critique of liberal group-blind conceptions of political representation by speculating that her alternative approach 'offers a reconceptualization of autonomy that contributes more than it takes away from liberal views of fairness' (1998: 239), and, referring specifically to socialism, I once endorsed the project (and still do) of 'superseding' liberal democracy in a technical, Hegelian sense where among other things this means reorienting its core elements instead of simply discarding them (Cunningham 1987: ch. 8).

Chapter 5

Classic pluralism

'Whatever the explanation for conflict may be,' Robert Dahl writes, 'its exis-tence is one of the prime facts of all community life' (1967: 6). Dahl is not so much identifying conflict as a problem for democracy as he is situating democracy within the framework of what he sees as unavoidable and perva-sive conflict in political society. Even more, the tone of his discussions suggests that conflict should be welcomed, that, as Seymour Martin Lipset put it, conflict is 'democracy's lifeblood' (1960: 83). Dahl and Lipset reflect the core idea of a school that dominated political theory, at least in the US, for over two decades beginning in the 1950s and, as David Held notes (1996: 202), still infuses journalistic and other non-academic portrayals of demo-cratic politics. The theory comprises both an explanatory and a prescriptive dimension.

Like 'realists' in the Schumpeterian tradition, classic pluralists maintain that their approach to democracy is anchored in truths discovered by empir-ical study. But unlike the Schumpeterians, who take as their point of orientation electoral contests among political parties, pluralists focus on con-flict among a society's 'interest groups,' and their methodology and putative empirical results are in this respect broadly Hobbesist. In Chapter 3, liberal-democratic pluralism was described as permitting individuals as far as possible to pursue their own goods in their own ways. Employing Held's terminology, the pluralist theorists discussed in this chapter are called 'classic,' to differ-entiate them from those who favour this normative pluralism generally (and also from the radical pluralists to be discussed in Chapter 10). This does not mean that classic pluralists, who consider themselves liberal democrats, disagree with normative pluralism, but their main concern is to make recom-mendations about how, consistently with democracy, to maintain stability and peace in conflict-ridden societies. In this respect, the normative dimen-sion of classic pluralism is opposed to the antidemocratic prescriptions of Hobbes and more in keeping with the views of James Madison, to whom these pluralists often refer.

Neo-Hobbesist political sociology

Hobbes began his famous political treatise, *Leviathan*, by applying physical laws of the sort advanced by his early contemporary, Galileo, first to human sensation and thought and then to society and politics. Just as bodies in motion keep moving in a given direction until deflected by encounter with other bodies, so individuals use all their powers to maintain their lives, tempering such use only when this is necessitated by interactions with other individuals motivated in the same way (1968 [1651]: pt 1). The pluralist picture, especially in its earliest expressions, is similar. Societies are composed of conflicting groups, each exercising the powers at its disposal to further interests proper to itself. When political scientists have identified the groups of a society, know their interests (thus also knowing where interests conflict), and have ascertained how much power each group possesses, they can make predictions about group interactions by a sort of vector analysis.

Interest groups

The basic units of analysis in this approach are interest groups, and despite the narrowly empirical pretenses of classic pluralists, the characterization of these groups depends upon contestable and contested theory. An interest group is comprised of people who are organized to pursue interests they share. A theoretical complexity in this apparently simple picture recognized by pluralists themselves is that since the people making up an interest group share some interests (those by reference to which the group is identified) but not others, it is misleading to think of such a group in terms of individuals. For this reason David Truman describes an interest group as 'a standardized pattern of interaction rather than as a collection of human units' (1951: 508, and see the descriptions by the influential forerunner of classic pluralism, Arthur Bentley 1967 [1908]: 176–7, 206–17). A related feature of pluralist theory is highlighted by its focus on interest groups as the basic building blocks of the theory. On this approach individuals can actively enjoy the political efficacy to advance their interests only by engagement with as many organizations as they have different interests. In addition to raising a question about how feasible this is, we shall see that it invites a charge that pluralism restricts the scope for democratic activity to those with access to often costly resources for political organization.

Interests

Another key theoretical concept in pluralist political sociology is 'interest.' By this term, pluralists mean 'subjective interests,' or what Truman prefers to call 'attitudes' (33–6, and see MacIver 1950, and for a behavioristic, or in the terminology of political-scientific empiricists of the time, 'behavioralist' interpretation, Lasswell and Kaplan 1950: 23). Interest groups include chambers of commerce and other organizations of business, trade unions, politically active religious or ethnic organizations, neighbourhood committees, parent-school associations, and other such collections of people explicitly organized to promote specific interests their members recognize themselves as sharing. Excluded are groups defined by reference to structural features of a society, such as economic classes, and/or people said to possess interests of which they may be unaware, for instance in virtue of their gender or ascribed race. In defending this restriction, pluralists often contrast their approach to those that appeal to 'objective interests' charging the latter with having totalitarian tendencies (for instance, Dahl 1967: 17).

The notion of objective interests admits of more than one interpretation. To illustrate two of these, imagine employers who successfully followed Bernard de Mandeville's advice that to enhance productivity and avoid discontent, the working poor should be induced to 'go through the fatigues and hardships' of their labour 'with cheerfulness and content' (1970 [1723]: 294). On one interpretation of objective interests, such labourers would be mistaken to be cheerful and content, because their arduous and subservient positions are out of keeping with a basic human need for meaningful or intrinsically rewarding work and other life activities. In this sense the labourers may be said to possess this need, even though they are unaware of it. A second sense of the term refers to preferences that the labourers *would* have were they in possession of relevant knowledge, for instance, about how their contentment had been cynically manipulated by their employers or about the long-range consequences of acquiescing in arduous labour. (This is the sense most in keeping with Mandeville's advice, which was that to make people happy 'under the meanest circumstances, it is requisite that great numbers of them should be ignorant as well as poor,' *ibid.*)

Appeal to objective interests in the first sense is clearly susceptible to authoritarian abuse, since it can be used for justification of imposed policies on the grounds that this is in the interests people really do have, even if they are unaware of them. The second conception is less subject to abuse since it invites education to provide knowledge that will, presumably, lead people to change their own preferences. But on the assumption that whatever else democracy is, it at least means that policies or leadership are responsive to the preferences that people recognize themselves as having rather than to those somebody else claims they would have under other circumstances, this concept is also subject to antidemocratic paternalism or worse. So the pluralists may well be right to resist appeal to objective interests in formulation of political policy.

This is a topic of ongoing debate among theorists who concern themselves with objective interests and the related concept of false consciousness (for instance, Macpherson 1977, Cunningham 1987: ch. 9, Eagleton 1991, Hyland 1995: ch. 8, and an exchange between Bay and Flathman 1980). However, even if pluralists are right to avoid basing policy recommendations

on objective interests, this does not mean they are also justified in identifying the major units of descriptive or explanatory political theory solely by
reference to subjective interests. Objective interests in one of the two senses
listed – for instance, interests common to all members of an economic class
or a gender – might be or be correlated with causes of individual or group
behaviour which could affect such crucial matters for the pluralist as which
interest groups form or fail to form and how unified and effective they are
at promoting their ends.

A third conception of objective interests does not challenge people's
existing preferences but holds that they might be mistaken about appropriate
means to satisfying them. Brian Barry employs this sense of objective interest
when he criticizes pluralists for leaving too little room for the political recognition and promotion of 'public interests.' Government-enforced price
controls may, for example, be 'in' the interests of workers and manufacturers
alike since it would broaden and secure consumer purchasing power, though
often neither group 'has' an active interest in pressuring for the controls due
to the short-term concern that this would lower wages or profits (Barry 1969).
As will be seen, pluralists provide some room for recognition of public interests in the prominent role they accord to group leaders (who in negotiation
with one another may be expected to seek areas of agreement), but their
main focus is on achieving stability among groups that pursue conflicting
ends rather than on promoting common goals.

Power

Deployment of another important term in pluralist theory, 'power,' exhibits
the same feature of superficial simplicity. Nelson Polsby defines it as: 'the
capacity of one actor to do something affecting another actor, which changes
the probable pattern of specified future events' (1963: 104). While no
pluralist would disagree with this definition as far as it goes, none thinks
that it goes far enough, and a survey of pluralist literature reveals several
supplementations (see Arnold Rose's survey and his own, disappointingly
vague, proposal, 1967: 43–53). Dahl adds that power should be regarded
power over some other persons or group that obliges them to do something
they would not otherwise do (1970b: 32). Harold Lasswell specifies that
power involves getting others to do things against their interests (1948: 229),
and he and others sometimes add that the behaviour induced in others by
the more powerful are the former's choices or decisions (Lasswell and Kaplan
1950: 19, Polsby 1963: 3–4). Steven Lukes sees these as permutations on
what he calls a 'one dimensional' conception according to which power is
no more than a matter of behaviour with respect to specific issues when
there is observable conflict of subjective interests (1974: ch. 2).

A general feature of power conceived this way is what might be called its
'discreteness.' This means, in the first instance, that, like interests, power

attaches to groups independently of their conflicting interactions with one another. Some pluralists recognize complications due to changing coalitions of interest groups where powers are combined (Polsby 1963) or cases where groups have power over each other (Lasswell 1948: 10). But these are ultimately reducible to individual groups each with its unique interests and independently derived power, much as the interactions of physical bodies in Galilean physics are analyzable into each of their velocities, masses, and directions of motion. Uneasily accommodated in this picture, if accommodatable at all, are situations where a group's interests are bred exclusively of its power relations with other groups or where a group derives its power in part from its domination over other groups. Indeed, if a famous analysis by Hegel of the relations between masters and slaves (1949 [1807]: B.iv.a) is credited, a position of inferiority may itself generate power, as the more powerful become dependent on those they dominate.

A related way that power is discrete in pluralist theory is that different sources of power are independent of one another. Thus, in his study of politics in New Haven, Connecticut (a favoured test-case jurisdiction due to the location there of Yale University, where several leading pluralists studied or held teaching positions) Dahl sorts origins of power into four major types – social standing, wealth, the ability to dispense political favours, and control over information – arguing that power made possible by one of these sources does not afford a group general power or automatically give it access to other sources of power. Dahl's main conclusion is that in a democratic community such access is widely dispersed (1961: bk 4). Like Polsby, Dahl concludes that this dispersal of power, combined with a prodemocratic political culture, makes New Haven about as democratic as one could expect a political society to be. It is likely that they would have adduced this town (before it fell on its current hard times of crime and racial strife) as an example toward the 'perfect' end of the democratic scale were they undertaking the exercise in Chapter 1.

Critics of pluralism see these conceptions of power as a failing since they overlook the ways that some sources of power derive from possession of other sources or that some groups owe their power to their positions of domination over other groups with which they are in conflict. Pluralists, by contrast, view the discrete approach to power as an advantage. Conceiving of the sources of power as independent of one another guards against what they consider simplistic, reductionistic, or unicausal accounts of political life, such as are offered in Marxist theory, which most pluralists have taken special effort to denigrate. Like Marxists, however, pluralists see their approach as the rigorous application of scientific method to politics, and in this connection advancing discrete analyses of power can be held important for discovering political-scientific laws (where power and interests are independent variables by reference to which conflict and political responses to it are the dependent variables to be explained).

The Madisonian heritage

In his contributions to *The Federalist Papers* Madison saw factional conflicts as the principal challenge to the new American democracy. 'A zeal for different opinions concerning religion, concerning government, and many other points' as well as class divisions based on a 'landed interest, a mercantile interest, a moneyed interest, with many lesser interests' are unavoidable and have 'divided mankind into parties, inflamed them with mutual animosity, and rendered them much more disposed to vex and oppress each other than to cooperate for their common good' (1987 [1788]: 124, no. 10). As noted in Chapter 2, the goal of federalism (Madison's term for constitutional, representative democracy) is to protect people from the divisive potentialities of conflict by regulating it.

Modern pluralists adopt a more benign view of factional conflict ('democracy's lifeblood') than did Madison, but they agree with him both on the central descriptive claim that it is inevitable and on the prescriptive one that the overriding aim of democratic politics is peacefully to regulate conflict. In some pluralist writings, as of Bentley and Truman, the descriptive and prescriptive views come together in a functionalist picture of societies as unstable equilibriums such that when conflicts among groups do not balance one another and 'disturbances are intense or prolonged' new groups emerge 'whose specialized function it is to facilitate the establishment of a new balance' (Truman 1951: 44 and see Hale, 1969, on Bentley). Like other pluralists, Truman both describes how relative stability is possible – multiple group membership on the part of individuals and wide dispersal of powers prominently figure – and recommends that active measures be taken to protect it. The main agents charged with taking such measures are the state and interest group leaders, who, however, cannot perform their stabilizing functions unless supported by appropriate values in popular political culture.

The state

Pluralists typically use the terms 'state' and 'government' interchangeably to refer to institutions and personnel performing legislative, executive, and judicial functions. According to William Connolly, government in this broad sense is sometimes pictured by pluralists as an 'arena' within which conflict takes place and sometimes as an 'umpire' which intervenes when conflict gets disruptive (1969: 8–13). Though in one of the *Federalist Papers* (no. 43) Madison refers to governments as 'umpires,' he was mainly concerned to explicate and defend the check and balance system laid down in the US Constitution as a structure for containing conflict, so in this way his approach is of the arena sort. Connolly classifies Dahl's view in this vein, and it is advanced as well by Harold Lasswell and Abraham Kaplan for whom the proper function of government or the state is to regulate conflict by rules with institutionalized methods for enforcing them (1950: 188). V.O. Key articulates a functionalistic version of the umpire – or more aptly described 'mediator' – view. When discontent on the part of one or more groups challenges social stability, Key maintains, 'the processes of politics go into operation to create a new equilibrium' and in such a process the 'politician finds himself in the middle – and belabored from all sides – as he seeks to contrive a formula to maintain peace among conflicting interests' (1958: 24). Each of these versions poses a problem for pluralist theory.

Constitutional and other 'arena'-structuring rules that enable the state to regulate conflict do not drop from the sky, but are created by political actors themselves, which for the pluralist are interest groups in conflict. So the question arises about why the most powerful interest groups would not ensure constitutional arrangements biased in their favour, as left-wing historical critics of Madison and other founding fathers of the US Constitution (most famously, Charles Beard 1986 [1913]) maintain actually happened. A reaction to such a challenge implicit in pluralist writings is that there *is* no guarantee that governmental arenas can avoid manipulation subversive of democracy, and whether they do avoid it depends upon a variety of contingencies. Thus Dahl in a chapter of *Democracy and Its Critics* entitled 'Why Polyarchy Developed in Some Countries and Not Others,' produces a list of conditions that are conducive to successful polyarchy (his term for pluralist democracy). These include: high average levels of wealth and economic growth, occupational diversity, a large urban population, numerous interest groups, a political culture favourable to pluralism, freedom from antipluralist foreign intervention, and other such factors (1989: ch. 18). The implication relevant to this problem is that when appropriate conditions are present it is difficult for an interest group to rig rules of the democratic game in its favour and there is less incentive to try than when the conditions are absent.

When political leaders are viewed as umpires, the evident question to ask is why they do not turn their roles to their own advantage or to that of interest groups of which they are members. Addressing this problem with respect to New Haven, Dahl notes, consistently with the 'contingency' approach just described, that sometimes this does occur, and not all cities in the US are as democratic as New Haven (1961: 313). In addition, he identifies a built-in disincentive for 'political entrepreneurs,' as he calls political leaders, to abuse their positions. To attain and keep leadership positions the political entrepreneur must, to be sure, possess a variety of skills, but these skills are of no use unless time is devoted to their exercise: 'the most important resource of the professional is his available labor time' (*ibid.*: 306, italics omitted). Citizens without political ambition also have 'slack' time over and above that needed for subsistence, but most choose not to devote it to political pursuits since for ordinary citizens 'politics is a sideshow in the great circus of life' (305). Dahl's explanation for why politicians do not usurp their positions is that 'nearly every citizen in [a] community has access to unused political resources' (309), specifically slack time, which political entrepreneurs know they will employ should they become very dissatisfied.

Leadership

Madison's contributions to *The Federalist Papers* describe a tension between promotion of popular 'liberty' and political 'stability,' where, for example the former calls for frequent elections, and this threatens the stability afforded by infrequent ones. Allowing that each of these is important, Madison argued against more participatory-democratic compatriots, such as Thomas Jefferson, in favour of less frequent elections (nos 37, 51, 52). Commentators on Madison's ideas are not in accord about just how he thought that this would promote stability. One view (Kramnick 1987: 45) emphasizes Madison's contention that in addition to keeping elected officials honest, 'every political constitution' should aim 'to obtain for rulers men who possess most wisdom to discern, and most virtue to pursue, the common good of society' (1987 [1788]: 343, no. 57). Another is that Madison had a thin conception of public goods at best and thought that elected politicians each of whom represents a specific group interest can maintain peace among groups in their bargaining and negotiations, provided that there are enough different groups represented (Williams 1998: 41–2). On this view it is supposed that relative longevity of legislative service is required for effective negotiation.

Contemporary pluralist treatments of political leadership suggest that these two interpretations can be brought together with respect to one public good, namely stability itself. Despite their group-focused sociology, all the pluralists emphasize the crucial role of leaders. For instance, central to Dahl's analysis of pluralism in New Haven is his distinction among 'leaders,' 'subleaders,' and 'followers' (1961: ch. 3), and Rose similarly employs a core classification of the political world into 'elites,' 'publics,' and 'groups' (1967: 6). In deploying these classifications, the pluralists extend the role of leaders from Madison's elected officials to include as well elected officials of chambers of commerce and unions, traditionally accepted heads of religious groups, and informally recognized spokespeople for ethnic or neighbourhood associations, and they also emphasize the importance of leaders internal to interest groups, as in Truman's account of how leaders maintain group cohesion (1951: 156–7). The prominent place pluralist theory gives to group leaders prompts Peter Bachrach to label it a species of 'democratic elitism' (1967). Pluralists do not see themselves in this light, as among their targets are the political and sociological 'elitists' both of the right (Gaetano Mosca, Vilfredo Pareto) and of the left, especially C. Wright Mills.

Political culture

Madison and the other authors of *The Federalist Papers* (Alexander Hamilton and John Jay) produced this work to defend the Constitution of 1787 against those who thought that in removing or weakening powers invested in individual states by the earlier Articles of Confederation, it gave too much authority to the federal government. Madison in particular pleaded that the Constitution's system of checks and balances among the legislative, executive, and judiciary branches of government and its bicameral congress offered protection against abuse of central-government power. However, in addition to these structural measures he cites the 'genius of the people of America, the spirit which actuates the State legislatures, and the principles which are incorporated with the political character of every class of citizens' as safeguards against federal 'tyranny or treachery,' which he could not imagine being permitted by the American people given their values (1987 [1788]: 337, no. 55).

In his *Preface to Democratic Theory* (1956), which introduces the core ideas of pluralist theory in the form of a commentary on the views of Madison, Dahl picks up on and more strongly emphasizes the latter's references to democracy-friendly political-cultural values, specifically noting the importance of broad consensus on them by members of otherwise competing groups (132–5). This emphasis, echoed by other pluralists, invites two challenges: that the values required for a properly functioning 'polyarchy' are inconsistent with the neo-Hobbesist theory of human nature employed in pluralist political sociology, and that it supposes a more politically engaged citizenry than pluralists recognize. One way to meet the first challenge would be to mute a Hobbesist conception and allow that in some times and places and for any of a variety of happy circumstances it is possible for the bulk of a population to be motived by genuine adherence to democratic values. Alternatively, it may be urged that it is of paramount importance for citizens to place a common value on political stability. This approach is most in accord with Madison's perspective, within which stability takes precedence over liberty, and it is also consistent with Hobbes' view according to which political authority generally is motivated by the desire to avoid perpetual conflict.

Some who criticize pluralist theory for sanctioning apathy (for instance, Macpherson 1977: 87–8, Held 1996: 204–5) acknowledge that this criticism is not seen as damaging by pluralists themselves, who believe a certain degree of public apathy is *unavoidable* (since, as Dahl notes in connection with his study of New Haven, political activity and engagement requires investment of time that not everyone is prepared or able to make) and democratically *acceptable* as long as people have the ability to vote should they be motivated to do so. Some pluralists consider a large measure of apathy in addition as *desirable* on the grounds they share with Schumpeter that widespread political participation unduly constrains political leaders and endangers social and political stability (Berelson, *et al.* 1954: ch. 14, Lipset 1960: 14–16). As will be seen in Chapter 7 on participatory democracy, acceptance, much less sanctioning, of political apathy is enough for some to dismiss this theory. Pluralists, themselves, do not share the participationist enthusiasm for universal political engagement and, in addition to requiring only that prodemocratic values be passively held, they need only insist that it is important for a minority of political activists to be motivated by them (see Dahl 1989: 264).

Pluralism and problems of democracy

The principal strength pluralists claim for their approach to democracy is that it directly addresses the problem of conflict and prescribes democratic forums to accommodate it. Some critics of this orientation, most emphatically participatory and deliberative democrats, see this orientation as at best pessimistic about prospects for overcoming conflict and at worst promotive of it. They and other critics also charge that classic pluralism is itself *implicated* in current-day conflicts by being biased in favour of the 'interest group,' big business. Subsequent chapters will survey pertinent views of participatory and deliberative democrats; the bias charge will be summarized later in this chapter.

First, another sort of criticism needs to be registered, namely that while pluralism may be able to accommodate conflicts among the multitude of a society's shifting and cross-cutting interest groups, it lacks resources for addressing persisting conflicts arising from such things as national or religious differences that divide entire populations. In more recent writings Dahl recognizes polyarchy-threatening conflicts that beset a society when it is 'segmented into strong and distinctive subcultures,' but maintains that pluralist democracy is still possible provided 'its leaders have succeeded in creating a consociational arrangement for managing subcultural conflicts' (1989: 263). This important tendency deserves more extended treatment than the other summary reactions to problems.

Consociational democracy

This approach evolved out of the practice in certain countries of Europe – the Netherlands, Austria, Belgium, and Switzerland – initially to find governmental forums and practices to accommodate their Catholic and Protestant populations and adopted to secular divisions as well, as between liberals and social democrats. The term was coined by the theory's major proponent, Arend Lijphart, who mainly defends it with reference to his experiences in the Netherlands (1968, and see the application to other countries in McRae 1974). Whether Dahl should be seen as extending classic pluralist theory to encompass consociational democracy, or the latter is sufficiently different from pluralism to be regarded an independent theory that might supplement it, is a matter of judgment.

Like classic pluralists, consociational democrats propose their theory as a realistic way to accommodate unavoidable conflicts, and they see its overriding goal to maintain peace and stability. Also like classic pluralism, leaders play an essential and important role in simultaneously promoting special interests of their constituencies and negotiating with one another to preserve the peace. Moreover, some of the conditions seen by consociational democrats as crucial for success in achieving their aims are those listed as well by classic pluralists. Thus, the 'cross cutting cleavages' that Lijphart identifies, such that, for instance, religious divisions do not coincide with class divisions (1977: 75–81), play the same role as what Truman designates 'multiple group membership.'

At the same time, there are differences between the two theories. Most importantly, the 'groups' consociational-democratic theory addresses – all a country's Catholics, those with social-democratic political values, and so on – are larger and less internally homogenous even with respect to their group-specific interests than prototypical pluralist interest groups, such as chambers of commerce or neighbourhood organizations. While the mainly US classic pluralists see their view as especially compatible with the presidential federalism advocated by Madison, the European Lijphart thinks that parliamentary democracy can be more easily accommodated to consociational practices and structures (1977: 33). (Though he also sees possibilities for elements of consociational democracy in the US, as in the model of 'concurrent majorities' proposed in the nineteenth century by John Calhoun 1953 [1850].) Further, while Lijphart agrees with the classic pluralists that diverse groups in a society must share some common commitments, he cites nationalism and even loyalties to a monarch (1977: 81–3, 33) instead of the republican values pluralists uphold for this purpose. In summarizing consociational democracy in this section, then, I do not mean to imply that it is simply a form of classic pluralism (indeed, Lijphart himself classifies it as a species of 'consensus' theory, 1984: preface). Still, the approach shares sufficient similarities to make Dahl's appeal to it consistent with his deployment of pluralist theory.

In a concise explication and defence of consociational democracy Lijphart (1977) pictures it as a model of democratic governance where 'the political leaders of all significant segments of the plural society cooperate in a grand coalition to govern the country' and contrasts it with an 'adversarial' or 'government-versus-opposition' model (25). Three principles ensure joint governing by 'segment' leaderships: on major matters of common concern each has veto power; representation in governing bodies is proportional to the size of the segment's population in the country (examples he gives include the Swiss Federal Council and the Austrian Cabinet); and autonomy is 'segmented' such that leaders have exclusive or heavily weighted authority over matters especially affecting the populations they represent (36–47). Lijphart anticipates main criticisms of this arrangement – that it threatens democracy by entrusting too many matters to the discretion of segment leaders, that veto power can be abused, that it can lead to stalemate or to partition of a country – by acknowledging these tendencies while arguing that there are ways of counteracting them and that in any case under 'the unfavorable circumstances of segmental cleavages, consociational democracy, though far from the abstract ideal, is the best kind of democracy that can realistically be expected' (48).

It is probably in this spirit that Dahl endorses consociational democracy: not as a generally applicable theory but as a prescription for maintaining stability in societies divided by 'strong and distinctive subcultures' (Dahl 1989: 264). Thus conceived, Brian Barry criticizes consociational views for what he sees as a contradiction. Reaching accord on consociational arrangements and sustaining ongoing mutual accommodations among group leaders is impossible in a deeply divided society, but it is for just such societies that consociational democracy is devised; so when consociational democracy is feasible it is not needed (1991a: ch. 5). Lijphart turns this challenge around by agreeing that 'a moderate attitude and a willingness to compromise' are required for consociational arrangements and maintaining that the very prospect of joint participation in government stimulates these attitudes by providing 'an important guarantee of political security' among parties 'that do not quite trust each other' (1977: 30). It is unlikely that theoretical considerations alone can determine whether Barry or Lijphart is right on this issue, and it is also unlikely that consociational democracy is equally realistic regarding all divided societies. It remains, however, a candidate for pluralists, as for other democratic theorists who address the problem of large-scale national or ethnic conflict.

Majority tyranny and the empty space

Returning now to the other problems and pluralist responses, the tyranny of the majority and the empty space problems may be treated together. A common solution to both these problems in classic pluralist theory might be seen as a version of Schumpeterianism, albeit one that is more democratically robust than that of Schumpeter himself. It will be recalled from the discussion in the introduction that he reconceptualized democracy to void it of the two pillars of the previously dominant notions of democracy, popular sovereignty and the public good. Majorities regarding some policy (or even entire populations in the rare circumstance that there is consensus among them) are in fact heterogeneous constellations of individuals or groups who may sometimes share common goals or visions of a single public good but who much more often have diverse motivations for agreeing on policy matters. In a society where people generally recognized this feature of 'popular will,' it would be impossible for anyone to claim to speak for 'the people as a whole,' since citizens would not believe that there is anything to represent.

Schumpeter's view about the heterogeneity of 'the people' applies also to majorities. Accordingly, it differs from Tocqueville's image of a majority as 'an individual with opinions, and usually with interests, contrary to those of another individual, called the minority' (1969 [1835–40]: 251), and it is shared by the pluralists, for whom, as Truman puts it, the 'pattern of government' is 'a protean complex of criss-crossing relationships that change in strength and direction with alterations in the power and standing of interests' (1951: 508). Focussing on situations where 'a relatively intense minority prefers an alternative opposed by a relatively apathetic majority' (1956: 119), Dahl allows that purely constitutional safeguards cannot prevent this form of majority tyranny, but he thinks that nonetheless minorities have means at their disposal to constrain majorities by threats 'to engage in "abnormal" political behavior' or to win over factions of majorities by appeal to the conditions for pluralist legitimacy (*ibid.*: 138). Like Truman, he thinks that this is made easier for minorities due to the fact that strictly speaking there is no such thing as a majority, which is only 'an arithmetic expression' applicable when several different minority interests converge in a vote, so what democracy really involves is 'minorities rule' (*ibid.*: 132–46, and see Held's elaboration, 1996: 201–8).

Truman and Dahl differ from Schumpeter, who recommended reducing citizen participation simply to voting, in urging an active role in politics (that is, power politics among interest groups) for nongovernmental agents. The difference between dictatorship and democracy in Dahl's formulation is between 'government by a minority and government by minorities' (*ibid.*). So the more competing interest groups there are, with their shifting coalitions and membership overlaps, the more secure democracy will be. One problem with this solution, to which critics have called attention (as for instance, Hyland 1995: 90), is that it depends upon the dubious belief that constellations of minorities will not foster permanent exclusion of other minorities and that pluralists lack theoretical resources for addressing such situations when they do arise. The solution also involves a bit of tightrope walking if it is to be brought into alignment with pluralist views on democratic culture and on the role of group leaders.

One might imagine a group leader justifying predominance of one group by claiming that it best embodies truly pluralist values. This would include, and indeed especially so, the preeminent pluralist value of stability, which is not infrequently appealed to by would-be authoritarians. To avert such a danger by pluralist recognition of the importance of values shared across interest groups, as Dahl suggests, stains the hard-headed, Hobbesist dimension of classic pluralist that attracts many to it. To prescribe meeting the authoritarian challenge by encouraging more participation could place more emphasis on general citizen activism than pluralists consider realistic or, since this can diminish the role of leaders, desirable. Critics might see here damaging inconsistencies in pluralist theory, ones, moreover, that also affect pluralist ability to address the 'effectiveness' problem (since leadership and cohesive values are required to for commonality of purpose in pursuing society-wide tasks). Pluralists themselves would most certainly see tensions endemic to democracy that are simply to be recognized and managed as skilfully as possible in actual political activity and policy formation.

Mask of minority domination

The most persistent and systematic criticisms of classic pluralism have come from the political left and have focused on its empirical claim that power in the US is widely dispersed. This is the task that William Domhoff set himself in a criticism of Rose (1970: ch. 9). He partly frames his challenge as a defence of C. Wright Mills' claim that the US is run by a 'power elite' (Mills 1956) against criticisms of Mills by the pluralists (Domhoff 1967: ch. 7). A demonstration that political power in the US is concentrated in a few hands certainly challenges classic pluralist empirical claims to the contrary, but by itself it does not disprove the pluralist theory of democracy, which only holds that dispersal of power is necessary for democracy not that power in every society calling itself democratic is in fact dispersed. It is for this reason that some have seen Mills' theory not as an alternative to pluralism, but as a special-case application of it where one interest group possesses a disproportionately large amount of power (Balbus 1971).

One way to strengthen the specifically theoretical aspect of this criticism is to argue not just that pluralism's analysis of democracy in the US is empirically flawed, but that its conception of democracy generally is parochially limited. David Held advances this criticism when he maintains that pluralist identification of democracy with power politics in Western countries means that questions that 'have been part of democratic theory from Athens to nineteenth Century England' such as the appropriate extent of citizen participation are 'put aside, or, rather, answered merely by reference to current practice' (1996: 209). Another criticism is that of E.E. Schattschneider who argues that in limiting itself to the analysis of pressure groups, pluralists are bound to arrive at a skewed picture of democratic politics, since relatively few can direct the requisite time or other resources into this activity: 'The flaw in the pluralist heaven is that the heavenly chorus sings with a strong upper-class accent. Probably 90 per cent of the people cannot get into the pressure system' (1960: 35).

In a critique of pluralism much cited by its detractors in the mid-1960s, (the late) Christian Bay linked the theory to the empiricist pretensions of the 'behavioralists.' Both schools, according to Bay, had lost sight of what is essential to politics, namely the articulation and defence of 'some conception of human welfare or the public good' and instead concerned themselves with 'pseudo-political' empirical studies of use only for 'promoting private or private interest group advantage' (Bay 1965: 40). A fourth criticism, levelled by Peter Bachrach and Morton Baratz, is that in focusing on the exercise of power, rather than analyzing its sources, pluralists overlook the way that power often resides in limiting the scope of interests that can get expressed in political arenas and provides no objective criteria 'for distinguishing between "important" and "unimportant" issues' (1969: 53–4).

Dahl's odyssey

A possible test case for helping to decide whether pluralism is endemically complicit in economic oppression is the development of Robert Dahl's thought, which has changed from an anti- or at least nonsocialist bent in the 1950s to some form of socialism in subsequent decades. A hint of this change can be seen by comparing his criticism of Marx as the 'prophet' of a cumulative theory of power in the 1963 publication of his *Modern Political Analysis* (78) with this book's second edition in 1970 from which this and most of the other explicit criticisms of Marxism are excised. Most striking is the contrast between *A Preface to Democratic Theory* (1956) and *A Preface to Economic Democracy* (1985).

In the first book Dahl cites Madison's famous claim in the *Federalist Paper* no. 10 that human societies are bound to be divided into factions, and he agrees with Madison that it is possible only to deal with the effects of factions, not to eliminate them at their source. Madison himself does not profess ignorance of the causes of factions but declares that 'the most common and durable sources of factions has been the various and unequal distribution of property' (1987 [1788]: 124). His justification for not attacking factionalism at its most common and durable source by equalizing property is that this would be an 'improper or wicked project' (128) since government has as 'its first object' protection of the diversity in men's faculties from which 'the possession of different degrees and kinds of property immediately results' (124). Dahl does not treat these views in his 30-page, axiomatically formal summary of Madison's arguments. In fact, in a later book when he extensively quotes from Paper no. 10, Dahl replaces the passage about unequal property being the most common source of factions with three omission dots (1967: 5–6).

In striking contrast, Dahl's *A Preface to Economic Democracy*, published in 1985, centrally addresses economic sources of inequalities in political resources, chief among which is 'ownership and control of firms' which 'contribute to the creation of great differences among citizens in wealth, income, status, skills, information, control over information and propaganda, access to political leaders' among other things, and these differences help 'to gener-ate significant inequalities among citizens in their capacities and opportuni-ties for participating as political equals in governing the state' (54–5, italics omitted). Moreover, contrary to Madison, he argues against the view that 'private property is a fundamental right' (82), so egalitarian constraints on property are not 'wicked,' and he devotes about half the book to describing a 'self-governing equal order' (a form of workers self-management) and defend-ing it as a realistic way to achieve economic egalitarian conditions conducive to democracy.

Assuming that mainstream classic pluralism is subject to the characteri-zations by antioppressive critics listed above, it may now be asked whether Dahl's recent writings escape these criticisms and do so in such a way that his theory can still be considered pluralist. It should be noted, however, that Dahl's socialist conversion is not unambiguously complete. Four years after writing A Preface to Economic Democracy he again cites the problems that economic inequalities pose for democracy, but maintains that its prospects are 'more seriously endangered' by political inequalities 'derived not from wealth or economic position but from special knowledge' (1989: 333). This stands in tension with the Preface passage which names the 'economic posi-tion,' ownership of firms, as a source of inequalities in information and control over it, which are surely central to acquiring relevant 'special knowl-edge.' Such wavering can be interpreted in different ways pertinent to the question at hand: Dahl may have become aware that he was straying too far from pluralist theory and corrected for it (evidence that in his eyes the theory is incompatible with an anticapitalist politics), or he may have been genuinely ambivalent over whether to adopt one or the other of two polit-ical stances, both of which are compatible with the core theory he has been instrumental in propounding.

On my reading, the issue of whether classic pluralism must support procap-italist exclusions destructive of democracy is inconclusive. Starting with the claim of Bachrach and Baratz that pluralism has these consequences due to ignoring or down playing the sources of interest group power, it is clear that at least in his later writings Dahl does not ignore such sources, even if he is ambivalent about their causal interrelations. So this marks a departure if agnosticism about sources is definitive of classic pluralism (and if, of course, identification of structured, antidemocratic inequalities and other forms of exclusion requires investigation into sources).

As to Bay's claim that pluralists abjure conceptions of the public good, Dahl's 1989 book, Democracy and its Critics stands as a possible counter example, since this is a recurring theme in it. His view, in brief, is that common goods are the informed interests that individuals share and that 'the rights and opportunities of the democratic process are elements of the common good' because informed people would realize that these are neces-sary, among other things, for them to gain the enlightenment required to know what is in their interests (306–8). In one respect, this conception is close to that of the classic pluralists, since there is no guarantee that even informed interests will converge on substantive goals shared by all members of a society, as the 'traditionalists' whom Dahl criticizes (ch. 20) would have it. Whether Dahl's reliance on informed interests is also compat-ible with classic pluralism depends upon how far it is thought to depart from the latter theory's focus on subjective interests. On the one hand, the concept is rooted in subjective interests, since informed interests are people's subjective ones plus those they would have and minus those they would not were they properly informed. On the other hand, Dahl is clearly employing one concep-tion of 'objective interests' as summarized above, and although it is arguably the most innocuous version, pluralists, including Dahl himself in earlier writings, typically avoid accommodation of objective interests in any form.

Determination by pluralists to maintain their empirical, 'realist' creden-tials probably does impede speculation about institutions and the articulation of visions very far removed from the actual democratic practices and values they see in their countries, thus opening them to Held's parochialism charge. However, this does not preclude their taking a broader view of what those practices and values are than was typical of their early writings. Thus Dahl appends an epilogue to his book on economic democracy by speculating about whether its recommendations might receive a sympathetic hearing from his compatriots in the US. He concludes that this is hard to predict since they are 'torn between two conflicting visions of what American society is and ought to be,' where one is of 'the world's first and grandest attempt to realize democracy, political equality, and political liberty' while the other is of 'a country where unrestricted liberty to acquire unlimited wealth would produce the world's most prosperous society' (162). As in the case of Dahl's interpretation of interests, this conception strains the neo-Hobbesist theory of human nature on which classic pluralist political sociology is modelled, but perhaps it can be made to fit within it.

Dahl's proposal of a system of self-governing firms is partly advanced to expand the number of people who can be politically active, both within their workplaces and in broader political arenas thanks to resources and expe-rience gained in the firms. This is one way that he addresses the criticism of pluralism that it sanctions narrowing access to democratic politics to those who have the time and resources to be parts of interest groups. Here, he may be on stronger classic pluralist ground. It is true that the theory's neo-Hobbesist *descriptive* theory remains confined to existing interest groups (though Truman wished to introduce 'potential groups' into this dimension of pluralism, 1951: 51, 505), but on its Madisonian, *prescriptive* side there is nothing to prevent making recommendations for ways to multiply interest groups and access to them, since this is the surest way to guarantee stability. Where there may be a problem is in the intersection of pluralist descriptive and prescriptive theory. If, in keeping with the functionalism expressed by some pluralists, it is assumed that destabilizing power imbalances will adjust themselves, recommendations for corrective group activity should not be necessary.

This problem is viewed as especially severe by Melissa Williams. Liberal democracies such as the US depend upon the joint functioning of an equal franchise and interest-group competition, where the former provides formal democratic equality for individuals and the latter ensures group-sensitive equity in securing just governmental representation of citizen interests. Essential to achieving this goal is that equity-challenging, oppressive injustices will prompt the formation of politically active interest groups by disaffected people. In her *Voice, Trust, and Memory*, Williams cites Schattschneider and argues that inequality of resources, especially money, renders such action impossible for groups of people whose unjust circumstances, for instance due to ethnic, racial, or gender discrimination, denies them both access to governmental representation and the resources necessary to break into the ranks of established interest groups (1998: ch. 2). Her critique is not just of classic pluralism but of 'liberal representation' generally, to which she sees pluralism as integral. Accordingly, a discussion appended to this chapter is an appropriate place to survey some discussions by democratic theorists about representation.

DISCUSSION: REPRESENTATION

Bernard Manin, Adam Przeworski, and Susan Stokes probably reflect the stance of most authors who address the question of representation in assuming that, if for no other reason than the size and complexity of modern societies and for better or for worse, representative democracy 'is our form of government' (1999: 1). Their aim and that of the other authors included in their collection on this topic, is to identify features of electoral systems that defeat responsiveness and accountability of representatives to an electorate. These treatments implicate abstract debates over the meaning of the term 'representation' itself, and they call to mind concrete recommendations by feminists and other social activists for opening representative institutions to previously excluded categories of people. In this discussion, primary attention will be devoted to these two topics, but first it should be registered that not all theorists take it for granted that representation is democratically acceptable.

For and against representative democracy

Democracy, according to Andrew Levine, crucially involves 'choosing for oneself among alternative options for collective choice' on the part of all citizens; so 'the transformation of the citizen from direct legislator to conferrer of consent upon the choices of others, fundamentally violates' democracy (1981: 150). A prodemocrat from the Rousseauean left, Levine sees this transformation as essential to a liberal-democratic agenda where matters of vital common interest have been increasingly removed from the realm of collective decision-making and consigned to the tender mercies of a capitalist-dominated market. An analogous criticism, but coming from the extreme right, was that of Carl Schmitt. He also set democracy against liberalism, which he saw as based on contradictory principles. The ideal of democracy is thoroughgoing self-determination by a collective of people, which requires homogeneity of values among them; while the liberal principle assumes heterogeneous values and opinions. Parliaments in Schmitt's view are nothing but liberal arenas in which contesting viewpoints are argued over with the (stated if always frustrated) aim of discovering some truths in the process. Because they are premised on heterogeneity, parliaments cannot represent homogenous democratic publics and the pretense to do so impedes formations of the latter (1988 [1923]: ch. 2).

David Beetham allows that representation 'constitutes a substantial surrender or diminution of citizens' autonomy,' but he further maintains: that this is unavoidable due to the impossible demands that direct participation would place on their time; that by focusing debate on issues of broad and pressing concern elections have the advantage of inviting and coordinating public political activity; and that disadvantages of representation can be compensated for by equalizing resources needed for access to representative forums and by the measures for opening them to politically excluded groups urged by the pro-social activist theorists shortly to be discussed (1993: 63–6). A similar defence is offered by Carol Gould, who argues that democratic 'authority' may be devolved on representatives by members of a political society provided it is 'instituted, delimited, and revocable by the members themselves, and is exercised in their interests' (1988: 225). In criticizing Schmitt, Chantal Mouffe maintains that parliamentary representation can be made consistent with democracy provided some measure of concurrence on broadly defined democratic values can be achieved in each domain while acknowledging that democratic publics, no less than representative assemblies, are marked by unemendable conflict (1993: ch. 8). Chapter 7 will pursue debates between representative and participatory democrats; in Chapter 10 the views of Schmitt and Mouffe will be further discussed.

The nature of representation

As with many other core conundrums of democratic theory, the question about how properly to conceive of representation was well put by John Stuart Mill: 'Should a member of the Legislature be bound by the instructions of his constituents? Should he be the organ of their sentiments, or of his own? their ambassador to a congress, or their professional agent, empowered not only to act for them but to judge for them what ought to be done?' (1991a [1861]: 373). Mill is here expressing what Hanna Pitkin calls the 'mandate-independence controversy' (1967: 145), sometimes also expressed as the question of whether elected representatives should function as 'delegates' or as 'trustees' for those who elected them.

Though tangled up with his suspicion of the ability of ordinary voters to make wise decisions and his concomitant recommendation of voting rules to ensure election of a large number of educated representatives, Mill's prescribed solution was to nurture a 'political morality' that gives wide discretion to representatives to act as they think is in the best interests of their constituencies. To this he added the important provisions that representatives should honestly represent their viewpoints to voters and be ultimately accountable to them (especially to poor voters who would not likely have many from their own ranks in a government) and that on matters involving 'fundamental convictions' or basic political and social philosophies (Tory or Liberal, Churchman or Rationalist, and so on) voters should select representatives as mandated delegates and not as trustees with a large scope for independent judgment (1991a [1861]: ch. 12).

Pitkin's classifications

Pitkin defends an interpretation akin to that of Mill in her *The Concept of Representation*, a book often referred to due to its skilful deployment of linguistic analysis and its wealth of historical applications. Her basic classification (1967: ch. 3) provides a useful picture of some ways to conceptualize representation (see Figure 2).

Formal conceptions of representation address the relation between representative and represented abstractly and have two emphases depending upon whether those represented authorize a representative to act for them or representatives are accountable to those they are to represent (or both, since the categories are not mutually exclusive). Pitkin gives as an example of a pure 'authorization' theorist, Hobbes, for whom a contract between citizens and government leaders empowers the latter to govern as they see fit. An example

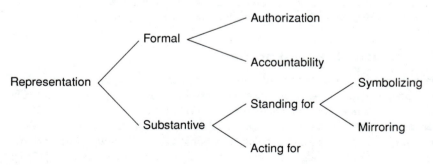

Figure 2

of a pure accountability theorist (though not one Pitkin cites) would be Riker, for whom the principal relation government officials have with a public is that they may be voted out of office in an election and in this sense are accountable. Pitkin favours a combination of authorization and accountability, but by themselves she considers these formal notions insufficiently concrete for useful application in actual politics.

Hence she adds two 'substantive' categories. In the category, 'standing for,' either representatives are considered as a 'symbol' of a constituency, as the Pope is of the Church or a king is of his country, or representative bodies are a 'miniature of the people at large' (ibid.: 60, quoting John Adams). Pitkin sees the latter way that representatives may stand for a constituency (also called 'mirroring' or 'descriptive' by her) as more relevant to modern democracies than symbolic representation. It often informs those who complain that a representative assembly does not reflect categories of people in a population (for instance, having few or no women to stand for their 51 per cent of the population or being overloaded with people from the upper and middle classes). Her other main substantive category ('acting for') looks not to who representatives are but to what they do. Pitkin thinks that this category is the best suited for thinking about political representation, but she also recognizes that it confronts the 'mandate-independence controversy,' since representatives may act for citizens as delegates and hence be bound to follow their instructions or as trustees, whose 'acting for' is a matter of doing what they think best for those they represent.

The scope of representation

This controversy is better described, Pitkin maintains, as a paradox embodied in the very conception of 'representation,' where there is something represented, but at the same time that which does the representing must have characteristics of its own. Hence, the best one can do is establish limits to political representation to determine its proper scope. This means ruling out situations at one extreme where someone is in fact no better than an oligarch whose actions are unrelated to the wishes of a constituency and those at another where the representative is simply a tool, with no room for independent discretion.

To ascertain the scope of representation within these broad limits Pitkin invokes as guidelines that representatives be free to exercise discretion, but that they strive to do so in the interests of their constituents, who for their part are thought of as also capable of independent judgment and not just as charges to be taken care of. Since the (objective) interests of people and their (subjective) wishes tend to coincide, representatives ought not to stray too far or too often from constituents' wishes, but when they do persistently stray they are obliged to explain and justify this to the constituents (ch. 7, and the summary at 209–10). In making judgments about whether the right balance between delegation and trusteeship has been struck, there is room for further theoretical debate, especially between those with more or less 'objective' conceptions of interests (Pitkin discusses Edmund Burke and James Madison).

Pitkin's views on this matter are not uncontested. One problem is to decide what is a matter of theoretical debate *within* the limits of proper representation and what is a debate over these limits. An example is a difference between Mill and Pitkin regarding basic values of one's social philosophy. Mill wanted to exempt such 'fundamental convictions' from representative discretion, but these are, presumably, among the things subject to theoretical debate within acceptably representationalist viewpoints for Pitkin. Of course, there could also be debate about what exactly constitutes a fundamental conviction on Mill's account. A response by Thomas Christiano is that legislative representatives should engage in far-reaching deliberation about *means* to socially determined ends, but that with respect to the ends themselves, they should act as citizens' delegates (1996: 215–19).

For Christiano, this means that representation with respect to social goals is a matter of being mandated by an electorate to deliberate (including to negotiate) with other representatives about the best means to carry out voters' chosen ends. Because different voters will often favour different ends, this raises a question about what Christiano calls the 'object of responsibility' of a representative, which might be those who voted for him or her, or all those in the representative's voting district, or all the society's citizens (214–15). Assuming that it is clear what the mandated end is, it will also be clear on his view that representatives should be responsible to those who voted for them to carry out that mandate. This is feasible in practice, he thinks, if people vote for political parties, each running on platforms that conform to alternative ends, and if seats allocated to a legislative assembly are proportional to the percentage of votes received by each party (227–9).

Christiano's view is in tension with that of Pitkin, for whom proportional representation is a form of the static 'standing for' conception to which she opposes her active view of representation (1967: 60–6). It is also in tension with critics of 'mandated' conceptions of representation generally, such as Przeworski. Drawing on the same decision-theoretical literature that, as noted in Chapter 4, made William Riker sceptical about discerning a popular will (and hence identifying mandates) and noting that in 'no existing democracy are representatives subject to binding instructions' (1999: 35), Przeworski recommends rejecting a 'mandated' concept of representation for the 'accountability' conception according to which a government is deemed to have represented a public if it survives a test of re-election (1999, and see the introduction to the 1999 collection he coedited with Manin and Stokes and their lead article in it). This criticism of proportional representation is, it should be noted, by no means similar to that of Pitkin, whose views Przeworski regards as 'incoherent' because, while representation for her requires conformity of representatives' actions to citizens' interests, she rejects the only two methods he allows for ascertaining this conformity, namely government action in accord with voters' instructions or electoral survival (1999: 33).

The objects of representation

Yet another aspect of attempts to characterize representation concerns the question of *what* should be represented. For Pitkin the objects of representation are people's interests, but interests may be held by different sorts of agents. As Ross Harrison reports, in classic Whig thinking interests were held by social groupings (one thinks of mercantile interests, agricultural interests, and so on), thus putting them at odds with utilitarians such as Bentham and James Mill for whom interests were held by individual people (Harrison 1993: 100). It might be thought that group interests can always be analyzed into individual interests, but (in keeping with Truman's concerns on this score) to do this would lose sight of the interests specific to a group, and it is these interests, rather than the very large number of interests that might be held by any one individual, to which, on Truman's view, democratic political policies and actions can and should be sensitive.

Whatever is taken as the bearer of interests, it is not clear just what interests are (as this discussion of objective interests should make clear) or that interests are the only or most important objects for democratic representation. Thus, Iris Young distinguishes among *interests* ('what affects or is important to the life prospects of individuals, or the goals of organization'), *opinions* (a person's 'principles, values, and priorities'), and *perspectives* (in virtue of which 'differently positioned people have different experience, history, and social knowledge') (2000: 135–6). All of these objects merit representation, according to Young, but each in its own way. In particular, while 'liberal principles of free speech and association ought to govern the representation of interests and opinions' (147), proactive public measures are sometimes needed to ensure the representation of social perspectives.

Special group representation

The concern of Young and other advocates of special group representation is not a general one about how to ensure that all the ways that individuals may have special needs or interests attain government representation. Such a 'mirror' view would hardly be realistic, except, perhaps, in such small democratic jurisdictions that direct democratic participation could obviate the need for any but minimum representative structures. Also, the mirror result would be more easily achieved by choosing representatives by lot, as indeed one contemporary theorist, John Burnheim, recommends (1985: ch. 3). Their recommendations are instead for measures specifically designed to address what they variously describe as persisting marginalization, oppression, or exclusion of people in virtue of their membership in categories of people, such as of women or racial minorities, which membership does not justify enduring these disadvantages. Due to 'the myriad and subtle ways in which ostensibly fair principles and procedures can reproduce structural inequalities,' as Williams puts it, such situations call for special measures (1998: 194).

People structurally or systemically excluded or marginalized are, the theorists in question insist, caught in downward spirals where underrepresentation in government due to discriminatory attitudes and lack of access to political resources facilitates government inattention to their economic, educational, and other needs, and this in turn makes it even more difficult for them to acquire political resources and further feeds discrimination. Accordingly, special group representation is seen as part of campaigns to arrest these downward spirals and replace them with upwards ones. On the question of whether special representation, should it succeed in this venture, ought then to be dismantled, theorists are not of one mind.

Types of groups

Kymlicka distinguishes between national minorities, such as aboriginal people or franco-Quebeckers in Canada, whose aspirations to maintain their national culture and integrity is impeded by their minority status within a bi- or multi-nation state and who require some measure of autonomous self-government to overcome this impediment, on the one hand, and disadvantaged ethnic, gender, or racial groups who seldom seek self-government and could not exercise it if they did, on the other. Provision for national self-government is appropriate to the first category of people, and it might be expected to persist in some form of permanent consociational arrangement. Special measures for other sorts of group representation, however, are needed only to the extent and for the length of time required to free people of systemic barriers to effective equality in group-blind political processes (1995: ch. 7).

Young is wary of self-determination claims when they are associated with national groups, fearing that this can foment nationalistic sentiments and policies in which the needs and perspectives of a variety of different groupings of 'peoples' gets submerged (2000: 251–5). At the same time, her position is more conducive than Kymlicka's to some form of permanent group representation in public arenas. Even though she says that the principle she favours 'calls for specific representation only of oppressed or disadvantaged groups' (1990: 187), Young resists an ideal vision of 'liberation as the transcendence of group difference' (ibid.: 168), and defends group representation positively for bringing alternative perspectives to a 'heterogeneous public' for which, presumably, provision would need to be secured even in a post-oppression world (ibid.: 190).

Modes of group representation

As to the ways that groups might be represented, Williams provides a list of the most common recommendations (1998: 221–33). Some measures apply to elections and comprise: proportional representation; holding reserved seats in legislative bodies for members of underrepresented marginalized groups; redrawing of electoral boundaries when underrepresented groups are concentrated in geographically determined ridings or providing for multimember districts when appropriate; and providing for quotas for underrepresented groups in political party candidate lists. Other measures are especially designed to encourage inclusive deliberation within legislative assemblies. In contrast to Pitkin, who regards symbolic 'standing for' as a largely impractical form of representation, Williams maintains that the mere presence of people from marginalized groups in a legislative forum goes some way toward encouraging inclusive deliberation. More proactive measures are the encouragement of coalitions of representatives of several marginalized groups and voting rules requiring more than a simple majority. Williams does not endorse a recommendation suggested by Young in her influential, *Justice and the Politics of Difference* (1990: 184, though not in her more recent *Inclusion and Democracy*, 2000), to give veto power to representatives of marginalized groups, as this would be internally divisive of the groups.

William's third category of modes of representation concerns the relation of representatives to their constituencies. Like other antioppressive theorists (for instance, Phillips 1991: 77–83), she sees this as problematic due to heterogeneity within systemically excluded groups, such that, women are of different economic class backgrounds and ascribed races, working-class people are of different nationalities and genders, and so on. According to Williams, neither a model whereby representatives are accountable to constituencies but not their strict delegates (Pitkin's view) nor the model (favoured by Mill and Christiano) where they are delegated to represent their constituencies' fundamental values or favoured goals suffices. Instead, she recommends promoting forums like town-hall meetings or electronic focus groups where representatives or potential representatives and others from their groups could mutually shape conceptions both of goals and means to be taken into legislative assemblies (231–2).

Challenges to group representation

In addition to posing the problem of which groups merit representation, a blanket criticism of special group representation is that it violates the democratic principle of individual equality. As Nathan Glazer puts it regarding legally enforced affirmative action programmes on racial or ethnic bases, 'individual claims to consideration on the basis of justice and equity' are replaced with 'a concern for rights for publicly determined and delimited racial and ethnic groups' (1975: 197). This concern is usually rejected by advocates of group representation on the grounds that no method of voting in a representative system can be utterly neutral regarding who gets how much representation. For instance, proportional representation voting rules in a multiparty system will provide higher representation of minority interests than will first past the post, single-member district majority voting in a two-party one. Selecting representatives from geographical districts seldom maps the size of district populations, and what interests or groups get represented depends in large part on how district boundaries are drawn (Williams 1998: 26, Young 2000: 143; Kymlicka 1995: 135). The problem of deciding which groups merit special representation is met, as indicated, by using a criterion that refers to continuing and systemic disadvantage.

All proponents of special group representation acknowledge that there are merits to criticisms directed against specific proposals, and they accordingly qualify their recommendations, for instance, to insist that measures for special representation be implemented only when there are no acceptable alternatives and that they not be employed longer than necessary. Of the specific criticisms three, related ones recur: that special representation Balkanizes people; that it 'essentializes' people by thinking of them just in terms of one of their group identifications; and that it faces the problem of the relation between group representatives and the groups they are to represent.

One way that group representation is thought to run the risk of Balkanization is by legitimizing marginalization: giving groups official recognition undermines a major aim that special group representation is supposed to overcome, namely, the stigmatization of being singled out (see Young's summary and references, 1990: 169). Another manifestation of Balkanization is addressed by Kymlicka (1995: 139–40) when he notes a tendency for special group representation to lead people from relatively privileged groups (for instance, men or middle-class people) to feel themselves exonerated from taking account of the needs of the less privileged and, conversely, for people from specially represented groups to attend only to their own interests. It is feared that Balkanization in this sense leads to a form of power politics where no representatives concern themselves with the common good (Elshtain 1993: chs 2,3, Phillips 1995: 24). The essentialism charge is that in granting special representation on the basis of one characteristic, for instance gender, it is falsely assumed that all members of the group exclusively or primarily identify with that characteristic and that they share the same values (see Young's summary and references 2000: 87–92).

Phillips sees an essentialist assumption as well in what she calls 'the politics of presence' or the view that by getting (in her example) women included in government, women's interests will be represented by them (1995: ch. 3). This raises the challenge of how the specially represented and their representatives are to be related. One way to underline the problem here is to compare a method of reserving places in governmental bodies for people from marginalized groups with the alternative method of ensuring that at least some political party platforms feature marginalized group interests (this would be one form of what Phillips calls 'the politics of ideas'). The first strategy guarantees that people from underrepresented groups are in government, but it has to be allowed that they might not strive to represent interests specific to their groups. Party discipline makes it easier to hold elected representatives to account on the second strategy, but even with proportional representation, there is no guarantee of electoral success. Nor, unless the parties included group lists, is there a guarantee that those elected are from a relevant marginalized group (see Kymlicka 1995: 147–9 for an analogous discussion).

Full review of ongoing debates sparked by these challenges is beyond the scope of this discussion, which will conclude by indicating first-response counter arguments by defenders of special group representation. Williams' reaction to the stigmatization charge is probably typical when she counters that group marginalization is already a stigmatizing fact in contemporary societies not created by political recognition of special needs and interests of the marginalized (1998: 211). Moreover, as Kymlicka argues, such practices as drawing electoral boundaries to coincide with constituencies with common needs (for instance, rural and agricultural) are not at all new to democratic politics, but what is new is that there are now demands to introduce measures like these for underrepresented groups, such as blacks in the US (1995: 135–6). A similar reaction is expressed by Young to the other Balkanization charge that group representation turns politics away from seeking the common good when she maintains that in political forums as currently structured 'greater privilege and dominant position allows some groups to articulate the "common good" in terms influenced by their particular perspective and interests' (1990: 118).

In her more recent book Young reiterates this view and supplements it to insist that the presence of heretofore silenced voices in governmental forums contributes to the potential of these forums to pursue common goods, since when deliberation is sincerely directed to this end, deliberative bodies need to draw on the experiences and perspectives of all citizens (2000: 82–3). Kymlicka meets the charge in a way that is meant to turn the table, at least on those who level it from a liberal-democratic stance. The main thrust of his argument is that special group representation is not alone in confronting theoretical and practical difficulties, and that it is not 'inherently illiberal or undemocratic' (1995: 151). In a similar table-turning argument, Williams addresses theorists who are concerned that common goods be sought within democratic forums and argues that a conception of 'the common good toward which public policy should aim must incorporate a conscious focus on the goods of groups whose good has been systematically overlooked in the past' (195).

To meet the other criticisms, theorists have recommended reorientations in the way that representation generally is regarded. Thus, Young introduces her distinction among interests, opinions, and perspectives to meet the charge that special status essentializes groups accorded it. While women, working-class people, blacks, and other such groups contain people within each group of widely varying interests, group identifications, and opinions, they all share certain perspectives in virtue of their 'structural social positions,' and this is especially so when people 'are situated on different sides of relations of structural inequality' (2000: 136). On traditional theories representation is either of persons or of the (objective) interests or (subjective) opinions thought common to a represented constituency. By shifting primary attention to perspectives, Young thinks that she can avoid the pitfalls of any of these alternatives, since perspectives are common to groups of people who are otherwise individually complex and hence have a variety of sometimes divergent interests and opinions.

A similar shift in thinking may be seen in the approaches of Phillips and Williams to the problem Phillips herself raises about how marginalized groups are to be represented without either assuming an unrealistic essentialism or losing the advantage of having accountable representatives from these groups in legislative forums. Phillips speculates that the problems of accountability derive from setting a 'politics of presence' and a 'politics of ideas' in opposition to one another such that either 'ideas are treated as totally separate from the people who carry them out' or 'people dominate attention, with no thought given to their policies and ideas' (1995: 25). Her solution is to recommend simultaneous pursuit of both sorts of politics. This suggests a pragmatic approach in which, for example, whether one or the other or some combination of the reserved seat or the party-platform strategies already described is employed depends on local circumstances. For Williams, the key change in thinking about representation is to pay primary attention to the interactions between represented and representative in which they have the potential to change one another. This, in turn, displaces an abstract debate about the nature of representation and accountability to the practical ground of facilitating 'communication between representatives and constituents' (1998: 231, and Young: 2000: 129).

All the authors cited who support special group representation concur that neither group-blind governmental forums and procedures nor conflict among traditional interest groups suffices to make for an equitably representative democracy. While they agree with the classic pluralists that democratic theory should not just concern itself with formal structures of government but should attend to formations and activities of people in civil society, the activities they have in mind are not those of power politics around self-interest but more akin to the transformative activities favoured by participatory democrats. We turn to these theorists in Chapter 7 after surveying a school even further removed from theorists who focus on oppressed groups than classic pluralists.

Chapter 6

Catallaxy

A survey of current democratic-theoretical literature would likely reveal, at least in the English-speaking world, a predominance of work by deliberative democrats and by social (or 'public' or 'collective') choice theorists. Deliberative democracy will be the subject of Chapter 9. Social choice literature, however, does not exactly constitute a unique *theory* of democracy. Rather, it employs techniques supposed to explain any behaviour where individuals collectively make decisions and applies them to democratic practices – in particular those associated with majority voting by citizens or legislators – by employing an ideal model of political behaviour. The aim is to identify problems (such as the cyclical majority problem discussed in Chapter 2) and sometimes to make recommendations about how to meet them. Depending upon how confident theorists are that actual political actors match the model, they may try to make predictions as well.

Social choice theory is a species of more general 'rational choice' theory and is sometimes simply referred to by this name when it is understood that collective decisions are being addressed. Social choice theorists concerned with political behaviour agree on the core of their ideal model: a rational individual comes to a political situation calling for a collective decision with ranked preferences over possible outcomes and chooses that course of action (usually, to vote one way or another or to abstain from voting) deemed likely to realize the most highly ranked of his or her preferences possible given the decision-making rules in place, the anticipated behaviour of other individuals, and other such constraints.

One guiding methodological postulate of social choice theory is that rationality has only to do with whether people take appropriate means to their preferred ends. The ends themselves are neither rational nor irrational, but are simply taken as given for evaluating the rationality of those who take actions to further them. A second major postulate is that individuals are the basic units of analysis, so when the 'rationality' of groups is discussed, it is understood that group behaviour can be analyzed into that of a group's members. Applications of social choice theory to democratic politics share with classic pluralism the 'realist' assumptions that politics has to do mainly

with conflicts among self-interested political actors and democracy with electoral competition, but this 'methodological individualist' postulate creates
an important difference expressed by Mancur Olson's critique of Bentley,
Truman, and other pluralists for making interest groups their basic units
of analysis. He sees a fatal flaw in their approach: groups are supposed to
act to advance the common interests of the individuals who make them up,
but among these interests is the 'economic' one to minimize costs required to
provide resources for the group as a whole, so each individual will try to avoid
incurring these costs and will not 'voluntarily make any sacrifices to help their
group attain its political (public or collective) objectives' (1971: 126).

Refinements and explications of social choice theory exhibit complexities
(for instance, insisting that to preserve rationality, preference rankings must
be transitive) and reveal differences among rational choice theorists (for
example, over whether altruistic preferences may be taken into account).
Among the advantages seen by social choice theorists to their approach is
that it lends itself to formalization and graphic representations. When reconstructing or projecting the rational decisions of two or more individuals who
are strategically anticipating one another's calculations, social choice theorists avail themselves of the techniques of game theory, which are especially
designed for such situations. The summaries of rational and social choice
theories by Donald Green and Ian Shapiro (1994: ch. 2) and contributions
and to collections edited by Jon Elster (1986a) and Hylland Aanund and
Elster (1986) survey some of these complexities. They also provide points
of entry into an extensive literature, as do the texts by Russell Hardin (1982)
and, specifically on game theory, by Peter Ordeshook (1992).

The catallactic theorists

Later in this chapter I shall return to the question of whether deployment
of some such model and use of rational-choice techniques commits one to
a unique democratic theory. There is evidence that it does not in the diversity of orientations among those who are at home in this approach, including
political conservatives such as David Gauthier and theorists on the political
left such as Elster or John Roemer. However, if one focuses on the imme-
diate ancestors of contemporary social choice practitioners a more unified
approach is clear. These are in what Dennis Mueller calls the 'first generation' of 'public choice' theorists as distinguished (though not consistently)
from 'social choice' theorists and from the nineteenth-century forerunners,
Condorcet and Borda, referred to in Chapter 4. This is in Mueller's introduction to a useful collection of essays on different aspects of public choice
theory (1997). These ancestral public choice theorists are directly in the
line of Schumpeter, whose conception of democracy they take as a starting
place. Chief among them are Anthony Downs, James Buchanan, and Gordon
Tullock.

The approach they develop is sometimes called 'catallactic' with reference to a term appropriated by Friedrich Hayek (1976: ch. 10) from a nineteenth-century economic theorist, Richard Whatley, who adopted the Greek verb, 'exchange,' to describe the essence of political economy. (The approach is also sometimes attributed to the 'Virgina School' in recognition of Tullock's presence at the Thomas Jefferson Center at the University of Virginia when collaborating there with Buchanan.) The remarkable feature of human societies of any size beyond the tribe for Hayek is that without face-to-face meetings to agree upon the distribution of goods and services, mutually acceptable distributions are nonetheless made by people with a wide variety of life aims who are strangers to one another. This is possible due to exchange in impersonal markets, and Hayek used the term 'catallactics' to describe the science of exchange *per se*. This science 'describes the only overall order that comprehends nearly all of mankind' (113). Subsequently 'catallaxy' has been used to refer to the application of economic theories and methods to the study of politics.

This fits the orientation of Downs, who in his *An Economic Theory of Democracy* set out to apply the methods of economic theory to politics to discover 'a generalized yet realistic behavior rule for a rational government similar to the rules traditionally used for rational consumers and producers' (1957: 3). A government is rational on this approach for the same reason that an individual may be rational on the rational choice model, namely when it pursues appropriate means to a given end. This end is not difficult to locate for Downs: following Schumpeter, he avers that since the 'political function of elections in a democracy ... is to select a government [therefore] rational behavior in connection with elections is behavior oriented toward this end and no other' (7).

Political parties

Because it is political parties that compete in elections, to understand the 'rule of government' is to understand the behaviour of political parties. These in turn are made up of politicians, who do not seek office in order to implement favoured policies, but act only 'to attain the income, prestige, and power that comes from being in office,' for which purpose they join with others in a political party to compete for the spoils of government (24–31). Downs thus describes his 'main thesis' as that 'parties in democratic politics are analogous to entrepreneurs in a profit-seeking economy' in formulating 'whatever policies they believe will gain the most votes just as entrepreneurs produce whatever products they believe will gain the most profits' (295). Governments must perform certain social functions (collect taxes, maintain public services, look to national defence, and so on) and a governing party must keep enough voters sufficiently satisfied to be re-elected, so in the exchange the citizenry gets something in return for its votes. But these benefits are 'by-products' of the motivating goal of getting elected and staying in power (28–9) in the same way as providing a customer with a functioning car is a by-product of an auto dealer's effort to make a sale.

One of the conclusions Downs draws from this catallactic model of politics concerns the distribution of ideologies among a country's political parties. While some voters analyze the specific policies of a party competing for their votes and evaluate its candidates, many, if not most, do not take the time or effort to do this (quite rationally for Downs, as will shortly be seen); rather, they follow the less time-consuming practice of voting for or against a party on the basis of its stated ideology – that is, its image of a good society and how to attain it as projected in its platform and campaign slogans (96). Knowing this, parties publicize ideologies as advertisements. Since the aim of a party is just to get elected, its leaders do not care about the intrinsic worth of ideologies, but publicize one they think will attract the largest number of voters.

Against this background Downs adopts a simplified model and its graphic representation from an earlier economist (Harold Hotelling), which takes as its prototype the observation that in towns with only two grocery stores, these are usually very close together and near the town centre. The evident explanation is that a store near the centre of town would attract more walk-in customers than one further from the centre, so each store owner will try to move as close to the centre as possible with the result that the stores are next to each other. A society with a large middle class and shared, moderate political values in the majority of the population, Downs maintains, is analogous to Hotelling's model, and the result is that one can expect two major political parties, espousing distinguishable but vague and similar ideologies. Not only will this attract the maximum number of voters for each party, but no matter which one wins an election it will be able to satisfy its voters without greatly alienating the bulk of supporters of the other party, and government will be stable.

By contrast, if a society is ideologically polarized, two parties will again be the norm, but they will be so far apart in ideology that once elected a party cannot both keep its voters and the large minority that voted against it satisfied, and government will be unstable to the point of inviting revolution. Or, again, in a country where people are attracted to several ideologies in more or less equal numbers, a multiparty system will result, each party appealing to a different segment of the population. Ideologies in such a system will be sharply defined, but in part for this reason, the coalitions needed to govern will find it hard to pursue policies acceptable both to their core voters and other voters, and government will be ineffective (Chapters 8 and 9). Downs attributes the political stability of the US to its approximation to the two grocery stores model: were he responding to the exercise in Chapter 1, he would have no hesitation in adducing it as the best example of an electoral democracy.

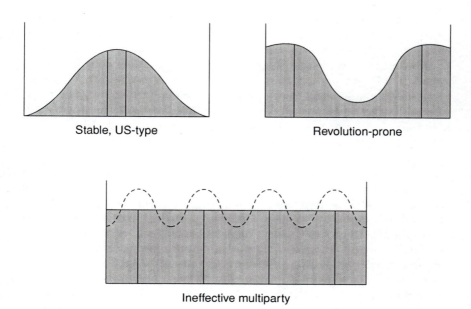

Stable, US-type   Revolution-prone

Ineffective multiparty

Figure 3

Note: Shaded areas represent the distribution of voters by ideological inclination. Vertical lines represent political parties.

Voter abstention

As the US approached its year 2000 presidential election (itself grist for several democratic-theoretical mills), a Midwest newspaper invited high school students to send it letters about voter apathy. Most of the responses cited uninspiring or otherwise off-putting qualities of elected leaders. Some referred to discouragement due to broken campaign promises and suspicion that politicians serve powerful, minority interests, and others blamed the media or their parents for bad mouthing elected leaders. One person identified voter attitudes themselves as the cause and admonished citizens to change their ways: 'Many people don't feel they can make a difference [however] voting doesn't cost you anything, but if you don't, it can cost you everything' (*Indianapolis Star* May 26, 2000).

Downs devotes a chapter of his seminal book to this topic and agrees with the view of the quoted student except in one respect. He notes that voting takes 'time to register, to discover what parties are running, to deliberate, to go to the polls, and to mark the ballot' and since 'time is a scarce resource, voting is inherently costly' (1957: 265). For some people, such as those without cars or who will lose job pay to vote, these costs are higher than for others, and this adds a disincentive to vote. Also, some people are indifferent as among parties or candidates, and they too will be loathe to go to the polls. These two variables – relative cost and degree of indifference – are central to Downs' explanation of the rationality of voter abstention: 'when citizens balance their costs and returns, some vote and others abstain' (274). Assuming that rational agents in general wish to maximize gains and minimize losses, someone who is indifferent to an election's outcome will suffer a net loss by taking time to vote; a person who is not indifferent may also suffer a loss if his or her cost of voting is high, which is why voter turnout among the poor is low.

To this basic account, Downs adds two twists (267–72). Citizens have a stake in maintaining electoral democracy, as this is the only peaceful way to change government leaders, and since the perpetuation of this system requires that at least someone votes, even voters indifferent to a specific electoral outcome have a reason to cast a ballot. This reason can be outweighed if the cost of voting is high, but, to add the second twist, it can also be outweighed by what other theorists in the rational choice tradition call 'free-rider' considerations. In one sense citizens are right to doubt that 'they can make a difference' because the chance of any one voters having the deciding ballot is very low. This is especially true when the outcome in question is simply that enough people vote to keep the electoral system from atrophying. Hence, rational citizens will calculate that the benefits of this system will accrue to them without incurring the costs of voting. Downs alludes to the paradoxical nature of this calculation that in a society of rational citizens nobody would vote unless they thought that nobody else would, but if everyone thought this way then each, again, would think that others would vote and so it would be rational to abstain. He then sets this conundrum aside to reiterate his conclusion that voting is a matter of weighing relative costs and benefits.

Democratic decision-making

Buchanan and Tullock begin their book, *The Calculus of Consent* (1962), by noting a disparity between economics and traditional political theory. Economists assume that trade is a way for individuals with different interests to cooperate and aim to explain how this takes place, while political theorists assume that there is some 'truth' in politics, in particular about what is in the general public interest, and seek ways that democratic (or nondemocratic) methods of decision-making can discover or promote this interest. Like Schumpeter, they deny that there is any such thing as the public interest over and above mutual advantages to be gained by cooperating, so in catallactic fashion Buchanan and Tullock recommend modelling political theory on economics where no assumption of a social goal is required.

Using Daniel Defoe's story of Robinson Crusoe and Friday as the human occupants of an island, Buchanan and Tullock illustrate the parity between economics and politics they have in mind. Crusoe is best at fishing and Friday at coconut collection, so the two 'find it is mutually advantageous ... to specialize and to enter into exchange': this is an economic relation. At the same time, each recognizes the advantage of living in a common fortress so they enter into a 'political' exchange and cooperate in its construction and maintenance (1962: 19). A major task of political theory informed by this model is to address the 'constitutional' problem of determining the rules for such cooperation. For the Schumpeterian public choice theorist, this means figuring out what voting rule rational individuals would select in specified circumstances – unanimity, majority rule, or any other proportion of votes required for a binding decision.

Being a two-person society the Crusoe/Friday island offers few alternatives. (Buchanan and Tullock abstract from the fact that in Defoe's story, Friday is Crusoe's servant, which would simply make Crusoe a dictator, unless Friday's ability to strike is as threatening to Crusoe as whatever power Crusoe holds that maintains him as the 'master' is to Friday.) In larger societies, the voting rule rational individuals would agree to will be a function of the number of people required to make a decision and two categories of cost. If one person can make binding decisions, the costs to all other individuals expected

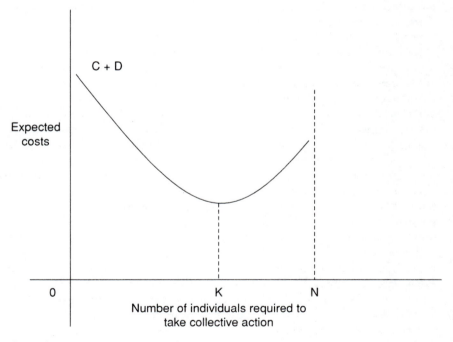

Figure 4

to result from their lack of control over an outcome ('external costs') will be very high. If unanimity is required, this cost will be reduced to nothing since each individual will have veto power over unwanted outcomes, but the cost of devoting time and other resources to trying to convince all the others to vote with one ('decision-making costs') will be very high. In between these extremes (and abstracting from the intensity of preferences), the two sorts of cost will vary in proportion to the number of people required to make a decision. The rational person will thus opt for a rule that minimizes the sum of the two costs.

Prescriptive implications

Ostensively the catallactic theorists employ an idealized model of rational behaviour for explanatory, as opposed to prescriptive, purposes. C.B. Macpherson both recognizes this purport and grants that by and large the views of theorists like Downs and others in the tradition of Schumpeter accurately represent what transpires under the name of democratic politics in competitive, market societies. His conclusion is that it is so much the worse for such societies that they breed these politics (Macpherson 1977: ch. 4). Whatever the empirical merits of the catallactic theorists, it is not too difficult to see that in their accounts, descriptive or explanatory focuses shade into prescriptive recommendations. One place this is evident is in Downs' discussions of uncertainty and information.

Rational agents wish to be informed so as to remove as much as possible uncertainty about how best to further their ends (that is, to get the most out of government and one another on the part of voters, and to maintain themselves in political power for governments). But at the same time both voters and governments will wish to avoid the costs required to acquire information. Since in the social division of labour, not to mention due to disparities of income, it will be easier and less costly for some individuals than for others to acquire politically relevant information, there will be unavoidable inequalities among abilities to use information to influence government or, indeed, to know how to vote. From its side, political uncertainty within governments, that is, uncertainty about what parts of the population it is most important for it to please in order to maximize chances for re-election, will lead them to shape policy in reaction to the most vigorous and powerful 'representatives' of the population. Even knowing that lobbyists and leaders of labour, business, and other such organizations will try to exaggerate the strength of their support, the uncertainty of governments and parties aspiring to government about popular sentiment makes preferential reaction to the most vigorous of these representatives the most cost-effective way for it to comport itself.

Downs reiterates versions of this view in several places in his book. One summary is: 'Hence rationality under conditions of uncertainty leads government to construct policies often aimed more at the good of a few voters than at the good of all, or even of a majority' (1957: 93). Taken literally, this is another descriptive, not prescriptive, account. So is the announcement in the quoted passage's next sentence that 'to act otherwise would be irrational,' as are the claims that any 'concept of democracy based on an electorate of equally well-informed citizens' presupposes that they 'behave irrationally' and that the 'foundations of differential political power in a democracy are rooted in the very nature of society' (236) or that 'it is irrational for a democratic government to treat all men as though they were politically equal' (83). A strained reading might be that Downs wishes democracy could treat people as political equals and laments the fact that this flies in the face of rationality, but unless he intends to be recommending irrationality in politics, the prescriptive implications of his view must be to resist efforts to promote political equality.

Similar descriptive conclusions with evident prescriptive implications run through *The Calculus of Consent* (Buchanan and Tullock 1962). Democratic decisions are appropriate when it is rational to take collective actions: if raw materials were so abundant on Crusoe and Friday's island that the organizational efforts required to cooperate in building a common fortress plus the time lost for devotion to other projects ('opportunity' costs) outweighed the cost to each of building his own fortress, it would be irrational to engage in the joint effort. Since one of the costs of democratic decision-making depends upon the size of the relevant population ('N' in Figure 4), this means that an increase in this number will not only bear on the rationality of what voting rule to select, but on whether it is rational to engage in democratic collective action at all: '*ceteris paribus*, the larger the size of the group, the smaller should be the set of activities undertaken collectively' (1962: 81).

Another implication concerns majority rule. Once dictatorship and unanimity are departed from, the most rational voting rule will depend upon the sum of 'external' and 'decision' costs ('K' in Figure 4) and Buchanan and Tullock emphasize that 'there is nothing in the analysis that points to any uniqueness in the rule that requires a simple majority to be decisive' (*ibid.*). The commonly held opinion that gives pride of place to majority rule derives from the fact that most previous democratic theory has been developed in 'noneconomic, nonindividualistic, nonpositivistic terms' (82). Buchanan later described one of 'the main purposes of *The Calculus of Consent*' as the 'removal of the sacrosanct status accorded to majority vote' (1986: 243), and in this respect the prescriptive implications of this theory depart from a standard liberal-democratic presumption in favour of majority rule. In another respect, however, the approach endorses a liberal-democratic emphasis on representative, rather than participatory democracy. The reason for this is that the 'decision costs' of direct democracy are prohibitive in any but very small groups, and delegating representatives to negotiate among one another is therefore cost effective for citizens by contrast with trying to do this among one another (Buchanan and Tullock 1962: 213–14).

Downs' model stipulates that the rational individual is also selfish while recognizing that this is an ideal construct (27). Buchanan and Tullock deny that people are motivated to enter into market-like exchanges or otherwise interact with one another solely for selfish motives; however, insofar as people's political behaviour is like economic exchange they should be assumed to take only their own interests into account (17–18). This has a certain plausibility in the case of economic behaviour in the ordinary sense. One does not normally pay more for an item than necessary out of concern for the well-being of its manufacturer or salesperson. But the point of catallaxy is to extend the economic model to democratic political behaviour, so when someone votes, runs for office, or pursues certain policies when in office, this is assumed not to be done out of concern for the public good.

In the last chapter of their book, 'The Politics of the Good Society,' Buchanan and Tullock justify this approach in a way that probably lays bare the underlying normative strategy of catallactic theory. They allow that pursuit of the golden rule or promotion of equal freedom are morally worthwhile. However, if the individual is to be a free agent it 'cannot be assured that he will always follow the moral rules agreed on by the philosophers as being necessary for harmonious social life.' This, they maintain, 'brings us squarely to the central issue' of whether 'society should be organized to allow moral deviants to gain at the expense of their fellows' or whether institutions or 'organizational norms' should be constructed with the always present possibility of selfish behaviour in mind so that it 'can be channeled in such a direction that it becomes beneficial rather than detrimental to the interests of all members of the community.' Economic markets achieve this result in part because they are premised on the assumption of purely self-regarding behaviour. By implication, the political arrangements recommended by catallactic theorists have the same result for the reason that they are also premised on this assumption (303–4).

Neoliberalism

In defence of the 'self-interest axiom' Downs approvingly quotes Adam Smith's view that mutual benefit is not necessarily the result of mutual altruism: 'It is not from the benevolence of the butcher, the brewer, or the baker, that we expect our dinner, but from their regard to their own interest.' Smith's reasoning, Downs adds 'applies equally well to politics' (Downs 1957: 28, Smith 1937 [1776]: 14). Smith thus foreshadowed 'neoliberal' thinking during the Reagan and Thatcher years and its revival after the collapse of communism in the Soviet Union and Eastern Europe. According to Hayek, once the notion is abandoned that public policies can be ranked by reference to some overall public good, government's role should be seen as facilitating the pursuit by individuals of their various interests, which he vigorously argues is best achieved by allowing the market to function free from state interference.

The resulting free market is described by Hayek as 'the game of catallaxy' where, as in other games, the outcome for any player is determined by a 'mixture of skill and chance.' Though competitive and subject to bad luck, the catallactic game is not a 'zero-sum game' where some must lose if others are to gain, but a 'wealth-creating game' where in principle everyone can gain and in any case has a better chance of gaining than under either feudalism or in a democracy with an interventionist state. This is true even if the intervention is supposed to compensate for chance, including the bad luck of being born into disadvantaged circumstances since intervention will grow, and even this degree of it will interfere with the functioning of a free market (Hayek 1976: ch. 10, 1979: ch. 15). In addition to policing, national defence, and enforcing contracts (plus raising taxes for these purposes) the role of the state should be minimal.

Macpherson sees an intimate historical connection between catallactic and similar 'realist' views about democracy and advocacy of Smithian capitalism: these will generally be regarded plausible when there is relative prosperity, class divisions are submerged, and dominance of an economy by competitive market relations promotes a political culture of possessive individualism (1977: ch. 4). This might explain why and when people who are attracted to catallaxy are also attracted to neoliberalism (and in my classroom experiences I have seen an invariable association on the part of students), but it does not establish a necessary, conceptual connection between them. To *model* politics after economics is not automatically to advocate replacing political relations with economic ones. In fact, both Downs (1957: 22–3) and Buchanan and Tullock (1962: 65–6, ch. 14, Buchanan 1975: ch. 6) allow for some government intervention. So does Hayek, but he stipulates that intervention must be free-market friendly; for instance, government should fund universal education by providing vouchers for use at private schools and certify that such things as food products or medical services are safe but not prohibit the sale of uncertified goods or services (1979: 61–2).

Government predation

One way to establish a tight connection between catallaxy and neoliberalism is to justify a *presumption* against more than minimal government intervention in human affairs. This approach is invited by the structure of Buchanan and Tullock's overall argument, which crucially involves performing cost/benefit analyses on alternative political arrangements. Thus they point out that collective (that is, state) action is agreed to in order to reduce 'external' costs; for instance, to regulate a plant with a smoking chimney that imposes 'external costs on the individual by soiling his laundry' but hasten to add that 'this cost is no more external to the individual's own private calculus than the tax cost imposed upon him unwillingly to finance this and other public services' (65–6). As noted earlier, the larger a decision-making body is, the higher the 'decision costs' of time and effort are to individuals in it; so, as these costs are added to external tax costs, compensating benefits of state regulatory or other actions will be increasingly outweighed.

This consideration does not automatically establish a presumption against state action, since it might be that external costs that can only be met by collective intervention are so high that they would seldom if ever be offset by other costs, also, as Tullock later opined, the cost of government can be reduced by 'improved governmental design' (1970: 128). However, another view of Tullock and Buchanan could be invoked to tip the scales. Tullock in particular is well known and revered among economic theorists of a catallactic persuasion for developing a concept technically labelled by others 'rent seeking' to describe what he saw as an essentially wasteful aspect of any government (Tullock: 1980 [1967], and see Tollison's summary, 1997).

Expenditures by entrepreneurs to secure access to privately owned goods or services and the renting of these resources by those who own them are normal, profit-seeking activities, which through time create value by stimulating initiative and prompting efficient allocation of resources. However, when entrepreneurs must compete for access to resources over which a government has monopolistic control, the rents they pay are 'artificial' adding 'nothing to social product' and their 'opportunity cost constitutes lost production to society' (Tollison 1982: 576). A favoured example is the cost of lobbying. This not only has the direct opportunity cost to those competing for government favours of denying resources they could put to productive use, but it also creates long-term, wasteful social costs as the jobs provided to lawyers by lobbying needs 'will generate a disequilibrium in the market for lawyers, with the implication that there will be excessive entry into the legal system' (ibid.: 578, and see Tollison 1997).

Tullock's original statement of government monopolies that occasion rent-seeking behaviour described the rent extracted as a form of theft, and one theorist approvingly cites this essay as an 'examination of government as an instrument of predation' (Wagner: 1987). In keeping with the deliberately amoral stance of catallactic theorists, such terms as 'theft' and 'predation' should be taken as technical, economic ones. Otherwise, moral or ethical cost/benefit analyses would muddy the waters. If, however, one agrees with Tullock's claim that government intervention in the form of regulation or monopolization of goods or services is bound to be socially wasteful, this might be enough to create a presumption against such intervention, so the burden of argument would always be on the shoulders of advocates of collective, state action, and one kind of connection between catallaxy and neoliberalism would be established.

The rational impossibility of state action

A second way to establish the strong connection between catallaxy and neoliberalism is not one that the catallactic theorists surveyed in this chapter would welcome, but their reliance on rational decision theory invites it. In reconstructing the calculations of rational individuals, they distinguish between decisions to adopt some specific voting rules ('constitutional decisions') and the exercise of those rules once decided on. While the specific rules may mandate majority vote or more or less than this, a decision about which of these rules to adopt must be unanimous if a specific rule is to be reliably followed. Buchanan and Tullock are not arguing that people submit themselves to a general, originating social contract, as theorists like Hobbes held, but that rational individuals will all see it as in their long-run interests to bind themselves to some specific rules.

Citing David Hume for support, Buchanan argues that adherence to a constitutional rule will be secure even if individuals know that it will sometimes be to their advantage to break it since 'each individual must recognize that were he free to violate convention, others must be similarly free' and he will accordingly choose to accept restrictions on his own behaviour to avoid the resulting chaos (appendix to Buchanan and Tullock 1962: 314–15, Hume 1978 [1740]: bk 3, sec. 3). But this runs afoul of the famous decision-theoretical problem of the prisoners' dilemma: two prisoners charged with committing a crime together are given the option to confess or not to confess knowing that if neither confesses they will both get light sentences, if one confesses and the other does not, the one that confesses will get off and the other will receive a very heavy sentence, and if both confess each will receive a medium-heavy sentence. In this circumstance each prisoner will conclude that it is only rational to confess (to avoid getting a heavy sentence if the other confesses or to get off if the other does not confess). Therefore, both will confess thus receiving harder sentences than they know would be available if neither did. The point is to show how rationality can knowingly lead to suboptimal results.

Catallactic theorists cannot appeal to such things as custom or social encouragement of trust to escape the dilemma, since they explicitly set aside such 'psychological' considerations (Downs 1957: 7). If there is no solution to this problem in the catallactic models, it might be argued that collective action is rationally impossible and should be replaced by the purely individual actions of the market. This, recall from Chapter 4, was the sort of argument that Russell Hardin, citing voters' paradoxes and the free-rider problem, gave for 'anomic capitalism' as an alternative to democracy in confronting ethnic conflicts. To be sure, the arguments that collective, government action cannot escape this dilemma and that purely individual, free-market driven behaviour is feasible and void of analogously damning problems involve several steps, but their soundness would provide another conceptual link between catallaxy and neoliberalism.

Rationality in the service of competition

Yet another argument connecting catallaxy and neoliberalism proceeds by an historical, evolutionary argument of Hayek's that links market competition and rationality (1979: 75–6). On the story he sketches, the few people who are skilful at taking appropriate means to achieve their given ends (that is, skilful at rational thought) will make gains in competition thus obliging others to 'emulate them in order to prevail' so that 'rational methods will progressively be developed and spread by imitation': it is not 'rationality which is required to make competition work, but competition . . . which will produce rational behaviour.' This development, however, supposes that a 'traditionalist majority' cannot stifle competition, which according to Hayek is 'always a process in which a small number makes it necessary for large numbers to do what they do not like.' Thus, not only economic innovation but the nurturing of rationality itself requires devolution as much as possible to unconstrained market interactions.

Full defence of this viewpoint, like the one derived from the prisoners' dilemma, would require many steps and involve several assumptions about the nature and evolution of human economic and political practices and of rationality. Indeed, if public choice theories are suspect from a social-scientific point of view (as, for instance Lars Udehn argues, 1996), they would do well to avoid causal hypotheses such as Hayek's in favour of the more guarded claim that they are offering a model designed to illuminate one aspect of human behaviour (Downs 1957: 6–7). Also, even if it were accepted that human rationality is a product of economic competition, it would still have to be shown that this justifies libertarian restrictions on the scope of democracy, since it might be that though rationality in this purely instrumental sense had competitive origins, it can be dialectically turned to cooperative use. The argument also raises questions about the relation of catallaxy to social choice theory generally.

Social choice theory and catallaxy

Allusion has already been made to one way that social choice theory might commit one to catallaxy. If democracy is considered nothing other than self-interested voting, the voters' paradoxes and the prisoners' dilemma are especially threatening problems. If there are no ways to meet them, then it might be argued that the only alternatives left for the coordination of human activities are submission to dictatorial authority (Hobbes' unpalatable solution), uncritical following of tradition (too late in the modern world), or relying on free market, invisible hand 'regulation,' that is, on catallaxy of a neoliberal variety.

The paradoxes and the dilemma certainly do pose problems for rational choice theorists concerning themselves with collective action, that is for social or public choice theories. Their import, however, will differ depending on whether social choice theory is regarded normatively or descriptively. As an effort to explain or predict the behaviour of voters or legislators, the dilemma and paradoxes function as *parts of* explanations to identify circumstances in which collective action will be forgone, erratic, or stymied. Social choice theorists have been strikingly undaunted by demonstrations, as by Donald Green and Ian Shapiro (1994), of the many predictive and other empirical failures of their approach thus deployed.

A justification for this stance is to classify predictive failures not as defeats but as provocations for innovation either in the characterization of rationality or in identification of circumstances allowing for rational action. An example of the first innovation is a suggestion broached by Buchanan (1986: 233–6) that voting is mainly a matter of expressing sentiments (see Christiano's discussion of this 'expressive' theory of voting, 1996: 157–9). The second sort of innovation is exemplified in Gerald Strom's refinements (for instance to take into account vote trading, agenda control, and alternative distributions of preference rankings) when confronted with the fact that legislative voting more closely approximates majority preferences than theory predicts (Strom 1990).

Like most rational decision theorists who address collective action, Elster insists that the approach is primarily normative (1986b: 1). As such the dilemmas and paradoxes pose more grave threats, since it is of dubious value to recommend to people that they act in ways that, though rational from an individual standpoint, will unavoidably have socially irrational consequences (likely to rebound to the detriment of the individuals themselves and hence irrational for them to undertake after all). The question here being addressed, however, is whether the problems must lead a social choice theorist to catallaxy, and the answer partly depends upon what the aim of such a theorist is.

One commentator, Emily Hauptmann, distinguishes between 'public choice theory,' and 'social choice theory' by noting that while each is modelled on economics, they follow different approaches to economics and have different aims (1996: 2). On her view the aim of public choice theorists like Buchanan and Tullock is to analyze democratic institutions on the model of free market economics with an eye to transforming the institutions in a neoliberal direction. Social choice theorists, or at least those who are most worried about the paradoxes of democratic decision-making, regard rational choice theory as potentially helpful in a utilitarian effort to achieve the satisfaction by each person in a society of his or her highest ranked preferences compatibly with others enjoying the same success. They thus seek ways to attain 'Pareto optimality' (named after the Italian economic theorist, Vilfredo Pareto, to describe situations that cannot be changed to satisfy anyone's higher ranked preference without thwarting a preference of someone else already satisfied in the situation) and model their approach on welfare economics. These social choice theorists ask whether majority vote can aggregate preferences to achieve this result.

Such theorists might interpret political behaviour in a catallactic manner and they might even conclude from the putative intractability of constitutional dilemmas and voting paradoxes that free markets make anything but limited government unnecessary since they can achieve Pareto optimality alone, but if their aim is strictly welfarist, they may not need to concern themselves with any general theory of political behaviour or draw these neoliberal conclusions. For example, they could argue that experts should be entrusted with the task of figuring out what the optimal distribution of goods is and that constitutions do not require an imagined, much less real, contract among all voters but can be crafted out of existing political resources by informed public leaders motivated by concern for the long-range well-being of the body politic. This is more or less Mill's approach to representative government, and a version of it is expressed by Jonathan Riley in his use of rational choice theory to defend 'liberal utilitarianism' when he argues that some of Arrow's rules for a democratic collective decision should be broken to ensure choices that are 'competent and just from a liberal point of view' (1988: 300).

Whether some such stance is available to social choice theorists depends upon how they conceive of human nature and upon how 'totalistic' they think rational choice theory must be. Someone who thinks that humans are self-interested by nature or who thinks that only self-interested behaviour is rational and who also thinks that only a social theory focused on the adoption of appropriate means to these self-interested ends can provide an adequate base for making political prescriptions will probably be driven either to libertarian catallaxy or despair. Regarding the Millian recommendation, for instance, such a theorist will see the experts and public leaders as either altruistic but irrational or rational but not concerned with the public good. As to constitutions, it might be acknowledged that they typically draw upon preexisting political habits and norms and are forged by informally recognized leaders, but for the totalistic rational choice theorist, historical and sociological explanations of these things are both incomplete and inadequate to ground political prescriptions until they are reduced to or at least supplemented with reconstructions of self-interested instrumentally rational decisions on the part of individuals.

Elster (1986c: 127) seems to have the narrow and totalistic conception in mind when he remarks that the economic theory of democracy underlies social choice theory (used in the sense Hauptmann wants to reserve for public choice theory). But even on this conception, Elster suggests a way that pubic choice theorists might avoid full catallaxy. He contrasts two conceptions of political democracy, 'the market' and 'the forum.' On a market conception the purpose of democracy and of politics generally is 'economic,' that is, aimed at advancing individuals' interests, and the normal functioning of politics is for each to vote on these interests, typically by secret ballot and hence 'privately.' The purpose of democracy in a forum, by contrast, is the non-instrumental one of encouraging public participation itself. Such democracy functions by public discussion in the expectation that people's interests may change as a result and with the aim of reaching consensus. Elster's favoured approach to politics would mix the forum and the market, whereas it is central to full-blown catallaxy that citizen involvement in democratic politics be no more than voting on preexisting interests.

Though distinguishing between social and public choice theories, Hauptmann is equally critical of each and considers their similarities with respect to democratic theory more striking than their differences. Her focus is on the central role they accord to choice. On either application of rational choice theory, democracy is centrally a matter of a society making collective choices, and these choices are, again, analyzed and valued in terms of the choices of individuals. In her book, *Putting Choice Before Democracy*, she maintains this orientation supposes that 'democracy is valuable because it honors individual choice' but provides no motivation 'to make political choices worth making' (1996: 12). As evidence of this she notes that Buchanan and Tullock sanction logrolling or vote trading, which, as they acknowledge, constitutes the buying and selling of votes; so, the very heart of democracy for them, the individual choice to vote becomes a commodity (Hauptmann 1996: 26–6, Buchanan and Tullock 1962: 122–3, ch. 10). A compatible criticism is levelled against liberalism generally by Samuel Bowles and Herbert Gintis for seeing human action as exclusively a matter of 'choosing' rather than 'learning' (1986: ch. 5).

In addition to arguing that rational choice theorists lack the ability to guide and justify choices, Hauptmann also maintains that the specifically democratic choice endorsed by these theorists, namely, the ability to vote, is of secondary importance, and may even be dispensed with in the case of selection of legislators who can be selected by lottery (ch. 3, and see Burnheim 1985). On her alternative view, democracy is to be valued for encouraging 'popular participation and passionate political commitment' (90). It might be retorted that though not mandated, such an aspiration is permitted in rational choice theory, since it does not rule out the wish to engage in political activity with others as a top priority of some or even all members of a political society. This retort is not likely to be satisfactory to anyone sympathetic to Hauptmann's criticism, which rejects the entire paradigm of rational choice theory in favour of the participatory-democratic orientation that will be the subject of Chapter. 7

Problems of democracy

Notwithstanding the complexity of their arguments and calculations, the catallactic theorists work with a simple conception of democracy: the ability of people to vote for or against legislators and that of legislators to vote for or against proposed legislation plus, in the case of Buchanan and Tullock, constitutional endorsement of specific voting rules. Whatever the loss in power to accommodate what champions of more robust orientations toward democracy claim to be of value in it (creation of civic spirit, promotion of dialogue and deliberation, education to the virtues and skills of participation, promotion of politically egalitarian values and policies), this parsimonious conception provides some straightforward means for meeting standard problems and objections to democracy. For instance, regarding the problem of ineffectiveness, it will be recalled that for Schumpeter governance is the most effective when citizens involve themselves very little in politics. For the catallactic theorists it is rational for citizens to do this, because costs are incurred by concerning oneself with politics. A rational population of voters, therefore, will let those who were good enough at governing to get elected or re-elected do so with little interference.

Irrationality and conflict

Some responses to these problems were summarized in Chapter 4. Riker meets the charge that democracy is irrational due to such things as the voter's paradoxes by maintaining that they would only be damaging if the aim of voting is to aggregate preferences, but they are not damaging if, in accord with Schumpeter's view of democracy, the aim of voting is just to maintain a threat to defeat political leaders at the polls. Hardin offers as a solution to the problem of ethnic conflict, global 'anomic capitalism.' Neither of these solutions, however, is itself problem free. In Chapter 4 some misgivings were expressed about the anomic capitalism solution to ethnic conflict. Those who agree with these misgivings will wish to avoid the neoliberal premises on which they are based and will accordingly either try to prevent catallaxy or rational choice theory generally from leading one to neoliberalism or reject these approaches in order to avoid this commitment. Even classified as a species of public choice theory that does not aim at preference aggregation, critics note that Riker's theory does not entirely escape the 'irrationality' problem (Coleman and Ferejohn 1986). In a multiparty system, cyclicality could still plague elections for leaders, as it would even in a two-party system at the level of party nominations.

Tyranny of the majority

As to the other problems of democracy, whether or how well the catallactic approach can address them depends in part on the distribution of preferences and political values among a voting population. Majority tyranny would be the most grave if one of the two modes in the 'revolution-prone' distribution depicted in Figure 3 were much higher than the other (in which case the danger would be of a minority *putsch*). Majority tyranny problems exist for those represented at the two tails of the bell curve in the 'stable' distribution, but in addition to affecting few people, this distribution is supposed to be found in societies lacking deep ideological differences of the sort that inhibit such things as vote-trading coalitions by means of which a minority can keep from being completely shut out. Attributing this 'solution' to Buchanan and Tullock, James Hyland identifies it as a version of the classic pluralist reaction to majority tyranny referred to in Chapter 5. The deficiency of both approaches, according to Hyland, is that they do not address situations when minorities are not in a position to engage in logrolling or otherwise to influence those in a majority, which are just the situations when the problem of the tyranny of the majority is most in need of a solution (Hyland 1995: 90–1).

Demagoguery

As noted in Chapter 4, Riker advised that citizens should be educated in rational choice theory so that they will understand that the concept of popular sovereignty is incoherent. To the extent that such a project succeeded it would certainly avert the problem of demagogues claiming to represent the people as a whole. A by-product of this campaign, apparently not recognized by Riker, could be to exacerbate one dimension of the 'massification of popular culture' problem that worried Tocqueville. This would be the case if attitudes of self-interested calculation and a punitive stance toward political leadership spilled over into popular culture generally, affecting people's views of their friends, family, and fellow citizens and fomenting an instrumental orientation where cultural products are primarily viewed in terms of their costs or of the profits they might command. As to whether the campaign Riker recommends could succeed, the impediment should be recognized that politicians would not see it as in their interests. Rationality for them might well dictate using the special powers of the state to promote a certain measure of irrationality among a population including belief in popular sovereignty. It is less costly for electoral purposes to claim to represent 'the people' than to try figuring out which constellation of specific self-interested preferences to serve.

This prospect highlights a feature of catallactic and public choice theory generally that some have seen as questionable. On such theory preferences and the presence or absence of rationality in action on them are regarded parts of a given background against which political cost/benefit calculations are made. In this way the preferences and rational habits are outside of or 'exogenous' to political processes. But if political activity itself can internally, or 'endogenously,' affect preferences and rationality, this assumption is challenged. Introduction of sophistications such as learning through repeated efforts to make a collective decision (called participation in 'iterated strategic games') can account for some changes internal to political processes, but it is not clear how this could accommodate changes in given

preference rankings or in how rational one is. Moreover, even this complication detracts from the descriptive simplicity and prescriptive neatness that
attracts many to the catallactic approach. (A pertinent treatment of endogenous preference formation in economic markets with reference to democracy
is in Bowles and Gintis 1993.)

Against this challenge, public choice theorists can claim that from the
point of view of the citizen confronted with policy options, the preferences
that one has at the time of voting must be taken as fixed, at least by the
voter. Otherwise people would always be second guessing themselves about
what their preferences might be as a result of voting one way or another. In
addition to this being unrealistic, it would render decision making extraordinarily difficult if not impossible. Meanwhile, from the point of view of
government, thinking in terms of endogenous preferences is an invitation
to try to manipulate them or to excuse undemocratic behaviour by claiming
that it responds not to what people's preference are but to what they will
become. (If pursued, I suspect that this debate would quickly lead into metaphysical realms having to do with the nature of a person, not unlike disputes about whether a material object can be identified independently of its
relations to other things or processes.)

Oppressive rule

Critics of catallaxy on the left, such as Macpherson, see it as not only ill-
equipped to head off oppressive rule by a minority, but as complicit in
capitalist domination. That the sentiments of leading catallactic theorists
have been procapitalistic there can be no doubt. Buchanan and Tullock
consider government claims to individual property the 'most basic threat' to
liberty (1962: 56, 97). Like Friedman and Hayek, they journeyed to Chile
after the 1973 coup there to give economic advice to the military government. Indeed, General Pinochet held a personal meeting with Hayek,
and Buchanan gave a talk at the headquarters of the Admiralty in Vena
del Mar where the coup (proximately) originated (reported, respectively,
in *La Tercera*, January 18, 1978 and *El Mercurio*, May 7, 1980). William
Scheuerman (1999a: ch. 7) argues that Schumpeter located himself on the
left only because he feared the demise of capitalism as inevitable and
thought that he could best slow this down as a catallactic social democrat.
(Scheuerman cites a 1920 essay by Schumpeter for support along with references of praise by him for Franco and criticism of the German press for being
too hard on Hitler before the latter took power, 324.)

These observations alone do not prove that catallaxy inherently sanctions
or masks oppression as this requires reasons beyond biography. The discussion in Chapter 4 about whether liberal democracy and socialism are
compatible is pertinent here. In extending the remarks in that chapter to
catallaxy, some of the same complexities about how catallaxy and socialism

or capitalism are to be interpreted apply, as do assumptions about whether capitalism is indeed oppressive or whether a less oppressive socialist alternative is available. Thus, a theorist like Hayek will have no problems endorsing a neoliberal extension of catallaxy on the grounds that this is the least disadvantaging form of human organization and, if free market forces work the way they should, it may not disadvantage anyone at all. Motives of citizens and politicians on the neoliberal scheme may still be interpreted on a economic model, but since the state is minimal for the neoliberal, the burden of their claim will stand or fall with their economic, not political, theories. On this interpretation, democratic motives could be attributed even to support for the Chilean coup. Acknowledging that it violently deposed a democratically elected government and used extraordinarily brutal measures to suppress opposition, the coup could be justified in the name of democracy on the grounds that it was required to prevent socialist planning from blocking the truly democratic functioning of a free market. This would be a sort of procapitalist analogue of defences of socialist authoritarianism as necessary to attain the superior democracy of a classless society. On this benign interpretation of the catallactic theorists' motives in this case, they may still be faulted for not learning the lesson of the earlier, left-wing experience that taking one democratic step backwards in anticipation of later taking two forward falsely assumes that democracy is like tap water that can be turned off and then on again without severe damage to it. It is noteworthy that praise of Chile since the resignation of Pinochet mainly focuses on its so-called economic achievements. (For a critical assessment of these achievements see Collins and Lear 1995.)

Different considerations pertain to a theorist who endorses the catallactic method, but wants it to stop short of neoliberalism. The reasons to want more than a mere caretaker state are: to maintain goods or services that the private sector cannot or will not affordably provide; to regulate private and public sector enterprises in the public interest; and to prevent monopolization from upsetting fair competition. (Like most neoliberals, Hayek recognizes the presumptive need only of the latter task, but thinks this should be done not by constraining monopolies but by laying down impartial rules for competition, 1979: 85.) For catallactic theorists consistently to recommend these things, certain claims of Downs and of Buchanan and Tullock would have to be abandoned. In particular Downs' implied sanctioning of preferential treatment by government officials for those with something special to offer them is an obvious invitation for the rich to buy government favours. This should be described as *antidemocratic*, not as a normal part of democratic functioning. Similarly, since government provision of goods, services, and protections is usually more important in large-scale societies than small ones, the recommendation of Buchanan and Tullock that government action is less appropriate the larger a society should also be dropped.

Having made such adjustments, some reasons come to mind for thinking that catallaxy is still in some way supportive of oppressive activities by a minority of powerful interests. One argument is that catallaxy justifies the most oppression-prone features of liberal democracy. It will be recalled that antioppressive theorists fear that oppression by powerful, minority interests is facilitated when liberal democracy restricts itself to no more than formal endorsement of democratic rights and discourages participation in favour of tenuously accountable representative democracy. Catallaxy endorses just such a restricted conception and in addition gives reasons to justify thin accountability and voter apathy.

Another misgiving pertains to political culture. To think of democratic politics in terms of the self-interested calculations of individuals is to debase the way democracy is regarded and invite its subversion. Citizens for whom democratic politics is just trying to figure out whether it is worth their while to vote for someone who might give them something in return or to punish somebody who has displeased them are not likely to be sufficiently committed to democracy to defend it (even in this narrow Schumpeterian sense) against challenges or to resist antidemocratic measures that might benefit them. Politicians for whom democracy is just an opportunity to aggrandize themselves will similarly have little incentive to defend or preserve it if the rewards for selling democracy out are high enough. Against these considerations, one might cite the claim of Buchanan and Tullock, referred to earlier, that since some people will in fact think this way, it is safest to gear democratic institutions and policies to them. Bowles and Gintis (1993), like most other critics from the left, see this as another instance of the endogenous creation of preferences and retort that designing politics for the worst people will bring out the worst in people.

Related to the argument about political culture is the claim that at the same time catallaxy promotes a pernicious political culture, it discourages the nurturing of an alternative culture that places civic commitment to public goods and enthusiastic involvement in public affairs at its centre. This is the core objection to catallaxy and several other approaches to democracy on the part of the participatory democrats, to whose views we now turn.

Chapter 7

Participatory democracy

Participatory-democratic theory is the polar opposite of catallaxy, and it set itself as well against all versions of liberal democracy that see active politics as the domain of government and (as in the case of the classic pluralists) interest group leaders. While these approaches view a large measure of apathy and political inactivity on the part of ordinary citizens essential to democracy, participatory democrats consider breaking down apathy and maximizing active citizen engagement a main task of democrats. Like other theorists informed by the realist school of Schumpeter and his followers, democracy for the catallactic and what Peter Bachrach called 'democratic elitist' school (1967) is just voting, while for the participatory democrats, representation and competitive voting in formal elections are viewed as necessary evils at best, which they aim to replace when possible with decision-making by discussion leading to consensus. While Hayek disparages 'unitedness in pursuit of known common goals' as a vestige of tribalism (1976: 111), participatory democrats applaud the forging of solidarity as a principal virtue of democracy.

Participatory democracy is not only conceptually at odds with catallaxy and democratic elitism but also its historical opponent. According to Jane Mansbridge the term 'participatory democracy' was coined by Arnold Kaufman in 1960 (Mansbridge 1995: 5). This was on the eve of the student power movements in the US, the aims of which were set down in a document, the 'Port Huron Statement,' prepared by radical students at the University of Michigan (Kaufman was one of their advisors) and serving as a reference point for students across the country and beyond. These students were simultaneously demanding participation in university and other sites of governance and criticizing the antiparticipatory views of their professors, among whom the neo-Schumpeterians were prominent (Teodori 1969: 163–72, Kaufman 1969 [1960]).

Rousseau

Almost without exception participatory-democratic theorists have appealed to the works of Jean-Jacques Rousseau, and in particular his *The Social*

Contract (published in 1762) for support. Rousseau stood against the earlier modern contract theorists, especially Hobbes. On Hobbes' view self-interested individuals in a natural state are motivated by mutual fear to submit themselves to a sovereign authority in exchange for security. Observing that for Hobbes, as for Locke, personal liberty is the prime motive for entering into a compact, and submission to a sovereign authority, whether a king or, as in Locke's version, a majority government, is its result, Rousseau asked how liberty and submission can be reconciled: 'if the force and liberty of each man are the chief instruments of his self-preservation how can he pledge them without harming his own interests . . .?' This poses the guiding problem of *The Social Contract*, namely to 'find a form of association . . . in which each, while uniting himself with all, may still obey himself alone and remain as free as before' (Rousseau 1950a [1762]: 13–14, bk I. ch. vi).

While most challenges to Hobbes by other contract theorists questioned his view that the sovereign should be an absolute monarch, Rousseau focused on the prior act whereby individuals in the state of nature agree to submit themselves to any form of political authority. He argued that in order to be legitimately binding this agreement must be unanimous and that to achieve its aims people must give up all their powers, since if anything were left outside of potential public control, it could be insisted that other things should be exempted and the point of the contract to create a public authority would be defeated. Together these conditions mean that a legitimate and effective contract involves each person giving up all of his powers to everyone else. The effect is to create a 'moral and collective body, composed of as many members as the assembly contains voters, and receiving from this act its unity, its common identity, its life and its will' (15, I.vi).

The will that this body politic or 'public person' acquires is the famous (or for Rousseau's critics, infamous) 'general will,' and it is by reference to this that Rousseau thought he could solve the problem he had set himself. The key is that the general will embodies a moral imperative for people to promote common interests. Just how (or whether) this mandate is derived from the originating contract is a matter of ongoing dispute among scholars concerning themselves with Rousseau's theory, but assuming it makes sense to say that in giving their powers over to each other people undertake to promote and preserve their common interests, Rousseau can claim that they are simultaneously *bound* to one another (in looking to the common good) and *free* (since the imperative to act in this way is something they have willingly created themselves).

The political prescriptions Rousseau drew from this theory were meant to apply to city states, such as the cantons of his native Switzerland. Indeed, these cities would have to be 'very small,' since they would be governed by a legislature made up of the people as a whole meeting periodically (90–1, 96, III.xiii, xvi). Rousseau usually reserved the term 'democracy' to refer just to one possible composition of an executive (where the entire people or a majority thereof executes laws as well as founding them). Democratic execution of laws is at best only approximated, and the larger a state the less feasible it is (63–6, III.iii, iv). Using the term 'democracy' loosely with respect to this technical sense to refer to government leaders selected by the population (rather than leadership by aristocrats or monarchs), Rousseau thinks that ideally selection by lot is superior to elections (107–9, IV.iii), and in any case governments are strictly mandated just to carry out the will of the legislature and hence have only administrative powers (93–6, III.xvi). When the people are in legislative mode a majority vote carries the day, and it is assumed that majority will expresses the general will (106–7, IV.ii).

A critical reading of Rousseau sees in his conception of a general will the seeds of totalitarianism (for instance, Talmon 1970). In particular, this conception is said to be especially susceptible to the dangers provided by the 'empty space' of democracy described in Chapter 2. The critics invariably seize upon a central thesis of Rousseau that one can be 'forced to be free.' He allowed that people's actions are not always in accord with the general will since 'each individual, as a man, may have a particular will contrary or dissimilar to the general will which he has as a citizen,' and if he refuses to obey the general will he may be 'compelled to do so by the whole body.' In such a case he is denied freedom to pursue his particular interests, but as a citizen his freedom has been enhanced (17–18, I.vii).

Rousseau and participationism

Rousseau's thesis does, indeed, seem hard to square with the strongly democratic views of participationists; nor can it be dismissed as inessential to his theory. In this respect it arguably differs from Rousseau's sexism, which led him to exclude women from the social contract (hence the use of gendered pronouns in the summary above) on the grounds that they are only suited to the service of men (Rousseau 1979 [1762]: bk V). So Carole Pateman, a feminist and a leading participatory-democratic theorist, can appeal to his core theory while regarding his sexism an aberration (Pateman 1985: 157–8). If Rousseau's views are to be consistently drawn on by participatory democrats, this must be because they can interpret his theories in ways useful to their ends, and in fact a case can be made that several of his theses, including the one about forcing people to be free, do admit of such interpretation. So, notwithstanding the democratically problematic nature of some of his notions and setting aside questions of interpretation such as Andrew Levine's thesis that there is a systematic tension between an apolitical, abstract ethics and prefiguration of more concrete Marxist political theory in *The Social Contract* (Levine 1993 and 1987), the rest of this chapter will explicate participatory-democratic theory against a Rousseauean setting.

Sovereign people and delegated government

Anarchists are participatory democrats who think full democracy requires that people directly govern themselves without the mediation of state agencies or officials (for instance, Michael Taylor 1982, and the contributions to Benello and Roussopoulos 1972). Pateman more closely represents most participatory democrats in stopping short of anarchism, from which she explicitly distances herself (1985: 134–42). Instead she endorses Rousseau's view that government is delegated to carry out the wishes of the people and is thus nothing but an administrative tool (150–2). This clearly puts her view and Rousseau's at odds with the catallactic theorists and liberal democrats in the tradition of Schumpeter, such as Riker, for whom governments are elected on the understanding that they will have a nearly free hand in governing as they see fit. As well, there are theoretical differences with more robust versions of liberal democracy.

Participationists' objection to representative democracy is stronger than the complaint that government representatives normally break campaign promises and pay little attention to citizen concerns except in superficial ways and then only as elections approach. These complaints are often voiced by liberal-democratic supporters of representative democracy. Similarly, among the several participatory measures discussed by Joseph Zimmerman are referenda, recall, and citizen-initiated legislation (1986); however by contrast to the other measures Zimmerman addresses (town hall legislative assemblies and voluntary neighbourhood administration), these are more ways of accomplishing what elected representatives ought to be doing and keeping them honest than they are alternatives to representative government. The fundamental participationist objection to any theory for which representative democracy is central echoes Rousseau's views that sovereignty 'cannot be represented' (1950a: 94, III.xv) and that there can be no contract between the governed and the government (96–8, III.xvi).

On the participatory-democratic perspective, democracy is control by citizens of their own affairs, which sometimes though not always involves instructing governmental bodies to carry out citizens' wishes. This perspective connotes a relation of continuity between people and government which is broken when the latter is regarded a representative of the former. It is then a short step to conceive of government as a body with its own interests and in charge of special state powers and with which citizens must negotiate or make contracts. The result is reflected in the title of Philip Resnick's critique of democracy in Canada, *Parliament vs. People*, where he argues that a section of the Canadian Constitution's Charter of Rights and Freedoms entitled, 'Democratic Rights,' should be retitled, 'voter's Rights' or 'better still "The Rights of Parliament" ' (1984: 53).

State and civil society

An implication of the foregoing observations is that for participatory democrats state and civil society are not distinct entities; there is no line dividing a state that rules and citizens in civil society who are ruled. This is reflected in Rousseau's argument that there is only one contract, that which creates the body politic. In this body governed and governors are identical: the body politic 'is called by its members *State* when passive, *Sovereign* when active' (1950: 15, I.vi). The 'chief business' of citizens is public service, and the 'better the constitution of a State is, the more do public affairs encroach on private in the minds of the citizens' (93, III.xv). These and related passages have fueled the criticisms of Rousseau for being a proto-totalitarian, where the distinction between public and private is obliterated and people are expected to serve the state.

One participatory-democratic response is to gravitate toward an anarchist position and maintain that on the Rousseauean perspective there is very little of a state for people to serve. In retort the critics may argue that if there is anything of a state left, its officials can still exercise dictatorial powers in the name of the general will, or that if the state really is marginalized, then statist oppression will be replaced by that of public opinion in the manner of Tocqueville's tyranny of majority mores. These reactions will be pursued in due course. Participationists typically consider the statism charge more plausible in the abstract than in the concrete. Their principal concern is that democracy be promoted outside of formal government in all the institutions of civil society.

In keeping with the Port Huron Statement, a prime target of attention for early participationists was the universities, over which radical students urged and sometimes secured partial democratization by involving students in decision-making at the level of the classroom as well as in committees in such things as curricular and grading policies. Similarly, participatory democrats have proposed ways to democratize workplaces, the family (including formation of alternatives for living and child care to the traditional family), media, neighbourhoods, preuniversity schooling and day care, and decision-making about human relations to the natural environment. All these locations constitute 'political systems' in a broader sense than having to do with the state, and they are thus subject to democratization (Pateman 1970: 35, Bachrach 1967: 70–8).

Participationist reaction to the criticism that few people are interested in devoting time to workplace councils or neighbourhood committees highlights a second group of concrete recommendations pertinent to the current topic. Citing empirical studies for support (Almond and Verba 1965, Verba and Nie 1972), participatory democrats argue that public reluctance to become directly involved in local activities is largely a function of the unavailability or the ineffectiveness of forums through which to exercise this ability. As Benjamin Barber puts it, people are 'apathetic because they are powerless, not powerless because they are apathetic' (1984: 272). In discussing 'democracy in industry' Pateman illustrates this claim when she distinguishes between 'partial' and 'full' participation, where in the former management consults with workers without any obligation to heed their advice, while in full participation 'each individual member of a decision-making body has equal power to determine the outcome of decisions' (1970: 71). Apathy might still persist even with opportunities for full participation at the level of the shop floor if decisions there can be overturned or are severely constrained by levels of higher management, which is why Pateman echoes many participationists in urging full workers' self-management (85).

In her discussion of workers' self-management in (the former) communist Yugoslavia – the main place it had been tried on a large scale – Pateman observes that the evidence for its beneficial effects on worker attitudes and effectiveness is inconclusive due to that country's top-down governmental structure (1970: ch. 5). This highlights a dimension of participationist recommendations pertaining to decision-making. Democracy is appropriate when alternative solutions to problematic situations are available, but democratic decision-making is of limited value when problems or alternative solutions are defined by people other than those who are supposed to address them and/or when there is little control over how or whether agreed upon solutions will be implemented.

Workers' self-managed firms in the former Yugoslavia often found that they were constrained in one or both of these ways by a state that was at best only slightly democratically responsive. Full participation thus requires citizen involvement at all stages of democratic decision-making. Referring specifically to environmental problems, Arthur Schafer (1974) identifies six of these stages: identification and definition of a problem, canvassing alternative solutions, proposing a specific solution, deciding whether or not to adopt the proposal, formulating a plan of implementation, and implementing the plan. His main point is that exclusion of people confronting the problem in question from decision-making in any one of these stages will weaken effective participation and enthusiasm to participate in the others. Similar considerations are raised by participatory democrats as cautions against proposals for 'direct democracy' by means of the extensive use of referenda aided by electronic balloting technology. 'Somebody,' as Macpherson puts it, 'must ask the questions' (1977: 95 and see Barber 1984: 289–90; for qualified defence of electronically aided direct democracy see McLean 1990 and Budge 1993).

The general will and the will of all

In a central passage of *The Social Contract* Rousseau announces that there is 'often a great deal of difference between the will of all and the general will' explaining that 'the latter considers only the common interest' while the former 'is no more than a sum of particular wills' (1950a: 26, II.iii). This passage makes it impossible to interpret the general will simply as what everyone might agree to or what the majority votes in favour of. Rousseau does remark that the general will is the opinion of the majority, but this obtains only when citizens are using their votes to express an opinion about whether the proposal 'is in accord with the general will' and only when 'all the qualities of the general will still reside in the majority' (106–7, IV.ii). Nor could the general will simply be that upon which there is unanimous agreement, since this might be reached by people each looking only to private interests but leading to a common result, such as the fear-driven contract in Hobbes' scheme (Harrison 1993: 55).

In Chapter 4 it was noted that although not all liberal democrats see it as the goal of democracy to aggregate interests, there is an inescapable element of aggregation in liberal-democratic theory: in accord with pluralism, people are assumed to vote on antecedently and usually diverse interests the mix of which will determine the distribution of votes. For Rousseau, such results reflect no more than the will of all, since people who simply vote on their preferences, even on many altruistic preferences, are not 'acting in accord with the general will,' which obliges them to try to ascertain what the common good requires when voting or otherwise making collective decisions. Rousseau is justly classified in the civic republican tradition (see Chapter 4) in his view that citizens ought to look first to common goods and that in doing so they constitute themselves as 'associations' as opposed to 'aggregations' (12, I.v). Democratic collective decision-making for Rousseau is, therefore, just this undertaking to find out and promote the public good. In form, such decision-making is best seen as an effort in consensus building, rather than as a contest among voters for whom democratic procedures are like the rules of a game each hopes to win. It is for this reason that Mansbridge entitles her book on this subject *Beyond Adversary Democracy* and that participatory democrats see constructive deliberation to attain consensus a superior way of making democratic decisions to voting, which Barber calls 'the least significant act of citizenship in a democracy' (Mansbridge 1983: 187 and see Pateman 1985: 185).

Levine illustrates the difference between a Rousseauean association and an aggregation with the example of people trying to decide where a road to connect two cities should be built (1993: 156–7). On what Mansbridge calls the adversarial model and Levine the mainstream, liberal-democratic view, citizens of the relevant jurisdiction will cast a vote each according to prior preferences and the outcome will be deemed democratic even if it is not the best place to build the road, for instance from an ecological or long-term demographic point of view. Utilitarians differ, albeit slightly, from the mainstream view since they have an idea of where the road *ought* to be built, namely in that place which will satisfy the greatest number of people. Voting is not a sure way of ascertaining what this is, but unless impeded by cyclical majorities, free-rider abstention, or the like it is generally reliable for this purpose. On Rousseau's perspective, by contrast, voters will try to ascertain what is best for the community comprising the two cities and those living between them.

Levine, himself, is doubtful that there is always an answer to such questions, but Ross Harrison thinks he can construct a general answer out of the egalitarianism reflected in Rousseau's comment that 'the general will tends to equality' (Rousseau 1950a: 23, II.i). On Harrison's interpretation, for people to discover the common good of the community is for them to discover what would equally benefit everyone in it (1993: 56–7). One objection that comes readily to mind is that there may be several alternative benefits, so it is still necessary for the associated deliberators to single one out. For Pateman this is not a serious objection since it is enough to appeal to the general will interpreted in this egalitarian way to rule out certain alternatives, namely those with inegalitarian consequences (1985: 155–6). In particular, she seizes on Rousseau's criticisms of economic or material inequalities, eloquently defended in his *Discourse on the Origins of Inequality* (1950b [1755]) and appealed to in *The Social Contract* where he describes 'the greatest good of all' as liberty and equality, and where equality mandates that 'no citizen shall ever be rich enough to buy another, and none poor enough to be forced to sell himself' (1950a: 49–50, II.xi).

Another objection is that due to basic conflicts of interest there may be no common goods to be discovered and that due to scarcity of resources the substantive equality that participationists like Pateman see as a precondition for pursuit of common goods is unattainable. One response on the part of the participatory democrat is to deny that these problems are insurmountable. Conflicts of the zero-sum game sort are seen not as inevitable features of human society but as a result of insufficient community feeling and commitment to common goods, and this is in turn a result of the isolations perpetuated by lack of opportunity for effective and ongoing participation. Scarcity on the Rousseauean perspective is in large measure a matter of maldistribution of existing resources, but it is also caused by the inflated needs of consumerism, which, like an individualism void of community spirit, is also susceptible of being eroded by participation. Thus Pateman alleges that departure from 'possessive individualist ways of thought and action' (Macpherson's phrase to describe consumerism and self-centredness) is facilitated by a change in people's values that results from political participation itself (1985: 156).

Barber offers a variation of this defence of participationism. While Mansbridge distinguishes between two forms of democracy, adversarial and unitary, Barber offers a three-way classification. 'Representative democracy,' also disparagingly labelled 'thin' by Barber, is democracy on the Schumpeterian model: citizenship is only a legal matter; people are bound together by self-interested contracts; and they are politically passive. One alternative model Barber calls 'unitary democracy' according to which: people are bound together by blood or analogously prepolitical and intimate ties; the ideal of citizenship is brotherhood; and politics involves self-abnegating submission to the group. The third category is 'strong democracy,' the title of Barber's book, a main thesis of which is that critics mistakenly assume that participatory democracy must be of the unitary variety. In strong democracy citizens relate to one another as 'neighbours' bound together as active participants in shared activities (1984: ch. 9).

Each form of democracy is 'grounded' in consensus, but of radically different types. Thin democracy is sustained by a contract entered into out of anticipation of mutual, self-interested advantage. The ground for unitary democracy is 'substantive consensus' around community-defining values that predate government and give individuals their identities. This is to be distinguished from the 'creative consensus' of strong democracy which 'arises out of common talk, common decision, and common work,' and is premised on 'citizens' active and perennial participation in the transformation of conflict through the creation of common consciousness and political judgment' (Barber 1984: 224 and see Mansbridge 1983: ch. 18). Barber's conception of strong democracy is meant to provide participatory-democratic theory with a way to recognize diversity of interests. Citizens in whom 'the quality of the general will' reside will see divergences as problems to be worked through together by seeking a creative consensus.

Forced to be free

In a state of nature people are motivated by instinct and enjoy 'natural liberty' when they succeed in getting whatever their instincts prompt them to want. People who are citizens in a body politic are motivated by their sense of duty to promote the common good. Action out of duty is self-imposed or an instance of self-mastery, rather than being a result of 'the mere impulse of appetite' and hence constitutes a unique and superior kind of 'civil liberty' (Rousseau: 1950, 18–19, I.viii). This is the picture of human action in which the notion of being forced to be free is supposed to be given nonpernicious interpretation. Those who are obliged by the laws of the body politic to act against their natural liberty are thereby 'forced' to act as they would rather not, but in being obliged to act in accord with their civil liberty they are not just acting freely but truly freely. It should be obvious that this account is open to debate – and there has been a lot of it – about whether or to what extent Rousseau's picture opens the door to authoritarian abuse. The problem arises in a situation where people in possession of the power of a state (or in a nongovernmental association of informal levers of power) judge that its citizens are not motivated by civic duty and thus suspend what the leaders consider the citizens' mere natural liberties, while denying that this is an infraction of their freedom in its superior sense.

I know of no champion of participatory democracy who endorses such a version of paternalism, and this sort of situation is not what they focus on in Rousseau. Rather they are attracted to two themes suggested in his discussions around the 'forced to be free' thesis. One of these concerns the goals of participatory democracy. Commentators on this theory have correctly worried about how participation should be interpreted and valued. One of these, Donald Keim (1975), sees a basic difference between theorists such as Bachrach (1967) for whom participationism mainly requires that the domains within which people may (effectively) engage in collective decision-making be broadened and who value this for enhancing individual autonomy and those theorists (Keim cites Robert Pranger, 1968) who think that participation is essentially acting in mutually supportive concert with others thus creating a community around common goods and hence worthy of being valued 'for its own sake.' But, as George Kateb observes, the radical students of the Port Huron Statement were motivated by *both* the 'wish for self-mastery and the thirst for community' (1975: 93). One might say that they were pursuing goals consistent with both the Ciceronian and the Aristotelian strains of civic republicanism as these were described in Chapter 4. The attraction to the participationist theorists of Rousseau's 'forced to be free' idea was, then, that it sought a way of integrating these two goals.

The other theme attractive to the participationists in Rousseau's discussion concerns his views about *how* people come to escape their 'servitude to instinct' and acquire civic virtue. 'The passage,' as Rousseau begins his chapter about civic freedom, 'from the state of nature to the civil state produces a very remarkable change in man, by substituting justice for instinct in his conduct, and giving his actions the morality they had formerly lacked' (1950a: 18, I.viii). In the latter state people are still forced to be free, but in a more defensible way than described in the scenario above: someone who had previously only considered himself now finds he is 'forced to act on different principles, and to consult his reason before listening to his inclinations.' Pateman urges that the term 'forced' in this passaged be interpreted as 'strengthened,' where the strength to look to the common good 'is provided by the transformation of [citizen's] consciousness that is gradually brought about through the participatory process' (1985: 156). To mark yet another polar difference between catallaxy and participationism, preferences for Pateman, as for all participatory democrats, are formed within the political processes in which people are engaged (or 'endogenously' to them as this notion was discussed in Chapter 6).

Both components of Rousseau's views on this topic are central to participatory-democratic theory: the idea that people's values and motivations are subject to radical transformation and the thesis that political participation can effect this transformation as a sort of on-the-job democratic training programme. So most of Pateman's touchstone text on participatory democracy (1970) is devoted to highlighting these views in the works of earlier democratic theorists, including Mill and G.D.H. Cole as well as Rousseau, and to illustrating them in the cases of industrial democracy and workers' self-management.

The principal differences among the three kinds of democracy Barber addresses is that thin democracy 'leaves men as it finds them,' namely self-interested bargainers, while unitary democracy 'creates a common force, but it does so by destroying autonomy and individuality altogether.' Only in strong democracy are individuals transformed such that they pursue the common good while preserving their autonomy 'because their vision of their own freedom and interests has been enlarged to include others' (1984: 232). Formal pedagogy can help to achieve this transformation, as can participation in local, private-sphere activities as in schools, churches, families, social clubs, or cultural groups, while direct political participation in public affairs is the most effective venue of transformation, according to Barber, who cites Tocqueville as well as Mill and Rousseau for support (233–7). The prescriptions that follow from this perspective are clear: forums for participation should be encouraged wherever and whenever possible and inhibitors of participation, such as economic deprivation or lack of time and elitist or possessive-individualist values, should be identified and combated.

Problems of democracy

Oppression

The 'problem of democracy' participationists explicitly set out to address is that democratic procedures facilitate and provide cover for oppressive rule based on class, gender, race, or other domains of ongoing exclusion and subordination. The reasons they see for this are not that elected representatives can be bought and that most people have little effective control over the comportment of political parties and legislative agendas. Nor is it just that liberal-democratic arrangements leave oppressive structures in tact in private realms. Even more debilitating is that people whose experience in collective self-determination is confined mainly to voting acquire neither the knowledge, the skills, nor the expectations for taking charge of their lives, thus acquiescing in their own oppression. Direct participation, initially in small and localized arenas, is required to break the resulting cycle of political passivity and continuing subordination.

Irrationality

An effect of the recommended alternative to exclusively electoral, representative democracy is that some other problems of democracy are also addressed. One is its putative irrationality, since for participatory democrats this is a problem entirely self-imposed by those who equate democracy with voting, thought of as a procedure employed by self-interested citizens to produce social policy or elect governments. To the extent that this problem requires a solution, it is to facilitate the transformation of individuals to civic-minded citizens and to expand democracy from voting to collective efforts to reach consensus. On the participationist viewpoint, the problem of apathy ('anomic democracy' as the Trilateral Commission labelled it) also largely results from what they see as the depoliticizing effects of representative democracy. Such democracy also has built into it an adversarial political culture, which, unlike the impetus toward consensus seeking of participatory democracy, exacerbates conflict.

Majority tyranny and the empty space

These proffered solutions illustrate the way ideas about democracy are imbedded within conceptions of the nature of humans and society, since they are not likely to be seen as solutions except by someone who accepts central participatory-democratic tenets. Participatory-democratic solutions to the problems of the tyranny of the majority and democracy's empty space can also be located in this category. To some it is obvious that participatory democracy not only offers no solutions to these problems, but blatantly invites them. Minority dissent is easily taken to be evidence of a lack of will or ability to seek consensus and hence of being a bad citizen; so there would be enormous pressure to conform to majority sentiment in a participatory-democratic community. If these communities are supposed to aim at a common good, authoritarians can too easily claim to know what the good is and thus to speak on behalf of the true community.

For participatory-democratic theorists, however, these are not seen as overwhelming problems. This must be because for them silencing minority opinion or acquiescence to authoritative declarations of knowledge about community goods are incompatible with ongoing and transformative participation, and such participation is just what democracy is taken to be. In addition, there is an implied counter attack. In participatory-democratic literature very little attention is devoted to the topic of rights. Rights prominently figure in the approaches to politics of Hobbes and Locke for which Rousseau sought an alternative. When problems of social conflict must be settled by appeal to rights that protect some members of the society from others, this is both evidence that the society fails to be a genuine community and a perpetuating cause for people not striving to make it one, since in a political culture of rights people view one another as potential enemies and use rights as shields or as weapons. The implied counter argument is that focusing on the majority tyranny problem and orienting public politics around rights to meet it locks people into the very conflictual situations that create the problem of needing to protect people from one another. (Elements of this stance are suggested by Barber, 1984: 137, 160.)

Popular culture

Whether participatory democracy contains resources for adequately dealing with the (alleged) problem that democracy debases culture depends more on empirically than on theoretically contested claims. Implicit in the egalitarian dimension of a participatory-democratic perspective is not just a prescription for economic equality, but an assumption of relative equality in human abilities and talents: participation could not draw out the best in everyone if there was nothing worthwhile to draw out. Whether this is the case regarding cultural talents and powers of appreciation, is not the sort of thing that can be settled by a general theory of human nature, for instance, one that says that talent is a scarce resource. Mansbridge (1995) allows that systematic study of this question with respect to political talents is sparse, and appeals to her own experience in participatory democratic ventures as evidence in favour of the optimistic conclusion. A similar observation is no doubt applicable to cultural aptitudes. (I have noted that those who, like myself, were raised in towns small enough for some interaction on an equal footing among different sectors of their populations, for instance in mixed-class schools, are often more generous in their estimates of how widespread cultural talents are than those from more cloistered and elitist backgrounds.)

Effectiveness and social capital

As to the question of governmental effectiveness, a hypothesis that Robert Putnam takes over from James Coleman concerning 'social capital' is apt. By social capital they mean 'features of a social organization such as trust, norms, and networks, that can improve the efficiency of society by facilitating coordinated actions.' An example is an agricultural community where farmers trust one another and hence are more prone to share equipment and help each other with the harvest thus allowing each to accomplish more with less investment of time and expense than when trust is lacking (Putnam 1993: 167, Coleman 1990). This perspective is the opposite of that favoured by champions of *laissez-faire* capitalism in the tradition of Adam Smith according to which cooperative values breed laziness while rugged competitiveness is required for efficiency, but it is fully in the tradition of participationism, according to which cooperative citizen involvement in joint activities nurtures just those values conducive to the accumulation of social capital and hence, on the thesis of Putnam and Coleman, to effective undertaking of human projects.

Realism

The charge that participatory democracy is unrealistically utopian sometimes is premised on a theory of human nature such as the Smithian one just alluded to. Rousseau, himself, seems to be granting the charge when he announces that were there 'a people of gods, their government would be democratic,' but that so 'perfect a government is not for men' (1950a: 66, III.iv) or when he recommends the secret ballot on the grounds that in an imperfect political world a hedge against corrupt electoral procedures is required and, in an argument not unlike one of the catallactic theorists, Tullock and Buchanan, Rousseau attributes the longevity of Venetian democracy to its design of laws 'suitable only for men who are wicked' (1950a: 120, IV.iv).

These claims depend upon views of human nature that modern-day partici-pationists need not accept and that, moreover, many of them contest partly by invoking theories of Rousseau himself. More difficult for participationism from the point of view of realism is the problem of scale. Assuming that participatory-democratic theory has a viable approach to conflict within a society, its application to international conflicts is less clear, since its focus and forte is groups small enough to admit of direct interaction. This poses a problem also at the level of the state or in substate locales such as regions and even medium-sized municipalities.

Addressing this problem, Macpherson projects a 'pyramidal council system' where one starts with 'face-to-face discussion and decision by consensus or majority' at the local level of neighbourhood and/or workplace where dele-gates would be elected to 'make up a council at the next more inclusive level, say a city borough or ward or township' and so on to the level of the nation. This scheme would be similar to the system of soviets in the former Soviet Union (at least as projected) with the large exception that instead of being overlaid with a single, autocratic political party the council system would include competing political parties provided that the parties, them-selves, were open and internally democratic (Macpherson 1977: 108–14, and see Resnick 1984: ch. 9 and Callinicos 1993).

Less grandly, Barber concludes his book with a chapter listing what he sees as institutional measures required to arrive at strong democracy in the US including neighbourhood assemblies, local election by lottery, work-place democracy, and other such measures (1984: 307). Yet another approach, sometimes appealed to by participationists, is found in 'associative-democratic' theory, some current versions of which are sufficiently well worked out to merit more extended treatment.

Associative democracy

Far from seeing devolution of political power to local levels as utopian, the-orists calling themselves 'associative' or 'associational' democrats regard this as realistic and as a way to invigorate democracy generally, in large-scale polit-ical societies as in local institutions. Joshua Cohen and Joel Rogers report having coined the term 'associative democracy' (simultaneously and inde-pendently with John Mathews – Cohen and Rogers 1995: 8, Mathews 1989).

They explicate a version of the theory aimed at showing how strengthening the discretionary power of local, voluntary, and self-governing associations would enhance the way that democracies such as in the US function by combating the 'mischiefs of factions,' facilitating informed and legitimate state policies, and promoting social justice (1995: 11). Meanwhile, Paul Hirst (1994) articulates a less state-friendly version of this approach drawing upon nineteenth- and early twentieth-century forerunners. Just as consociational democracy cannot be straightforwardly classified as a species of classic pluralism, so it would be inaccurate to conceive of associationalism simply as an application of participationist theory. However, appeal to it might be attractive to those wishing to meet the charge that participatory democracy is unrealistic.

In the deep background of this theory, Hirst sees anarchist-leaning theorists and especially Pierre-Joseph Proudhon, who advocated a 'mutualist' reorganization of economies around worker or artisan cooperatives in federations of decentralized states (1979 [1863]). More recent are the British theorists, John Neville Figgis, Harold Laski, and G.D.H. Cole. In an introduction to his selection of writings by these authors (1989), Hirst draws three main themes from them: a critique of parliamentary sovereignty, 'functional' democracy, and anti-statism. The first theme represents a certain departure from Rousseau. According to Laski, the idea that the people of an entire society may collectively be possessed of sovereignty is, in Hirst's summary 'a myth that modern states inherited from early modern royal autocracies' so when parliaments purport to represent a sovereign people, they are reduplicating such autocracy in modern guise. Popular power cannot be represented by a single institution but 'is federative by nature' and must be sought in a society's several associations of common purpose and activity (Hirst 1994: 28, Laski 1921).

While classic representative democracy sends members to a legislative assembly ostensively to represent the interests of individuals in geographic electoral districts, the form of representation argued for by Cole is 'functional.' Focusing on industrial organization, Cole advocated retrieval of an analogue of the Medieval guilds where for him this meant that society-wide tasks, such as national defence, would be performed by assemblies to which are appointed delegates from each of the main industries of the society (hence representation is determined by industrial function) in what he called 'guild socialism' (Cole 1980 [1920], Hirst 1989: 30–9). In campaigns such as by Figgis (1914) that the churches and other institutions of civil society should be as far as possible independent of regulation or direction by a central state, Hirst sees an important difference between this sort of functional approach and that of the corporatists, such as Hegel and European Fascist theorists contemporary with Cole (Hirst 1989: 16–19, Hegel 1942 [1821]: 152–5, 200–2, parags 250–6, 200–2, and translator's note, 366). Corporatists share the notion that government should give power to major, functionally determined 'corporations' of society, most importantly labour and capital, but also such institutions as agricultural cooperatives, associations of small business, the churches, and cultural undertakings. What Cole and the others resisted was the further corporatist view that the activities of these institutions should be directed as well as coordinated by a strong central state.

Hirst does not agree with all the tenets of these forerunners. In particular he thinks that Cole's guild system ought to have made more allowance for regional representation, that he was too narrowly confined in a 'workerist' way to functions relating to industrial labour, and that even regarding industries he did not allow for new functional representations created by rapid changes in technology or divisions of labour (1994: 107, 1993: 126–8). Nonetheless, Hirst thinks it important and possible that associations gradually 'become the primary means of democratic governance of economic and social affairs' (1994: 20). The obvious link with participationism is that the associations he and others have in mind are voluntary and self-governing. Examples Hirst gives are: local unions, associations of owners of small firms, religious voluntary workers in inner cities, disadvantaged ethnic groups seeking economic development and community control, feminist and gay groups aiming to escape discrimination and create their own communities, and ecological advocacy groups (1994: 43). Other examples often mentioned by associative democrats are neighbourhood associations, consumer groups, and parent-teacher associations.

Associationists are loathe to prescribe detailed methods whereby such associations could assume governing responsibilities of a central state, because they consider this a highly context-sensitive matter. Hirst thinks that the ability of local, voluntary associations to solve social or economic problems better than either central state planning or the market will encourage states to facilitate their formation and to invest them with governing responsibilities (1994: 41). Cohen and Rogers give the examples of devising, interpreting, and administering policies regarding environmental standards, occupational health and safety, vocational training, and consumer protection, in all of which 'associative efforts can provide a welcome alternative or complement to public regulatory efforts' due to their superior ability to 'gather local information, monitor behavior, and promote cooperation' (1995: 44). As to just which associations are to acquire 'semi-public' powers and how they may secure necessary funding, Philippe Schmitter (1995) advances a suggestion, endorsed by Hirst (1994: 62), whereby individual citizens would be allotted vouchers which they could transfer to any associations they wished, provided the latter conformed to certain standards, including openness of membership, internal democracy, budgetary transparency, and prohibition of such things as violence, racism, or criminal behaviour.

Contemporary associationist democrats emphasize that they do not favour dismantling the central state or advocate minimal states in the manner of neoliberalism. The standards for associations just mentioned require central legislative and legal institutions to be set and enforced, and states are needed in the face of tasks of society-wide coordination or needs that no voluntary associations exist to serve. With these concerns in mind Hirst represents associative democracy not as an exclusive alternative but as 'a supplement and a healthy competitor' for what he sees as the 'current dominant forms of social organization: representative mass democracy, bureaucratic state welfare, and the big corporation' (1994: 42). This poses a problem for someone who wishes to appeal to associative democracy to show how participatory democracy could be realistic.

The problem is evident in Cohen and Roger's exposition and critical reactions to it (usefully included by them with their 1995 statement of the theory). The principal theoretical merits they claim for associative democracy is that it would strengthen popular sovereignty (in the 'whole society' sense about which Hirst, following Laski, is wary) and that it would promote political equality, distributive equality, and civic consciousness, in accord with values they consider liberal democratic and within liberal-democratic states (1995: 64–9). The practical, political advantages they see are to minimize factionalism and to facilitate economic efficiency and competent governance. To this end, they regard it as important to recognize that associations are 'artifactual,' which means that, though they are not simply political creations, government policies can affect the kinds of associations there will be (46–7). Since, moreover, such policy can help to mold the nature and distribution of a society's associations in good or in bad ways, 'the trick of associative democracy' is to use 'conventional policy tools to steer the group system toward one that, for particular problems, has the right sorts of qualitative features' (50), for them, therefore, one that promotes equality, civic consciousness, and the like.

Whatever success this portrayal may have in persuading liberal democrats (at least those with social-democratic leanings) of the realistic virtues of associative democracy, it was not well received by the more radical of Cohen and Roger's commentators. Schmitter and Iris Young fault them for downplaying the role of spontaneously formed social movements which, as Young insists, do have something 'natural' about them in not being artifacts of public policy (Young 1995: 210). The central and controlling role Cohen and Rogers assign the state leads Levine to see a worrisome element of corporatism in their approach (1995: 160). Hirst shares both concerns, particularly seeing in the approach echoes of Emile Durkheim's version of neocorporatism according to which democracy essentially involves effective communication between the state and organizations representing a society's main occupational groups (1995: 104, Durkheim 1957: chs 1–9).

Participationism as a project

One reaction of participatory democrats to this debate might be, of course, to side with Cohen and Rogers and classify associative democracy as a version of liberal democracy, albeit one that provides more space than other versions for citizen participation. Another is to try working out the details of a more thoroughly participatory-associational scheme capable of implementation in today's world. A third, more pragmatic orientation applies to any effort to give concrete interpretation to participatory-democratic theory. Macpherson classifies problems confronting an attempt to implement participationist ideas as challenges rather than as necessarily insurmountable obstacles – 'the main problem about participatory democracy is not how to run it but how to reach it' (1977: 98) – so the task of participatory democrats is to identify obstacles to realizing their prescriptions and to find opportunities for overcoming them.

The two main obstacles Macpherson sees are a public culture largely incorporating possessive-individualist values (hence citizens' acceptance of thin, representative government, provided they are kept well provided with consumer goods) and great economic inequalities, which further act as disincentives to participation even at local levels. This creates a vicious circle in which Macpherson seeks 'loopholes' that might offer grounds of hope, of which he identifies three. Degradation of the environment and threats to natural resources have made many people question the wisdom of indefinite economic growth and consumerism as the goal of life, and this erodes possessive individualist values. Failure of both private corporations and elected governments to confront problems affecting people where they live and work has led to the formation of voluntary, activist neigbourhood associations and pressure for workplace democracy. And the standard of living for increasing portions of populations has fallen in the face of growing and extreme minority wealth, thus prompting demands for policies in the direction of economic equality (1977: 98–108).

Barber takes a similar approach, identifying as analogues of Macpherson's loopholes what he sees as alternatives to the ethic of decision-making in traditional liberal-democratic politics. That ethic is adversarial – prototypically, voting for competing candidates or policies. One alternative Barber calls a 'consociational' model of decision-making based on amicable agreement and another is 'authoritative interpretation' where, for example, a chairperson's 'sense of the meeting' replaces votes and 'obviates the need for factions to form around adversary interests.' These practices point in the direction of a strong-democratic model where political decision-making is not seen as a matter of making the 'right choices' given one's preferences but as the undertaking to 'will into being a world that the community must experience in common' (1984: 199–200).

Informing these reactions to the utopianism charge is a general orientation toward the relations among the actual, the possible, and the desirable in politics. While theorists in the realist school see as the strength of their approach that it takes society and people as they are rather than as others may wish them to be, participationists view this stance as capitulation to the status quo. Pateman articulates an alternative perspective in her contrast between the Rousseauean social contract and what she sees as the antiparticipationist, liberal contracts of Hobbes or Locke. These serve to 'justify social relations and political institutions that already exist,' while the Rousseauean contract provides a 'foundation for a participatory political order of the future' (1985: 150).

Participationism in context

In keeping with the decision to bracket historical or political speculations about the origins of approaches to democratic theory, this chapter has focused on the content of participationism. However, it might be appropriate to conclude by noting that the principal North American expositions of participatory democracy were produced during a period of under two decades and were overtly inspired by oppositional political undertakings beginning in the mid 1960s. It is not hard to understand why this should be the case. The student, women's, civil rights, and peace movements of those times formed precisely because their members found the existing institutions of representative democracy inadequate as channels for effective political expression of their concerns. Moreover, the relative successes of these movements in interjecting these concerns into public consciousness and in reforming some private and public institutions was achieved by just the sorts of direct engagement of large numbers of people united in common causes generally prescribed by participatory-democratic theory.

Evidence that enthusiasm for participationism waxes and wanes with the popularity of such movements (as opposed to having purely theoretical origins) is that more current interest in it is expressed by partisans of environmentalism (for instance, Paehlke 1989, Naess 1989, Mason 1999). Also, echoes of participatory-democratic theory may be found in more recent approaches to democratic theory, such as on the part of some of the associationist democrats and the views of the deliberative democrats, where participationist themes are retrieved albeit in muted form and in a more institution-friendly way than in core participatory-democratic theory. Before turning to deliberative democracy (in Chapter 9), the pragmatic themes raised at the end of this chapter will be further pursued in Chapter 8.

Democratic pragmatism

In this chapter I shall flag a complication in theorizing about democracy additional to those noted in the first two chapters and fulfill the promise to explicate (a bit of) my own perspective in thinking about democracy. What I am calling democratic pragmatism is not so much a recognized theory of democracy in the way that, for instance, participatory democracy or classic pluralism are, as it is an orientation toward politics that may be integrated with elements of other theories. Accordingly, this chapter will follow a some-what different format from the others in not trying to apply pragmatism directly to the problems of democracy (although toward the end of Chapter 11, this orientation will be directly applied to the problematic dimensions of globalization).

The complications noted in Chapter 1 are that attempts to understand and appraise democratic theories cannot be completely abstracted from the historical and social settings in which they are propounded and that theo-ries differ not just in their conclusions but also in whether and how they place major emphasis on the evaluation of democracy, conceptions of its meaning, or views about how democracy actually functions. The additional complication is that working conceptions of democracy are bound to affect how theories about it are understood and critically accessed, thus raising the dangers of misperception and bias. I do not think these dangers can be entirely averted, but by describing the conceptions, at least readers can take them into account in making up their minds about the theories surveyed. The conceptions are called 'working' because they should be amenable to alteration in light of the examinations they initially guide; indeed, some aspects of my own earlier ideas about democracy and democratic theory have changed in preparing this book.

The thinking I bring to democracy and hence to democratic theories is largely influenced by C.B. Macpherson and John Dewey, and its main com-ponents may be labelled 'pragmatic' after the school of philosophy of which Dewey was a defining member. A brief summary of pertinent themes in Dewey's main work on democracy, *The Public and Its Problems* (1927), will serve to introduce these components. A 'public' in Dewey's usage is formed whenever people recognize that their actions have 'enduring and extensive' consequences for each other and for indefinite other people in the circumstances they share. 'Political democracy' exists to the extent that people thus constituted undertake collective measures to regulate these actions and their effects by appointing leaders to enact appropriate regulations (12–17). A public is deficient in political democracy when leaders or policies are imposed by force or unquestioningly accepted by custom or when, however selected, leaders use their positions to pursue private ends (ch. 3). Broader than political democracy is what Dewey calls 'democracy as a social idea,' which consists of people 'having a responsible share according to capacity in forming and directing' activities of the several overlapping groups to which each belongs (147).

Read one way, Dewey's notion of the public and its problems clearly involves taking substantive stands on specific matters of debate among democratic theorists. For example, participatory democrats must resist the important role he accords to political leadership, and catallactic and some classic pluralist theorists will reject the idea that democracy requires leaders to pursue public goods. I find myself sympathetic to Dewey on both these issues as I do regarding his (to my mind successful) efforts to avoid exclusive choices between Rousseauean collectivism or Lockean individualism in normative political theory (54: 87–8) or their social-scientific analogues in conceptualizing the relation between individuals and groups (23: 69). I am also in sympathy with his view, shared by Macpherson, that a democratically functioning group is to be valued especially for liberating development of the potentialities of all the individuals in it (Dewey 1927: 147; Macpherson 1973: ch. 3, 1977: ch. 3) and with the view of each theorist that egalitarian, and in Macpherson's case explicitly socialistic, policies are required for approximating this goal.

But these specific matters are not what I primarily draw from this approach as a useful perspective from which to approach democracy and democratic theory generally. Rather, within the theory are the following four theses that together define the orientation in question:

Democracy is of unlimited scope   With participationists, Dewey insists that political relations of publics and government leaders do not by any means exhaust democracy. On his view democracy is appropriate to 'all modes of human association, the family, the school, industry, religion,' or any other site of extensive and enduring mutually affecting interactions among people (143).

Democracy is context sensitive   Dewey's philosophical formation was initially Hegelian, and sometimes shades of Hegel's perfectionism can be detected in *The Public and Its Problems*. An example is a remark that were history to reach an end so that all the forms of state could be compared, a single, best form might be identified (33), but this is out of keeping with most of Dewey's discussion of variations in state forms, a survey of which shows, he maintains, that 'temporal and local diversification is a prime mark of political organizations' (47). Attempts by a public to regulate its common affairs (the core of political democracy for Dewey) are 'experimental' and will 'differ widely from epoch to epoch and from place to place' (65).

The point I draw from Dewey's discussion of state forms is that ways for achieving democratic progress or inhibiting regress depend on the circumstances (social, economic, cultural, and so on) within which this is important, and as these circumstances vary so will appropriate democratic institutions, policies, and practices. Such an orientation is central to Macpherson's influential published lectures, *The Real World of Democracy*, where he argued that each of the developed capitalist, socialist, and developing societies contained both democratic and antidemocratic features specific to them, thus presenting unique democratic challenges and possibilities (Macpherson 1965; and my discussion, 1994: ch. 1).

Democracy is a matter of degree   To say that democracy is a social idea is not to say that it is often or even ever attained in full (148–9), and Dewey allows that sometimes publics engage in socially harmful activities (15). This means that one can value democracy while recognizing that it might sometimes be in conflict with other values and that it might never be perfectly realized. Democracy on this view is an ideal in the sense of being a model by reference to which alternative (imperfect) democracy-enhancing practices and institutions might be identified. The essential methodological point here is that rather than regarding democracy as a quality that a social site either has or lacks, one should focus on 'publics' to ask how democratic (or undemocratic) they are, how democratic they might (or ought to) be, and how democracy within them can be enhanced.

Ian Shapiro notes that the unlimited scope and context sensitivity aspects of Dewey's approach mean that neither majority voting rules associated with formal elections nor the requirement of universal consent or unanimity for constituting democratic structures and rules is essential to democracy in all situations. As noted in Chapter 6, Buchanan and Tullock make a superficially similar point, but Shapiro observes that for them, as for contractarian theorists, the presumptive or default rule for those who limit democracy to formal voting is unanimous consent to the constitutional rules regulating it. He argues that in the relatively rare domains of social life where relations are created *ex nihilo* and cooperatively, unanimity is appropriate, but that usually the degree and nature of assent required for democratic decisions depends upon local circumstances (1999a: 31–9).

It might further be remarked that even formal constitution-making never takes place in a social or historical vacuum. Such endeavours instead grow out of and presuppose preexisting collective activities of relevant 'publics.' On a pragmatic perspective, a problem that has vexed some theorists of how constitutional democracy could ever get off the ground (see Mueller 1979: 268) is not seen as theoretically grave, as long as there are some democracy-friendly practices and attitudes on which to build, and this, according to Dewey, for whom democracy is 'the idea of community life itself' (1927: 148), will always be the case.

Democracy is problematic   A basic tenet of pragmatism is that human affairs are best seen as problem-solving processes, which, moreover, are unending because every solution creates new problems. This is no less true of politics than of science, education, art, and the interactions of everyday life. Continuing problems confronting 'publics' according to Dewey are for them to recognize themselves as publics and to regulate their common affairs in such a way as to liberate individuals' potentials. When this calls for political democracy, one problem created is to keep leaders honest and another is to entrust leaders with discretion without dampening citizen engagement and initiative. Efforts of everyone to exercise or develop their potentialities are not infrequently impeded by conflicts (for instance, over access to limited resources) so this is another problem. When Dewey says that it 'is not the business of political philosophy and science to determine what the state in general should or must be' (34), he means that political theorists ought to locate themselves *within* the ongoing processes of their societies and use their specialized skills to assist publics in their confrontation of problems by aiding in the creation of methods such that experimentation with solutions 'may go on less blindly, less at the mercy of accident, more intelligently, so that men may learn from their errors and profit from their successes' (34).

A radical interpretation of this orientation, forcefully expressed by Richard Rorty (1990), subordinates political philosophy entirely to politics so that the role of theorists is mainly to articulate existing values or goals of the societies in which they find themselves. A weaker and more palatable interpretation allows for critical interrogation of socially accepted goals and the projection of alternatives, but recognizes that if these are to have social or political effects they must draw upon aspects of values and tendencies already detectable within existing values and practices, even if these are in tension with other values and with alternative practices. Perhaps Michael Walzer's view of the way that political philosophy should be pursued 'within the cave' is of this weaker pragmatic variety (1983) as are the critical appropriations of Dewey by Richard Bernstein (1971: pt 3) and Cornell West (1989: ch. 3).

In previous writings of my own, I have tried to deploy the concepts of this orientation to address the problem of how economic egalitarian political projects might avoid the authoritarianism that plagued past socialisms by being integrated with efforts to defend and expand democracy (1987, 1994). I think that someone could accept most of the analyses of this book without agreeing with this left-wing political project, though it should be clear when I am assuming the accuracy of some of its key tenets. As noted in earlier chapters, this is especially evident in my assessments of the adequacy of theories to avoid the problem of democracy masking or perpetuating 'oppressions,' since as this term was defined in Chapter 2, it is mainly theorists on the left who consider this a problem at all.

A more intimate connection between my political views and democratic pragmatics is the conviction that with the resurgence of aggressive capitalism since the fall of communism in the former Soviet Union and Eastern Europe, not only do egalitarian values and politics need to be defended, or in Macpherson's phrase 'retrieved,' but commitment to and enthusiasm for democracy itself is in danger of atrophying due to public cynicism bred of obvious subversion of democratic forums and institutions by powerful, moneyed interests. This therefore poses another problem of democracy, namely that efforts are called for to maintain and spark interest in and to invite innovative thought about it.

Putting specific political viewpoints aside, the advantage I claim for the pragmatic orientation I have sketched is that it facilitates taking an ecumenical approach to democratic theories. One reason for this is that the orientation is not anchored in a single concept of democracy. This is because its core concept is not 'democracy' but 'more (or less) democratic.' I have therefore advanced different versions of an admittedly rough-edged definition according to which a site of mutually affecting interaction (a country, a neighbourhood, a region of the world, a trade union, a school or university, a city, a church, and so on – in short a Deweyan public or group) becomes more democratic when more of the people who make it up come to have effective control over what happens to and in it through joint actions they take to this end (1987: ch. 3, 1994 ch. 3).

On this perspective, an ideally democratic situation would be one where through their common actions people directly or indirectly bring aspects of their social environment into accord with their uncoerced wishes (whether those they bring with them to collective projects or those generated in the process of interaction) or where they negotiate a mutually acceptable compromise. An ideal democracy on one of these alternatives would still not be problem free. For one thing, achieving such democracy by one public may block or inhibit democratic efforts of other publics. Also, to preserve ongoing democracy, positive consensus must not be attained in such a way as to inhibit negotiation in the future, as when, for instance, communal living or working arrangements sometimes create pressures to feign agreement. Nor should negotiation impede future consensus, which sometimes happens when, for example, collective bargaining or legislative logrolling shut off avenues for future consensus-building or lock people into attitudes of mutual suspicion. Protecting the widest possible scope for democracy and keeping both the options of consensus and negotiation open are thus general problems of democracy.

When neither consensus nor negotiation of an acceptable resolution is possible, the overriding problem of democratic pragmatics is to identify methods for arriving at an outcome that, in the circumstances, would best promote or at least not inhibit consensus building or negotiation in other matters or for other people and in the future. Voting is one possibility, but so is leaving the decision to chance, for instance, by drawing lots or delegating decision-making to an independent party. (Indeed, even jousting or duelling, to take extreme examples illustrative of the open-endedness of this concept, could not be ruled out *in principle*, though it seems most likely that these methods would either make future consensus or negotiation extraordinarily difficult or, due to the death of one of the parties, too easy.)

Perhaps enough has been said about democracy as a context sensitive matter of degree, at least on my conception, to illustrate how some such notion provides a vantage point for seeing virtues in a variety of alternative theories of democracy, even those typically set against one another. For example, while voting does not exhaust democracy on this conception, in many contexts it is the most appropriate or only realistic way for making collective decisions. Social choice theorists for whom voting does exhaust democratic decision-making, have, to be sure, raised sceptical doubts about the coherence of voting procedures, but they have also usefully illuminated some pitfalls of voting, as in legislative assemblies, and indicated ways to avoid them. Meanwhile, participatory and deliberative democrats suggest ways of broadening the notion of collective action beyond just voting. The catallactic theorists might be faulted for harbouring an excessively narrow and mean-spirited view of the motives of politicians in representative-democratic politics, but nobody can doubt that they have illuminated some sobering facts about how such politics are often actually carried on.

Challenges to democratic progress

The nature of pragmatism as an orienting viewpoint on democracy and democratic theories may be clarified by referring to some arguments of Robert Dahl. A chapter of his *Dilemmas of Pluralist Democracy* (1982) entitled 'More Democracy?' questions a common viewpoint of prodemocrats, including Dewey (144), that problems confronting democracy, including ones caused by it, may be met by extending democracy itself. Dahl interprets this to mean that in a perfect democracy there would be no more problems to solve, and produces two examples to illustrate that an ideal democracy, even one inhabited only by prodemocratic citizens, would still present problems insurmountable by democratic means (Dahl 1982: ch. 5).

One of these is that such a democracy would require equal de facto as well as formal political power, but such power is exercised most effectively by organizations, and to give them equal power would require a utopian policy to equalize organizational resources, including leadership skills and levels of membership participation. The other problem is that when there is controversy over the appropriate boundaries determining which people have exclusive democratic decision-making rights over what geographical areas or issues, this cannot be decided democratically because any selection of those to make the decision will presuppose that the appropriate decision-making body is already known and would therefore be prejudiced in favour of one outcome.

Dahl's objections would have force against a 'democratist' theory holding that all social problems admit of complete resolution by means of expanding democracy, but the pragmatic orientation already outlined does not commit one to such democratism. Its principal force is to encourage flexibility when seeking democratic solutions, without assuming that all social problems can be adequately solved in this way or that a perfect democracy could ever be achieved. Flexibility means such things as looking to find democratic solutions specific to the circumstances of a problem (the 'context sensitive' component of this perspective) and avoiding all-or-nothing approaches according to which the circumstances or possible solutions are either entirely democratic or entirely undemocratic (the 'democracy as degrees' component).

Thus, from the pragmatic perspective it is futile to try stating a general solution to the problem of inequalities among organizations abstractly described. It matters, for instance, what the organizations are in actual social and political settings and whether they have potentially compatible goals, in which case democratic solutions might best be sought by dialogue among organization leaders as consociational democrats recommend, or, in keeping with the deliberative-democratic perspective to be summarized in Chapter 9, by discussion and debate within common public spaces by rank and file members of the organizations. If, however, organizational goals are in irreconcilable conflict, then negotiation of the sort that classic pluralism sees as the norm may be in order or, more ambitiously, prodemocrats in the organizations might pursue the project recommended by radical pluralists (to be discussed in Chapter 10) of interpreting organizational goals to their peers in such a way as to be compatible with a shared commitment to pluralist democracy itself. In no case, moreover, should it be thought either that any solution must be complete and permanent or that democratic shortcomings in a solution mean that it cannot be at all democratic.

Similar observations pertain to the problem of establishing boundaries, which will be less intractable in practice than as abstractly described. How solutions are to be sought will differ depending on whether one is trying to establish appropriate boundaries between federal and state or provincial powers (to decide, for example, which should set educational or health standards), generational boundaries (for instance, to establish a voting age), or boundaries between states and superstate regions (a problem to be addressed in Chapter 11). Dahl adduces each of these as examples of his concern, as if they were all solvable (or unsolvable) in the same way and to the same degree, but, as in the case of organizational powers, these problems admit of different sorts of attempts at (more or less) democratic solution. Moreover, to fix boundaries appropriate to some context is not to carve them in stone,

nor does it preclude there being more and less democratic ways of conduct-
ing politics within them, as Shapiro's discussion of 'governing children'
illustrates (1999a: ch. 4).

Like most modern-day democratic theorists, Dahl favours democracy and
thus sees the difficulties he recounts as unavoidable limitations to democracy, rather than as fuel for arguing against it. The Deweyan approach agrees
that democratic politics will always confront problematic limitations, but
sees each of them as challenges calling for creative thought and action to
be met. Perhaps there are some challenges that cannot be adequately met
democratically, or even at all. But on this perspective, abstract descriptions
of challenges cannot decide whether they are thus intractable; rather this
will be discovered only in concrete 'experimentation.' Where democratic
pragmatism emphatically agrees with Dahl is in its positive evaluation of
democracy, such that when and where possible democratic solutions to a
public's problems are to be preferred to alternatives.

Dewey's association with the term 'pragmatism,' should not detract from
his overridingly strong commitment to democracy. In a nontechnical sense
of the term to label something 'pragmatic' is to identify it as no better (or
worse) than any other means to some goal. This is not the sense that philosophical pragmatists like Dewey have in mind. In an early writing, he remarks
that when viewed 'externally' democracy can be seen as 'a piece of
machinery, to be maintained or thrown away . . . on the basis of its economy
and efficiency,' but viewed 'morally' democracy embodies the ideal of 'a good
which consists in the development of all the social capacities of every individual member of society' (Dewey and Tufts 1908: 474, and see 1985 [1932]:
348–50). Drawing on this conception, Macpherson also describes the 'basic
criterion of democracy' as 'the equal effective right of individuals to live as
fully as they may wish' (1973: 51).

Detailed analysis of this viewpoint and of alternative perspectives on the
main value of democracy is too ambitious a task for the confines of this book.
However, it is a major topic of democratic theory, so I shall say some things
about it in the following discussion.

DISCUSSION: THE VALUE OF DEMOCRACY

The thesis about equal development of potentials expressed by Dewey and
Macpherson is sometimes classified along with those of the participatory democrats surveyed in Chapter 7 as viewpoints which regard democracy as an 'end in
itself,' or as having 'intrinsic' as opposed to just 'instrumental' value (for instance,
Miller 1983: 151). One political motive for insisting that democracy be considered intrinsically valuable is to guard against its being sacrificed in the interests
of something to which it is thought instrumental, for instance to the market
if what is taken as intrinsically important is individual choice in free-market

exchanges, or to authoritarian state measures to ensure social order if this is the valued goal. Another political motive, often proposed by participationists, is to avoid what they see as the erosion of communal attitudes on the part of citizens should they come to think of democracy as a dispensable tool.

Critics of the 'intrinsic value' interpretation sometimes simply dismiss it as unrealistically out of keeping with how democratic politics are actually conducted or, in an unkind comment by Brian Barry, as a conceit of 'the radical chic of the Boston-Washington corridor and the London-Oxbridge triangle' (Barry 1978: 47). Political reasons to avoid an intrinsic value perspective are most often advanced by those who fear majority tyranny or despotism taking advantage of democracy's 'empty space' as this worry was explained in Chapter 2. If democracy is seen as valuable in itself, and especially if it is taken as the ultimate political value, this, it is feared, will help to justify overriding individual rights, and it will provide moral cover for demagogues claiming to embody the democratic will of people.

Fact, value, and meaning again

As a matter of strict analysis of the terms of this debate, it is too easily settled either for or against those who see democracy as an end in itself. If, for instance, democracy is regarded as being of intrinsic value when it involves direct and active participation, then what is valuable is whatever is considered worthy about participation – the solidarity or fellow feeling with which it imbues participants, its salutary effects on people's characters, and so on – and democracy is obviously valued not in itself but because it is conducive to these goals. This defeat of the intrinsic value position can, however, be averted by defining 'democracy' by reference to the goals implicated in participation, in which case democracy will be considered an end in itself for anyone who values these goals; but then the case has been won by definitional fiat. We thus confront once again the 'fact/value/meaning' triangle characteristic of approaches to democratic theory. In his treatment of democratic norms, Charles Beitz confines his attention to 'political equality' precisely to avoid the 'largely fruitless' debates over the definition of democracy (1989: 17, n. 22), but of course this just transposes the debate to the relation between democracy and political equality.

An alternative approach is to adopt a provisional definition in appraising alternative views about democracy's value, understanding that the results of an appraisal may lead to refining or even greatly altering the definition. For this purpose I shall employ a characterization by David Beetham (1999: 33 and 1993: 55), according to which democracy is 'a mode of decision-making about collectively binding rules and policies over which the people exercise control,' to which Beetham adds, consistently with a degrees of democracy perspective, that 'the most democratic arrangement [is] that where all members of the collectivity enjoy effective equal rights to take part in such decision-making directly.' Beetham too confidently represents this conception as 'incontestable,' but he recognizes that its generality leaves much room for debates about 'how much democracy is desirable or practicable, and how it might be realized in a sustainable institutional form;' so let us add to it that whatever other modes of participation may be properly regarded as democratic, it includes or may always fall back on voting in accord with formally or informally recognized procedures and voting rules.

Against the background of this conception (or some variant of it), theories about the value of democracy can be sorted in various ways. One strategy, employed by Carl Cohen, is to distinguish between 'vindicating' and 'justifying' arguments, where the former purport to show how democracy is conducive to desired consequences, while justifying arguments aim to demonstrate its 'rightness, based upon some principle or principles whose truth is evident or universally accepted' (1971: 241). A difficulty with this strategy (recognized by Cohen: 267) is that it invites classical sceptical foreclosure of arguments about democracy's value before any are advanced: vindicative arguments require justificatory ones, since to avoid an infinite regress of vindications the desirability of situations democracy is supposed to serve needs to be justified, but justification presupposes the claim that there are universal, philosophically foundational principles (and this claim has its own regress/circularity problems) as well as the doomed hope that everyone can be made to recognize the same first principles.

One way to stop a sceptical regress is to construct arguments based on beliefs that do not themselves require justification, as Descartes did when he appealed to belief in one's own existence to anchor a general philosophical system. James Hyland suggests such a path in one of his justifications of democracy, conceived of by him as 'the public recognition of equal status and the extension to everyone of the rights to be equal participants in political decision-making.' He maintains that viewed this way democracy is 'intrinsically valuable to people,' as is evidenced by noting that they would reject the contrary situation where they are 'publically proclaimed as inferiors, unfit for responsibility of self-government' (1995: 189–90). Persuasive as this argument for democracy's value may be to many, it lacks the force of Descartes' argument that one's own existence cannot be doubted, since there are examples of people who have sincerely (even if wrongly) harboured self-deprecating views about their fitness to govern.

Also, what the argument establishes is only that if democracy defined in this way is to have value, then this value will be in some sense intrinsic to it; so democracy would still have to be justified against antidemocratic elitists, who have no problem imagining that some people are unfit for self-government and therefore deny democracy's value, whether considered intrinsic to it or otherwise. Indeed, in addition to his appeal to 'the constitutively features of democracy,' Hyland, himself, gives other arguments appealing to its direct effect of satisfying people's preferences and to indirect consequences including promotion of governmental openness and development of individual autonomy (ch. 7).

Leaving Hyland's intrinsic value argument or alternative strategies for justifying democracy by invoking 'universally accepted' principles to readers disposed to seek and develop them, this discussion will instead classify arguments for democracy according to whether they appeal to extra-moral, 'prudential', or to normatively 'moral' considerations, where moral arguments may sometimes but not always invoke putative foundational ethical principles (such as that human happiness ought to be maximized or that individuals are equally worthy of respect). This distinction has the advantage of avoiding reduction of debates over the value of democracy to ones over whether such value is intrinsic or instrumental or over the merits of philosophical foundationalism, or at least it postpones such debates in the interests of cataloguing conceptions of democracy's value. Within each of the prudential and moral categories, arguments can be sorted into those that appeal to democracy's use or value for or to individuals and those appealing to group entities such as communities or states. Hence the arguments can be located (if not always neatly or exclusively) in one of the boxes represented in the following table.

	Prudential	Moral
Individual	A	C
Group	B	D

Reasons to value democracy

Figure 5

Best bet for most individuals

For Aristotle democracy is a deviant form of rule since it aims to promote the self-interest of a particular group, namely the majority. His evaluation of democracy as the least bad among other deviant manners of government is from the point of view of what is prudentially best for societies, but when he claims that the majority is always composed of the needy (1986 [c.320 BC]: 110, 1290b) he suggests another, common reason to favour democracy. It might be put by saying that anyone who is neither an autocrat nor rich enough to secure the services of one (or even who fears sometime being thus deprived) will be well advised to support democratic government. This would be unassailably good advice if, as Aristotle apparently thought, there were a homogenous class

interest of all members of the majority, but even given that there are conflicts within a majority such a person should still support democracy, because
other things being equal he or she will have a better chance of being in the
majority than in the minority with respect to specific issues. This is, therefore, a
justification in quadrant A.

One way to challenge this argument is to maintain that majorities might
oppress minorities. Given the moral connotation of 'oppress,' this is to marshal
a counter argument from quadrant C. A prudential reply is that members of a
majority might not be sufficiently educated or intelligent to vote in their best
interests, as Mill feared when he endorsed weighted voting for people from the
educated classes. Another prudential counter is that of libertarians, who claim
that this justification has force only in a minimal state, since government structures and activities beyond protecting life, property, and contracts are dis-
advantageous even to 'needy' individuals in the majority whose support for a
proactive state inhibits the economic growth that will eventually be to their
advantage. Those social choice theorists who doubt that majority voting can be
depended on to express majority will are sceptical of this argument on grounds
reviewed earlier (the cyclicality problem, agenda manipulation, absence of a
unique way to aggregate individual preferences).

Holding leaders to account

On the basis of this scepticism, William Riker (1982) and Adam Przeworski
(1999) endorse the Schumpeterian view that democracy is to be preferred to
alternatives due to its potential for holding elected officials accountable by the
threat of removing them from office. Perhaps this consideration could be considered a prudential one addressed to individuals, who are being told that they
have a better chance of getting rid of leaders they do not like in a democracy
than otherwise, but since the way to get rid of such leaders is by the vote,
the problem of the reliability of majority voting recurs. Riker acknowledges this
problem, but maintains that the mere fact that there will be elections, no matter
whether they must fail in aggregating the preferences of those in the majority,
suffices to impede self-serving behaviour on the part of elected officials. However, because some individuals will see their interests as in accord with those
of the leaders (and on the hypothesis of Riker's theory there is no way for
these individuals to know that voting will help keep officials or parties in office
any more than those who dislike the government know that voting will unseat
them) these considerations do not easily address individuals.

Maintains the peace

Przeworski's alternative deployment of the Schumpeterian view places it in quadrant B, since his main claim is that holding elected officials to account promotes
peace in a democratic society. Elections have this effect in part for the same

reason that tossing a coin every number of years to determine a government would: each contending party would be more inclined to take its chances on forming a government by election (or coin toss) than by employing violence to seize or retain power. Przeworski maintains that bloodshed is avoided 'by the mere fact that ... the political forces expect to take turns' (1999: 46). He further maintains that elections have the advantage not shared by coin tossing that they induce moderation on the part of governing agents, and they mitigate violence among an electorate by illustrating to contending parties the strength of potential opposition. It should be noted that theorists who advance this argument have in mind peace internal to a democratic community. They do not address the problem of governments that pursue bellicose foreign policies, whether in response to public sentiment, or in cynical efforts to deflect internal criticism, or in response to 'interest group' pressure as from armaments manufacturers.

Good leadership

It will be recalled that for Tocqueville one of the worst aspects of democracy is that it yields mediocrity in political leadership. Against this opinion are the stances of the participationists and of classic pluralists. For the pluralists democracy *permits* good leadership, due to public apathy or reluctance to engage in politics, while at the same time inhibiting incompetent or utterly self-serving leadership by keeping channels open for people to become politically active if motivated to do so. Participationists reject the elitism of Tocqueville's view and see as a main virtue of increased citizen participation that it energizes and draws upon the talents and experience of all of a society's population. In these ways pluralists and participationists offer additional arguments in category B, though based on quite different perspectives.

Wisdom in numbers

Aristotle raised a related argument when he critically examined (and did not entirely dismiss) a claim that majorities might make good rulers, not because any ordinary person is wise but due to the pooled experiences and knowledge of many individuals (87–8, 1281b). A similar putative advantage of democracy was proposed by the Marquis de Condorcet who defended the 'jury theorem' that on the assumptions there is some decision that would be objectively the best for a society to make and each of the society's voters has a better than 50 per cent chance of selecting it, the larger the majority of votes for a particular option the more likely it is that the best option will be voted for (see the summary of Condorcet's proof for this by David Estlund 1997: 202, n. 21). This theorem takes it name from voting in juries where jurors share the goal of reaching a correct verdict and vote according to their estimation of what this is.

Przeworski objects to Condorcet's theory for the reason that, unlike juries, modern democracies are marked by conflicts over goals themselves, so the assumption of an objective common good fails (1999: 26–9). Estlund (1997) introduces a pertinent distinction in this connection between situations where there is an objective, independent moral standard by reference to which disagreements over goals can be adjudicated and situations where there are no such standards. With respect to the latter situations, he argues that all one can expect is a fair procedure for arriving at a decision, and majority vote is one such procedure. When there are objective standards, 'epistemic procedures' are required of the sort that people can have confidence that following them will lead, though not infallibly, to discovery of the standards and of what satisfies them. These procedures include impartial public discussion which is at the centre of the deliberative-democratic theory to be reviewed in Chapter 9.

Stability

Classic pluralists consider it a main virtue of democracy that it promotes stability without requiring homogeneity of interests. But as the authors of the Trilateral Commission Report maintained (see Chapter 2) and the pluralists recognize, even when balanced or tempered by group overlaps, social conflicts still have destabilizing tendencies and hence more is needed than just trying to balance opposing interests. In particular, stability requires each citizen to be prepared to respect government, at least by obeying its laws even when it is acting against what the citizen takes as in his or her self-interests or when it is thought that the government is pursuing morally objectionable policies. In a society regulated by unquestioned tradition or in a hierarchical society where certain people, such as kings, are either thought to know best how the society should comport itself or, even if they are not thought to have special wisdom, citizens consider obedience to them as an overriding duty, this would not be a problem. But in a democracy, laws are supposed to derive their authority or, to use the term most often associated with this debate, their 'legitimacy,' from features of democracy itself. It is in part for this reason that the pluralists insist that democracy requires a prodemocratic political culture.

This view can be formulated as a prudential group-related defence of democracy: in a democratic society people are disposed to believe that government is legitimate, and this is required for stability-promoting obedience to law including rules governing democratic procedures themselves. Taken starkly it does not matter for someone advancing this argument whether democratic governments really are legitimate, just that people think they are legitimate. Hence to a counter argument, such as that of the philosophical anarchist Robert Paul Wolff (1976), that people are not justified in believing they have any obligation to obey a democratic state (or any other kind). It could, in principle, be retorted that this is irrelevant as long as people do not believe Wolff's conclusion. Anarchists typically maintain that government personnel and those in institutions that support what they see as objectionable statism, including the schools and the press, devote much of their efforts in a purely amoral, instrumental way to deluding people into believing in the legitimacy of the state. Democratic theorists, however, usually try to meet this challenge by giving moral arguments (in one or both of categories C or D) that democracy actually does confer legitimacy. When it ceases to perform this function, society is properly thrown into what Jürgen Habermas calls a 'legitimation crisis' (1975) as citizens withdraw their loyalty to the state.

Legitimacy

Wolff addresses those who think individual autonomy important, where autonomous action requires that people judge for themselves what to do. When they act out of obedience to commands of the state, he argues, people have not exercised such judgment and it is the state, not the individual, that is responsible for the actions they take. Wolff maintains this is the case whether the commands of the state have been dictatorially generated or arrived at by majority vote, or even if they have unanimous support, since at the point of action, people are forfeiting their autonomy by obeying a collective decision rather than acting on their own judgments. To say, in the tradition of Rousseau, that acting in accord with the democratic will of the people is the fullest realization of an individual's autonomy is to adopt a conception of autonomy quite different from Wolff's and one, indeed, he is especially concerned to criticize. A rejoinder closer to Wolff's perspective is that in a democracy people willingly agree to support decisions arrived at by majority vote or some other democratic procedure even when they do not agree with the content of these decisions. In Peter Singer's formulation, they give 'quasi-consent' to the outcomes of democratic procedures by the very act of voluntarily participating in them (1974: 47–50).

Some theorists see a paradox in this defence of democracy: if I vote on the basis of my moral or prudential opinions, I will think that government ought to enact the policies for which I vote, and if I am committed to democracy I will also believe that state policy should be whatever the majority decides; so when I am outvoted on a specific issue I must both favour and disfavour the outcome (Wolheim 1964, and see an evaluation by Goldstick 1973). In his summary and discussion of Wolff's challenge, Keith Graham (1982) points out that this is not a paradox but a sometimes unavoidable conflict between competing values. Political theorists who can live with tensions will be less troubled than others about this conflict, but any theorist who champions democracy will welcome arguments to show that one of the motivations that generates the 'paradox' – commitment to democracy – is justified. Such arguments will also serve, if not to eliminate a tension between autonomy in Wolff's sense and democracy, at least to provide reasons why democracy should be preserved even when it limits autonomy.

Maximizing welfare

The argument about democracy offering the best bet to an individual referred to earlier is a prudential one since it appeals only to the self-interest of the individual and there is nothing morally praiseworthy in itself about any person's or any number of persons' wishes being satisfied. The argument can, however, be recast as a moral social argument by adopting the utilitarian stance that the best society is one that maximizes social welfare. Among the many debates among utilitarian theorists (for instance over whether or how to distinguish between higher and lower pleasures or to take account of informed versus uninformed preferences) is one over how to interpret 'welfare.' Most democratic theorists who justify democracy on utilitarian grounds take this term to refer to the satisfaction of preferences and see voting as a way of revealing the aggregated preferences and therefore the welfare of a majority. This claim is the principal target of criticism by the social choice theorists referred to in Chapter 6 on the grounds that voting procedures cannot reliably aggregate or reveal preferences.

Tight shoes and empty stomachs

An analogue of the utilitarian argument, less beset with problems of defining 'welfare' and the like or confronting voter paradox-type conundrums is the 'tight shoes' argument that in a democracy the most dissatisfied in a society will at least have a way of making their discontent known (Carl Cohen 1971: 216). A similar argument is given by Jean Drèze and Armatya Sen in their book, *Hunger and Public Action* (1989), where they identify advantages to democracy for confronting hunger and poverty in general, especially in the developing world. Chief among these is that open political competition and a free press force accountability on governments. Unlike Riker and Prezworski, Sen and Drèze do not limit democracy to voting, but see active participation in local affairs as democratic exercizes as well. Such activity, they conclude, also helps to confront hunger and other such problems by nurturing people's will to collaborate with each other and governments to confront them (1989: 276–8, ch. 5).

Social justice

John Rawls maintains that his 'first principle of justice,' namely that people should enjoy equal rights to the most extensive liberty possible, both requires and is served by a constitution based on equal citizen participation and by maintaining equal formal opportunities for continuing political participation as well as substantive prerequisites for their effective use (1971: 224–8). He thereby exemplifies a second popular argument for democracy in quadrant D. As eloquently described by Tocqueville, democracy is associated with justice, where this is interpreted in one or more of three senses of equality. Access to the vote or to political office is to be distributed throughout the entire population of citizens instead of being the officially closed prerogative of, for instance, those of noble birth: this is *political equality*. *Social equality* prohibits *de facto* closure of such opportunities on the basis of such things as race or gender discrimination, and *economic equality* is sometimes added as a precondition for effective social and political equality.

Rawls sees a strong, theoretical connection between democracy and political equality, but just as he refuses to give concrete interpretation to his 'second principle of justice' – that social and economic inequalities should attach to offices or positions open to all and are permissible only if they benefit the worst off (1971: 60) – so he refrains from specifying just what the social and economic requirements for equal political participation are. The speculations of 'political sociology' he offers (for instance, about the ill effects for democracy of wide disparities of wealth or the need to ensure equitable campaign financing, 226) are in keeping with forms of social and economic egalitarianism more vigorously defended by other democratic theorists, as for example Amy Gutmann (1980) or Philip Green (1985, 1998) among many others.

Economic and social egalitarians typically assume agreement about the desirability of democracy and then try to show how certain kinds and measures of equality are prerequisites for it to function well. Rawls' argument can be construed as the inverse case that someone who agrees that justice requires people to have equal rights to liberty should also agree to democracy insofar as it alone essentially includes the right of citizens equally to enjoy important political liberties (for instance to vote or hold office). To make out a similar case regarding social and economic equality, a less direct argument is required. Assuming that these things are desirable, the question arises of how they can be attained or sustained without objectionable paternalism or, worse, self-serving manipulation of public policy, as state leaders or bureaucrats impose and administer social or economic policies. This is the challenge summarized in Chapter 3 that Robert Nozick puts to egalitarians who would prevent 'capitalist acts among consenting adults.' G.A. Cohen's response to Nozick is that this problem would not arise in an egalitarian society chosen as such by its citizens (Cohen 1995: ch. 1).

The implied argument regarding democracy is that those who favour social and economic justice but who recognize the dangers accompanying its imposition, should wish egalitarian measures to be freely chosen and monitored by citizens, which, since such measures are society-wide matters of public policy, requires democratic forms of government. Of course, this argument supposes that a democratically empowered populace can be persuaded to endorse egalitarian policies, about which egalitarians were once more sanguine than at the present time. When put together with democracy-based arguments for equality, the approach also confronts the chicken-and-egg problem that democracy requires equality and equality requires democracy. My own reaction to this problem hinges on regarding each of democracy and justice as matters of degree such that they might either support or militate against one another. From this angle, the problem can be redefined as a mandate to seek conditions conducive to their progressive mutual reinforcement (Cunningham 1997b, and see Shapiro 1999a: chs 1 and 2). It must, however, be recognized that this transposes a theoretical problem onto practical terrain in a way that pragmatic political theorists will find more attractive than others.

Moral claims about the value of democracy concerning the individual (quadrant C) defend or assume a viewpoint about morally desirable individual comportment or treatment and try to show that democracy realizes or facilitates it. One example is the argument of William Nelson that a main reason to favour democracy is that its system of open debate fosters 'the development of a public morality' (1980: 129). Another is a view of Singer's appealing to fairness in making compromises (1974: 30–41). The most common arguments of the C variety appeal either to some version of equality or of freedom. Each of these notions has long-standing associations with democracy in popular consciousness and in historical struggles, where democracy has been linked with and often defined as either justice when participating in collective affairs (equality) or self-determination of individuals by means of participation in collective actions (freedom). More than one argument for the value of democracy can be drawn from these associations, sometimes seen as complementary, sometimes in opposition depending on how equality and freedom are themselves interpreted. In what follows I shall summarize two arguments by way of illustration.

Equal respect

Thomas Christiano develops an argument from equality based on equal respect, or on what he calls 'equal consideration.' The core normative premise of the argument is that people's lives are equally important such that from a moral point of view there are no good reasons 'for arranging things so that some persons' lives will go better than others' (1996: 54). This means that people's interests in leading the lives they choose to live, including their interests in being able to make informed decisions in this regard, merit equal consideration. Christiano connects this to democracy through the notion of conflict over the distribution of public goods: because they affect the well-being of everyone in a society, such things as regulation of pollution or trade and distribution of educational or health care facilities call for collective policy-making, and since people's interests with respect to these matters differ, a question arises about whether some interests may be given special weight; on the principle that people's interests merit equal consideration, the answer must be that the interests should be equally weighted, and this is achieved only when collective decisions are democratically made (59–71).

When referring to economic and social (or 'civic') equality, Christiano allows that democratic decisions may have inegalitarian results, for instance, in sanctioning economic policies that maintain income disparities. However, democracy does not require accord on principles of economic justice, on which there 'will always be disagreement,' but it does require accord on the principles of democratic justice governing collective decisions. Essential is that 'even those who think that they have lost out will be able to see that their interests are being given equal consideration' in public decision-making (80–1). In this way his argument for democracy appeals to it as a *procedure* as opposed to its likely *outcomes*. For participatory democrats and for theorists like Dewey and Macpherson such procedural considerations do not express what is most valuable about democracy, namely that it promotes freedom in a certain, moral sense.

Positive liberty

The prudential argument referred to earlier that democracy gives (most) individuals the best chance to get the policies or leaders they prefer is based on a concept of freedom simply as the ability of people to do as they wish. Dewey and Macpherson have the alternative, 'positive' conception described in Chapter 3 in mind when they see democracy's value as facilitating the full development of people's potentials. Carol Gould elaborates an argument based on this concept of freedom parallel to Christiano's argument from equality of consideration. The central moral thesis in her approach is that people ought, as far as possible, to be enabled to develop their potentials or capacities. From this it follows that people should be provided with the means required to develop these potentials.

This includes social and economic resources, but it also has specifically democratic implications since, in accord with participationists, she holds that 'social or joint activity by agents is a fundamental way in which they attain their common, as well as individual purposes and through which they develop their capacities' (Gould 1988: 316). Equality of participation is justified by Gould because the one capacity that everyone shares, the bare ability to make choices, is equally possessed by everyone, so 'no agent has more of a right to the exercise of this agency than any other' (*ibid.* and 60–4). The value of democracy, especially in Beetham's characterization 'where all members of the collectivity enjoy effective equal rights to take part in ... decision-making directly,' is therefore its essential role in the development of everyone's potentials. (Beetham sees his characterization and justification of democracy as a combination of equality and autonomy, 1999: ch. 1.)

Christiano levels two criticisms at this defence of democracy by Macpherson and Gould: it does not explain why specifically political participation is required for self-development, because some may chose to avoid politics in order to develop their potentials, and democracy will be incompatible with the liberty of those who are outvoted in collective decision-making (1996: 19). Because Gould and Macpherson, in agreement with Dewey, hold that 'political' interaction takes place not just in formal electoral contexts but whenever people address tasks as a public, they would classify many more activities as democratic

than Christiano. Faced with people who avoid all forms of democratic participation, they could react that it is important to keep channels for participation
open so that as more people take advantage of them a society becomes more
democratic. The second objection cannot be so easily avoided, since conflicts
even in informal realms of family, school, neighbourhood, or workplace will
mean that almost any democratic decision will not be to all participants' liking.

One response is that democratic participation over time nurtures attitudes
of self-confidence, solidarity, tolerance, and the like which in the long run
encourage self-development more than it is discouraged by disappointments
when a decision does not go one's way. But such a response supposes that the
conflicts are not profound and recurrent. Macpherson's reaction is to maintain
that what he calls the 'truly human potentials' do not lend themselves to conflict.
In lieu of a proof, he produces a sample list of these potentials, including the
capacities for rational understanding, aesthetic creation or contemplation,
friendship, love, and religious experience, which have the 'staggering' property
that their exercise 'by each member of a society does not prevent other
members exercising theirs' (1973: 53–4). In one of his formulations of 'the
democratic ideal' Dewey anticipates a way to meet the obvious counter argument that even if truly human capacities can be generally exercised, there will
still be competition over scarce resources required for their development, for
instance, limited space in institutions of higher learning or short supplies of
medical facilities.

For Dewey, democracy includes both the right equally to share in making
collective decisions (the 'individual side' of democracy) and the mandate to
dismantle formal and informal obstacles to full human development, for instance
based on birth, wealth, gender, or race, and part of this 'social side' of democracy is to demand 'cooperation in place of coercion, voluntary sharing in a
process of mutual give and take, instead of authority imposed from above'
(Dewey and Tufts 1985 [1932]: 348–9). The relevance of this perspective for
the problem at hand is that for Dewey this side of democracy, 'like every true
ideal,' signifies 'something to be done rather than something already given' (350).
So rather than seeing competition as proof against the ability of democracy to
liberate individuals' potentials, the democratic process should be seen as
including an imperative to work away at counteracting institutions and attitudes
that promote conflicts that impede this liberation.

Perhaps this line of debate has been pursued far enough to illustrate complexities in arguing for the value of democracy. Even when alternative positions
share the same terrain (that is, take place within the same 'quadrant'), they
involve alternative views about what democracy is and what is realistic, and the
situation can be further complicated by differences over the appropriate quadrant on which to focus. In addition, the terms of debate are themselves
contested. Thus, proponents or critics of egalitarian defences of democracy
might have alternative conceptions of equality in mind, three of which (political, social, and economic) have been mentioned, and each of these is in turn

Chapter 9

Deliberative democracy

'The notion of a deliberative democracy,' according to Joshua Cohen, 'is rooted in the intuitive ideal of a democratic association in which the justification of the terms and conditions of association proceeds through public argument and reasoning among equal citizens' (1997b: 72). In describing deliberative democracy as 'a necessary condition for attaining legitimacy and rationality with regard to collective decision making' Seyla Benhabib (1996: 69), another prominent deliberative democrat, makes it clear that this is a *normative* conception, as does Cohen when he specifies that deliberation under the right conditions is an ideal model which democratic institutions ought to strive to approximate (*ibid.*: 73). A third central dimension is emphasized by Jürgen Habermas (regarded by many as the philosophical father of this theory) in describing legitimate decisions and institutions as the ones that would be agreed to by those involved in a democratic procedure 'if they could participate, as free and equal, in discursive will formation' (1979: 86).

The core theory

Allowing for variations, everyone in this currently popular school of democratic theory would agree that these formulations articulate the core of deliberative democracy. The contrasting approach – sometimes identified as 'liberal' and sometimes as that of social choice theory by deliberative democrats – pictures citizens entering a democratic political process with fixed preferences that they aim to further by use of democratic institutions and rules. These institutions and rules function to aggregate citizens' differing preferences and they are legitimate when people at least tacitly consent to being bound by them. The deliberative-democratic alternative takes issue with this picture regarding legitimation, fixed preferences, and aggregation.

Legitimation

It is not enough for the deliberative democrat simply that people consent to democratic processes, since this may be the result of a variety of motives including (and typically on the picture they resist) passive acquiescence or self-interested calculation. Rather, democratic processes are legitimate when they permit and encourage reasoned deliberation both over specific issues and also over 'the very rules of the discourse procedure and the way in which they are applied' (Benhabib 1996: 70, and see Manin 1987: 352). In order for such deliberation to confer legitimacy on democratic procedures and their results, reasons must be publicly given and exchanged in forums suitable for this purpose and participants must be able freely and equally to arrive at informed preferences and to acquire and exercise the abilities required for effective participation in the forums.

Fixed preferences

Democratic deliberation is called for when there is disagreement among citizens about what public policies should be or how they should be arrived at and enforced. This includes not just prudential disagreements about the best means for advancing common goals but also, and especially, moral disagreements about goals themselves (Gutmann and Thompson 1996: 40–1). Faced with disagreement, citizens may submit themselves to an impartial procedure, such as a vote, and hope their preferred outcomes will carry the day, or they may bargain with one another to arrive at an acceptable negotiated outcome. These two methods for confronting disagreements share the characteristic that people enter into voting or negotiation without any expectation that their preferences will change in these processes, and, indeed, the processes are not designed to encourage changes in preferences.

By contrast, those engaged in deliberative-democratic practices must be prepared to question and to change their own preferences and values. In such practices each gives reasons for his or her initially favoured views aiming thereby to persuade others to adopt them. Central to the theory is the thesis that this aspiration has what Amy Gutmann and Dennis Thompson (ch. 2) call 'reciprocity' built into it: I cannot expect you to entertain my reasons respectfully and with a mind open to changing your views unless I am prepared to entertain your reasons in the same spirit. As Cass Sunstein puts it, a 'well-functioning system of democracy rests not on preferences but on reasons' (1997: 94).

Aggregation

In Chapter 4 it was noted that not all liberal-democratic theorists hold that the goal of democracy is to aggregate preferences. This notion is associated, rather, with those utilitarian ethical theorists who value democracy for what they see as its potential to maximize overall utility, measured by reference to preference satisfaction. As also noted in Chapter 4, however, there is a *descriptive* sense in which as long as they restrict democracy just to voting, liberal democrats, utilitarian or otherwise, cannot avoid seeing it as a matter of preference aggregation: since the state is not supposed to force or indoctrinate people to live in accord with a common vision of a good life or society, but should facilitate pluralistic accommodation of people with different values, the result of voting will reflect the balance of the various preferences flowing, in part, from divergent values.

Deliberative democrats do not often distinguish between these two ways of regarding aggregation, but it is clear that they object to both claims. Sunstein explicitly links his criticism of preference-based views of democracy to aggregation, which, in taking preferences as given, fails 'to do what democracy should – that is to offer a system in which reasons are exchanged and evaluated' (*ibid.*: 94). The key point here is that democracy on the deliberative conception should be more than voting, and it should serve some purpose other than simply registering preferences. (A question of ethical theory not to be addressed here is whether this is compatible with utilitarianism, which would be possible if the deliberative democrat can sanction a scenario where citizens win each other over to utilitarianism and agree with respect to some if not all contested policy options to set aside deliberating about them and vote on preferences that have not been 'processed' by prior deliberation.)

Consensus and the common good

Viewing deliberative democracy, then, as a goal-directed activity, a question remains about what goal or goals it is supposed to serve. There are different responses to this question if it is interpreted to ask what deliberative democracy is supposed ultimately to achieve. Gutmann and Thompson value deliberative democracy for its ability to allow citizens and politicians 'to live with moral disagreement in a morally constructive way' (1996: 361). In some writings Habermas regards 'discourse politics' as required to overcome and prevent crises of political legitimation (1975), and more recently he specifies that 'deliberative politics' are essential for integrating the pragmatic, the moral, and the community/identity defining ('ethical') dimensions of life in a constitutional state (1998). Benhabib and Bernard Manin see deliberative democracy as central to legitimizing political arrangements and outcomes, but for Benhabib legitimacy is linked to rationality (1996: 72), while for Manin equal participation in deliberative processes confer legitimacy (1987: 359, and see Estlund 1997: 177–81).

Whatever differences there are among deliberative democrats about ultimate goals, they agree that, at least as a proximate goal, sincere democratic deliberation will encourage citizens to seek consensus over common goods. The process of articulating reasons and offering them in public forums 'forces the individual to think of what would count as a good reason for all others involved' (Benhabib 1996: 71–2). Cohen argues that this is incompatible with the presentation of self-serving arguments, since reasons must be given to show that a favoured outcome is in the interests of all (1997b: 75–7).

In one respect the charge of critics of deliberative democracy that it under-estimates irreconcilable conflicts is apt (Gould 1996: 174, Mouffe 2000: ch. 3, Shapiro 1999b). If intractable conflicts are widespread, then there are few common goods on which people could agree, and the scope of demo-cratic procedures encouraging people to seek consensus would be too limited to be of much use. But when critics imply that deliberative democrats ignore conflict or assume that people can always achieve consensus, they misinter-pret the theory. In explaining the claim that deliberation aims at consensus, Cohen allows that 'even under ideal conditions there is no promise that consensual reasons will be forthcoming,' so it may be necessary to take a vote, but in this circumstance 'the results of voting among those who are committed to finding reasons that are persuasive to all' will differ from those of people not so committed (1997b: 75).

Gutman and Thompson suggest what such difference may be when they list the main obstacles to reaching consensus. These are scarcity of resources, exclusive self-concern ('limited generosity'), basic moral disagree-ments, and 'incomplete understanding' of what is in individual and collec-tive best interests. They argue that sincerely *striving* to reach consensus by giving reasons, even when success is impeded in these ways, has the effects of: encouraging people to try to live civilly even while competing over scarce resources; taking broad perspectives that in turn makes people more generous to one another; inhibiting amoralism and immoral-ity while recognizing moral differences; and educating people to their true interests (1996: 41-4, and see also 1999: 248-50).

Weakened participationism/republicanism or fortified liberalism?

Among the several collections of essays on deliberative democracy is one edited by Jon Elster in which most of the contributors conceive of it prin-cipally as a way of making collective decisions through consensus-promoting discussion. For instance, in Elster's contribution he lists the circumstances that are conducive to deliberation and those that distract from it in making constitutional decisions (1998b: ch. 4). Adam Przeworski looks at impedi-ments to citizens making binding decisions created by such things as uncertainty about what decisions each other will make. On his view these difficulties confront people who otherwise agree on basic goals and are there-fore ignored by deliberative democrats, who he sees as mainly concerned with disagreements over goals (1998: ch. 6). Diego Gambetta (ch. 1) grants that deliberation has the advantage of promoting an informed citizenry but is critical of it for wasting time, giving an edge to the argumentatively eloquent, and failing to account for cultures in which people are quick to announce opinions and stubbornly reluctant to change them (he cites Italy and Latin America).

There may well be substance to some of these claims (though Gambetta does not document his, to my mind dubious, cultural generalizations), but they hinge on a conception of deliberative democracy as a device for generating public policy decisions. The main proponents of deliberative democracy would not deny it such a role, but nor do they portray deliberative democracy as primarily motivated by this aim. Indeed, one of the criticisms of Habermas is that decision-making as a central activity of self-government is obscured in it (Gould 1996: 176). Rather, the principal virtues of deliberative democracy as presented by its advocates are close to those of participationists and civic republicans: by encouraging people to seek common goods, deliberation nurtures and creates preferences that bind people cooperatively together and prompts equality and mutual respect. Embrace of these participationist and republican values is therefore contrary to one interpretation of deliberative democracy (also in the Elster collection) where the value of making people 'better citizens' or enhancing people's 'sense of shared community' is described as inadequate to justify deliberation unless they can be shown to 'improve policy outcomes' (Fearon 1998: 60).

Variations

At the same time, there are some differences between deliberative democrats, on the one hand, and both participationists and civic republicans, on the other. Whether the differences are significant enough to make deliberative democracy count as a version of liberal-democratic theory or a form of participationism and/or civic republicanism qualified by liberal-democratic principles is a matter on which opinion will no doubt differ. Also there are pertinent variations among deliberative democrats themselves that bear on this judgment.

One difference between a noted deliberative democrat and civic republicans is the view of Benhabib, who acknowledges that conflicts over values and visions of the good cannot be resolved 'by establishing a strong unified moral and religious code without forsaking fundamental liberties.' This stands in apparent tension with her claim that the 'challenge to democratic rationality' is to 'arrive at acceptable formulations of the common good.' The solution, according to Benhabib, is that agreement should be sought 'not at the level of substantive beliefs but at that of procedures, processes, and practices for attaining and revising beliefs' (1996: 73). Meanwhile, Cohen distinguishes his view from that of participationists who champion direct and local democracy by arguing that political parties (provided they are publicly funded) constitute superior arenas to those 'organized on local, sectional of special-issue lines' for carrying on deliberation (1997b: 84–5).

If deliberative democracy came down to the prescription just that political parties be encouraged to carry on wide-ranging policy discussions and that agreement should be sought on democratic procedures, there would be little to differentiate it from mainstream liberal-democratic opinion. However, few deliberative democrats hold such views without additions (for example, by Cohen's insistence on public funding for parties), and there are differences among the theorists over these matters. Gutmann and Thompson distinguish their conception of deliberation from what they see as Benhabib's excessively narrow proceduralism on the grounds that reasoned deliberation justifies and encourages acquiring substantive values, such as those favouring more than just formal freedom and equality (1996: 17, 366, n. 19), and in an essay addressing this question, 'Procedure and Substance in Deliberative Democracy' (1997b: ch. 13), Cohen argues that religious tolerance and other things not justified on democratic proceduralist grounds are engendered by deliberation.

Regarding forums for deliberation, few theorists restrict these to political parties, and this includes Cohen, himself, who as noted in Chapter 7 is a champion of associative democracy. Unless the associations he envisages are improbably regarded as internally lacking in differences of opinion, they are clearly candidates for being important arenas for deliberation. Legislatures and the courts are seen by most deliberative democrats as appropriate forums as well, as are nongovernmental arenas such as the media, places of work and living, professional associations, unions, cultural institutions, and social movements (Gutmann and Thompson 1996: 358–9, Benhabib 1996: 75).

Given its Janus-faced character, it is not surprising to find that the stronger criticisms of deliberative-democracy theory differ depending on which side of it they focus on. For instance, in a typical liberal-democratic manner, James Johnson criticizes deliberative democracy (though not entirely dismissively) for ignoring or supposing too much consensus over basic values (1998: 165–8); while William Scheuerman, targeting Habermas, complains in a way consistent with participatory-democratic theory that formal legislative, judicial, and executive institutions largely insulated from public deliberation, are still the effective political actors (1999b: 168–72). A similar criticism of Habermas is levelled by James Bohman (1996: 205–11). Bohman, however, is a fellow deliberative democrat and hence does not see this as a fatal weakness of the theory, but as a remediable shortcoming deriving from an unnecessarily rigid pairing by Habermas of public norms with civil society and political exigencies ('facts') with institutionalized administration. (The views criticized by Scheuerman and Bohman are in Habermas, *Between Facts and Norms*: 1998, especially Chapters 8 and 9.)

Transcendence of theoretical divides

There are also more and less charitable interpretations of the two-sided stance of deliberative democracy. An uncharitable viewpoint sees it as an effort to combine theories that are not combinable. The most charitable interpretation, given by leading deliberative democrats themselves, is that their approach *supersedes* traditional oppositions within democratic theory and that perception of tensions derives from inability to rise above them. Benhabib expresses this view when she describes deliberative democracy as 'transcending the stark opposition between liberal and democratic theory' (1996: 77). It is also the self-understanding by Gutmann and Thompson that their approach is an alternative both to the democratic proceduralism prototypically defended by Dahl and to liberal constitutionalism of the sort they see mainly expounded by Dworkin and Rawls (1996: 27–8, 361).

Habermas describes the 'discourse-theoretical' approach to democracy as an alternative to and a mean between liberalism and republicanism and spells out a way that deliberative democracy can be regarded as an effort to transcend these traditional oppositions in democratic theory. He draws the distinction between liberalism and republicanism in a way similar to Benjamin Barber's distinction (described in Chapter 7) between thin and unitary democracy: liberalism regards politics as the administration of competing private interests among citizens who possess exclusively negative rights, while republicanism tries to structure law and government to reach positive consensus on moral values and create solidarity among citizens. Habermas contrasts his alternative, deliberative view of democratic politics, with liberalism and republicanism regarding law, democracy, and popular sovereignty.

Rather than seeing law as no more than a way of regulating competition (liberalism) or as an expression of social solidarity (republicanism), the prime function of constitutions for Habermas is to institutionalize the conditions for deliberative communication. Democracy for the liberal just legitimizes the exercise of political power, while for the republican it is supposed to constitute a society as a political community. Democracy according to discourse theory is stronger than the first but weaker than the second in rendering the actions of state administration reasonable ('rationalizing' them). Finally, while popular sovereignty in the liberal conception is simply the exercise of duly authorized state authority, and for the republican it resides with a popular general will, the deliberative approach sees sovereignty as an ongoing process of 'interaction between legally institutionalized will formation and culturally mobilized publics' (Habermas 1996, reworked in 1998: 295–302).

Grounds for confidence

While these criticisms of liberalism and republicanism are similar to Barber's, Habermas' alternative differs from the latter's favoured 'strong democracy' in the prominent role he accords to government institutions acting to protect and promote constitutional law. Carol Gould raises a general problem for deliberative democrats here. As noted earlier, citizens for them are not supposed just to deliberate over specific policies but also over formal and informal democratic decision-making procedures and over values worthy of constitutional protection themselves. Referring specifically to Benhabib's formulation and focusing on constitutional rights, Gould sees a dilemma: if deliberation must take place within the constraints of rights already set down, then instead of people reasoning over important values, preexisting consensus about the values is assumed or they are imposed. On the other hand, if, as a result of public deliberation, 'the rights are really contestable, then one possibility has to be that they can be abrogated' (Gould 1996: 178). A similar dilemma can be constructed with respect to pro-cedures, for instance, to ask whether or not deliberation-independent cri-teria should dictate when negotiation or voting should replace striving for consensus.

Another way of posing this challenge is to ask whether the deliberative democrat presupposes some philosophically foundational theory of ethics by reference to which guidelines for deliberation should take place. Deliberative democrats resist tying their political prescriptions to foundational theory because they see it as a virtue of deliberative democracy that it allows for reasoned debate about normative matters without committing one to con-tested, foundational philosophical theory (Gutmann and Thompson 1996: 5, Sunstein 1997: 96). But even if philosophical foundationalism is currently out of favour among professional intellectuals, persisting and divisive debates among members of the public at large not infrequently involve 'parties who seek to challenge one another at a quite "fundamental" or even "existen-tial" level' (Johnson 1998: 165); so the question remains whether or how some such viewpoints should be excluded from deliberation for fear that they might carry the day. The deliberative democrat is thus up against a version of the 'paradox of tolerance' reviewed in Chapter 3.

Hypothetical consensus

One solution is suggested by Habermas' deployment of a 'discourse theory of ethics' (to be summarized more fully below) whereby appeal is made to the conditions for ideal communication in appraising actual modes of delib-eration. A deliberative-democratic approach drawing on such idealizations to address the problem at hand would be similar to classic social contract theory, which, for its part has both democratic and democracy-threatening, paternalistic dimensions. Notwithstanding the fact that the contract theo-rist, Thomas Hobbes, advocated absolute monarchy, the monarchs of his time (specifically Charles II) did not appreciate his views, since they wished their authority to be a result of divine will rather than resulting from a contract among the people. In this way, contract theory is protodemocratic. In another way, however, it is not democratic.

When the social contract is not unrealistically viewed as an historical event, but as an imagined agreement in ideal circumstances (between rational individuals who are ignorant of their lot in society as Rawls had it in his earlier expression of the theory, 1971, ch. 3), political recommendations flowing from it seldom reflect the opinions and preferences actually held by citizens, but those they would hold if they were living up to their rational potentials (and were properly informed). This provides a way of justifying political prescriptions on the grounds that they represent citizens' real interests, which, though it does not strictly entail antidemocratic paternalism, sets the stage for it. It is one thing to urge on the basis, for instance, of some ethical theory that people ought to pursue different interests than those they are pursuing, and another to maintain that properly conceived people really do have the interests a theorist maintains they should act in accord with.

Analogously to appeal to an ideal social contract, a deliberative-democratic model may be invoked to argue that if democratic deliberation were carried on in the spirit and under the conditions required by its ideal realization, then participants would support deliberative-democracy friendly institutions and policies. The problem with this approach is the same as the problem for ideal deployment of contract theory, namely to avoid paternalism. Institutional and policy recommendations are made in the name of the people, not as they are but as they would be in an ideal world. An example of this mode of thinking may be found in an argument by a legal theorist, Robert Howse, who uses deliberative-democratic language in defending political intervention by Canada's Supreme Court (in debates over possible Quebec secession). He describes the Court as 'the quintessence of the rational, deliberative element,' the unique role of which is to uphold rationality against 'the unruly passions of democracy' (1998: 46; for a contrasting view of the role of courts by a deliberative democrat see Sunstein 1998).

Limited application

An alternative reaction to the problem Gould raises is simply to stipulate, as Gutmann and Thompson do, that deliberative-democratic practices are only appropriate among those who are prepared to reason together in the right spirit. This would rule out the purely self-seeking amoralist and the intractable moral fanatic or fundamentalist. Regarding the first category of people, Gutmann and Thompson grant that deliberative-democratic recommendations do not apply to them (1996: 55). One justification for this exclusion is that this group is not as large as theorists who claim that humans are self-seeking bargainers by nature would have people believe. Another justification is that no political prescription, including one based on self-seeking bargaining itself, can reach the completely amoral person, so if normative political theory is to function at all, it must address a different audience. As to fundamentalist intractability, a virtue of Gutmann and Thompson's

Democracy and Disagreement is that it addresses practically relevant cases where protagonists are most likely to be locked into their positions with the aim of showing that respectful deliberation if not agreement is still possible.

For instance, regarding the abortion debate Gutmann and Thompson are prepared to grant that one confronts a moral disagreement (over whether the fetus is a human deserving constitutional protection) where it is not possible conclusively to prove that one side is right, so in this sense it is intractable. But deliberative democracy does not require that agreement can be reached, only that opposing parties offer and are open to reasons and respect one another (74–9). Someone is engaged in such deliberation when they are: consistent (for instance, guarantees against childhood poverty should be promoted by anyone who wants guarantees of the lives of fetuses); when they acknowledge their opponent's sincerity; and when they are prepared to make concessions, as Gutmann and Thompson think happened when the US Supreme Court in Roe vs. Wade, though refusing to make abortion illegal, allowed states to prohibit third trimester abortions or when foes of abortion make an exception for rape victims (82–90). The force of these considerations for the present purpose is to focus on what must finally be an empirical argument to show that the proportion of people in a society for whom deliberative democracy is unsuited is sufficiently small that this democratic theory has general application. The more (or fewer) people there are for every intractable issue of public debate who meet Gutmann and Thompson's criteria, the more (or less) applicable is the theory.

Reflective equilibrium

Yet another response to the problem under consideration, also advanced by Gutmann and Thompson, does not leave it to chance how many are suited to deliberation. This is to maintain that people can be deliberatively reasoned into deliberative reasoning. Deliberation requires that citizens give reasons to each other in public forums. Publicity obliges them to meet and hence attend to other's arguments. Debate often turns to the conditions of deliberation itself, which throws into relief the importance of mutual respect and equal access to the means for effective deliberation. All these things increasingly inculcate an ethos of reciprocal respect in a 'bootstrap' operation (Gutmann and Thompson 1996: 351–2). Of course, such an exercise will backfire if deliberative familiarity breeds contempt. This could happen if the principles to support reasons that opponents are publicly forced to adduce become partially definitive of their identities in such a way that they cannot back off from a position without humiliating loss of face or if the principles come to mark fixed boundaries between friend and enemy, as is not infrequently the case in, for instance, ethnic or national antagonisms.

Gutmann and Thompson do not have an argument conclusively to show that deliberation will engender respectful reason instead of backfiring, except to note that there are no decisive arguments to prove otherwise and that their view 'fits with considered judgments about particular cases' and 'provides a coherent and workable way of thinking about and practicing democratic politics' (1996: 353). The language here is that of Rawls' principle of 'reflective equilibrium.' On this principle, progress is achieved in political moral reasoning by testing theories against moral intuitions with the expectation that both the intuitions and the theories will change in reaction to one another as they are applied to concrete cases (Rawls 1971: 20–1). Gutmann and Thompson maintain that this form of reasoning is used by non-theorists in real political circumstances and for this reason deliberative-democratic theory is well suited to influence actual political actors (1996: 357–8). But whether deliberative democracy can thereby 'partly constitute its own practice' cannot depend just upon this form of reasoning. Ordinary citizens will not be open to persuasion by deliberative theory unless there is a basis for it in the values or modes of reasoning they already harbour or employ. Better suited than reflective equilibrium for those who seek iron-clad guarantees in this matter is some version of 'transcendental' argumentation.

Transcendentalism

When Cohen writes that deliberation 'carries with it a commitment to advance the common good and to respect individual autonomy' (1997a: 75), he does not mean this to be true by definition, which would claim an implausibly strong connection between deliberation and the values deliberative democrats expect of citizens. At the same time, given the crucial role deliberative democrats accord to pursuit of the common good, claiming that as a matter of empirical fact those who engage in deliberation are likely to acquire the right values is too weak a connection for many of them. Theoretical hypotheses of psychology or sociology might be employed to underwrite an empirical connection, though this would tie deliberative democracy to contested social-scientific theory. An alternative is 'transcendentalism' in the tradition of Kant, a variant of which is the approach of Habermas.

The central method Kant employed in his quest to save morality, science, and, more mundanely, the trust people put in their daily perceptive and reasoning powers and moral intuitions from sceptical doubts, especially those raised by David Hume, was transcendental argumentation. Rather than asking *whether* science, ordinary reasoning, or morality are possible (since there obviously are examples of successes in science and daily reasoning and of moral interactions among people), Kant asked *how* these things are possible. He concluded that science and ordinary reasoning are made possible by forms of perception and categories of understanding that are part of the human perceptual/reasoning apparatus such that, for instance, things are seen in spatial relation to one another and understood in terms of cause and effect.

Morality is possible because people are possessed of the ability to act in accord with rules that are not self-serving, but admit of general application and which they freely choose to submit themselves to. Hence that dependable causal and other general relations hold among things or that people can voluntarily act in moral ways are not hypotheses in need of empirical proof; rather, they are preconditions of thought and action themselves.

Since the late eighteenth century when Kant wrote them, the *Critiques* in which he performed 'transcendental deductions' to reveal these preconditions for reasoned thought and moral action (and a third critique which asked how the appreciation of beauty is possible) have arguably been the most influential, if problematic and difficult, philosophical texts of the modern world. Subsequent generations of philosophers have attempted to resolve questions Kant did not satisfactorily address, such as just what the relation is between the world 'as experienced' and as it is 'in itself' or how morality and science are related, and they have developed alternative conceptions of Kant's preconditions for human thought and action, most importantly for understanding Habermas' deployment of what he calls 'quasi' or 'weak' transcendentalism (1973: 8, 1990: 32) by multiplying them.

Critical social philosophy

Habermas has been a leading figure in the 'critical' school of social philosophy centred in Frankfurt, among whose founders were Max Horkheimer and Theodor Adorno. With the rise of Fascism in Europe, these theorists, like any thoughtful intellectual of the time, set themselves to seeking explanations for how a Europe, and particularly a Germany that prided itself on having achieved the promises of Enlightenment reason and morality and having constructed the short-lived Weimar Republic's liberal-democratic constitution (on which among the most gifted intellectuals of the times had worked) could descend into barbarism and totalitarianism.

In *Dialectic of Enlightenment* (1972 [1947]) Adorno and Horkheimer offered as part of an explanation that while the Enlightenment 'aimed at liberating men from fear and establishing their sovereignty' (3), these goals were thwarted due in large measure to a conception of reason and knowledge initially aimed at 'the mastery of nature' but soon generalized so that reason was simply regarded as a technocratic tool: 'Reason is the organ of calculation, of planning; it is neutral in regard to ends; its element is coordination' (88). In this way of thinking the only universal normative principle is that of self-preservation, so the 'burgher, in the successive forms of slaveowner, free entrepreneur, and administrator, is the logical subject of the Enlightenment' (83). Liberalism, on the view of Adorno and Horkheimer, is part and parcel of this mode of thought, since aside from self-preservation it avoids commitment to any ends and is thus no bulwark against the atavistic and (also in accord with Enlightenment thought) conformist values of totalitarianism (86–93, and see Bohman's summary, 1996: 193–7).

Horkheimer and Adorno do not frame their analysis of what the former labelled 'instrumental reason' (Horkheimer 1974 [1967]) as an exercise in transcendental deduction, though they come close in praising Kant for understanding that '*a priori*, the citizen sees the world as the matter from which he himself manufactures it,' thus foretelling 'what Hollywood consciously put into practice' (Adorno and Horkheimer 1972 [1947]: 84). However, their form of reasoning is consistent with that of the post-Kantian transcendentalists: conceiving the social and political world through the 'lens' of instrumental reason makes it possible to sanction amoral and manipulative practices even while applauding the emancipatory nature of reason and upholding the individual as a centre of autonomy. Adorno and particularly Horkheimer were pessimistic about the prospects for escaping instrumental reason, which, like their fellow member of the Frankfurt School, Herbert Marcuse, they saw as locking people into an oppressive (and auto-oppressive) 'one dimensional' life (Marcuse 1964). As the leading second generation scholar of this school, Habermas was less pessimistic (see his criticism of *Dialectic of Enlightenment*, 1987: ch. 5).

Communicative action

For Habermas the problem coming from the Enlightenment was not instrumental reasoning *per se*, which has its place when people are concerning themselves – in matters of politics, institutional organization, and everyday interactions as well as in scientific or technological matters – with planning to find or adjust appropriate means to accepted goals. But instrumental categories are not the only or the primary ones by which to orient thought and action. A main aim of Habermas has been to challenge the view of his senior colleagues, and of influential earlier thinkers like Max Weber, that politics must largely, if not exclusively, be pursued in accord with instrumental reason (or what Weber called 'goal rationality'). When instrumental reason is dominant, human projects and interactions become 'strategic': goals are not critically interrogated and people seek to manipulate or compel the behaviour of others. Throughout his extensive writings on this topic Habermas has (with impressive erudition and breathtaking complexity) explicated and defended an alternative way of thinking, sometimes called by him 'practical rationality' (for instance, 1975: 140–1) which is appropriate to 'communicative' as opposed to 'strategic' action.

The aim of communicative action is to reach agreement over facts about the world and over norms of social interaction and to achieve dependable mutual understanding by people about their unique world views and perceptions of themselves (Habermas 1984: 86, 1990: 136–7). Instrumental reasoning is inappropriate to communicative action where people 'are coordinated not through egocentric calculations of success but through acts of reaching understanding' and seek to 'pursue their individual goals under the condition that they can harmonize their plans of action' (285–6). The philosophical task Habermas sets himself is to show that such harmony is possible by identifying and justifying principles on which people can agree. Specifically referring to moral norms of social interactions, Habermas approvingly refers to Rawls' method of reflective equilibrium (1990: 116); however, noting that this method depends upon moral intuitions linked to specific cultures and therefore cannot justify universal norms, he argues for a broadened 'transcendental-pragmatic' method, though not a method with the immutable and directly demonstrated conclusions of Kant's deductions (see 1990: 62–8).

This quasi-transcendental demonstration of the possibility of communicative action proceeds through an analysis of everyday language, for which purpose Habermas makes use of work in the philosophy of language (particularly by John Austin and John Searle) to show that the most important principles of communicative action are presupposed in linguistic communication (1984: ch. 3). In one of many applications, Habermas takes the example of ordinary argumentation among people who sincerely wish to secure agreement (as opposed to strategically trying to bully or manipulate one another into accord). He thinks that linguistic analysis has shown that such people presuppose or are committed to certain 'rules of discourse' on pain of exposing themselves as insincere if they do not adhere to them. The rules he cites in this example are that all those who have the capacity to enter into argumentation may do so, that all may question any assertion by another and express their own opinions, desires or needs, and that 'no speaker may be prevented, by internal or external coercion, from exercising' these rights (1990: 89).

Habermas uses this method to justify a 'discourse theory of ethics' according to which an 'ideal speech situation' is imagined where participants are both willing and able to strive for agreement in accord with the rules implicit in language, and moral judgments are assessed according to whether they could be accepted by participants in such discourse. Because engaging in communicative action presupposes certain principles, namely that people are free and equal participants in it, these principles are transcendentally guaranteed as legitimate moral criteria: 'Anyone who participates in argumentation has already accepted these substantive normative conditions – there is no alternative to them' (1990: 130). Habermas recognizes that especially in politically charged controversies the ideal conditions for communicative discourse are seldom attained or sought by participants. Confronted with such 'distorted' discourse, the task of critical theory is practically to advocate conditions conducive to undistorted discourse such as availability of public spaces for deliberation and policies favouring appropriate freedoms and equality. Philosophically the theorist's task is to justify the rules to which people are committed, even if they do not recognize this commitment.

The application of Habermas' method specifically to democracy is most extensively carried out in his *Between Facts and Norms* (1998), which returns in several contexts to his (quasi-transcendentally deduced) principle that 'the only regulations and ways of acting that can claim legitimacy are those to which all who are possibly affected could assent in rational discourses' (1998: 458). Though open to input from nongovernmental bodies in the public sphere, deliberative democracy on his view should be thought of as restricted (in the way that perturbs Scheuerman and Bohman) to the 'regulations' side of this principle, namely as the formal procedures and constitutional rules within which people strive collectively to seek agreement about how to achieve common goals and resolve conflicts (Habermas 1998: 110, 158–9). Thus regarded, nearly all the preconditions identified by Cohen and other deliberative democrats are endorsed – full, equal, informed, and uncoerced political participation by people who enjoy the freedoms and opportunities necessary to this end (305–7).

In these ways transcendentalism offers a more secure ground for the kinds of consensus important to deliberative democracy than some alternatives, and it is more philosophically sophisticated than an analogue of ideal social contract theories. Whether it is prone to paternalism as (arguably) are the latter is a matter of debate. Also subject to controversy are the specifically philosophical merits of this approach, both regarding its 'quasi-transcendental' method (see criticisms of Cheryl Misak 2000: 42–5) and its philosophical content (critically assessed by David Rasmussen 1990: ch. 3).

Deliberative democracy and some problems

If deliberative-democratic theory is regarded as motivated to address one of democracy's 'problems,' it is that of conflict. Like classic liberal democrats and pluralists, deliberative democrats recognize persisting conflicts not just over such things as scarce resources but, more deeply, over matters where there are differences in moral values. When charged with unrealistic idealism, these theorists can retort that while the charge may apply to civic republicanism or participationism, their approach realistically addresses such conflict: by encouraging formal and informal forums conducive to the pursuit of agreement, by describing conditions that make the pursuit possible for everyone, and by identifying principles in accord with which deliberation should be conducted. This solution (if it is one) dovetails with implied or explicit approaches to other problems of democracy. These approaches all flow from what Gutmann and Thompson describe as deliberative democracy's 'moral conception of democracy' (1996: 7).

Tyranny of the majority

Specifically addressing freedom of expression, Cohen maintains that attempts in mainstream liberal-democratic theory to meet the tyranny of the majority problem by claiming that free expression is required for an informed public (as Mill argued) fail, since a majority may prefer restrictions to whatever benefits minority freedom may bring. Therefore, the liberal democrat must justify measures to protect a minority by extrademocratic, liberal measures. This problem arises because preferences are regarded as formed outside of democratic politics; whereas the 'deliberative conception construes politics as aiming in part at the formation of preferences' (Cohen 1997b: 83) in and by means of deliberation. Since among the conditions for free and equal deliberation is the ability of people to express their opinions without fear of formal or informal reprisal, minority rights in this respect are defended internally to deliberative democracy as one of its preconditions.

Benhabib generalizes this argument to apply to the other rights of individuals that lead liberals to worry about democratic majorities, and she maintains that deliberative democracy is well placed not just to defend liberal rights but to generate them. Democratic deliberation presupposes attitudes of 'universal respect' and 'egalitarian reciprocity' among participants in deliberation, but it does not presuppose that all the participants fully or firmly share these values or that there is a fixed list of specific freedom or equality rights that are appropriate to be enforced. Rather, processes of deliberation are self-building ones, and specification of rights is a matter over which deliberation takes place. In order for the processes to have these effects, individuals and minorities must be able freely to give (or withhold) consent; so, as long as deliberative-democratic practices are consistently followed, fear of majority tyranny is unfounded (1996: 78–9 and 93, n. 41).

Irrationality

It will be recalled that democracy regarded as making social choices by means of majority voting is supposed to be endemically unreliable due to such things as the ever-present possibility of a cyclical majority or because alternative voting procedures can yield different results. Like other deliberative democrats, David Miller grants that even a polity dedicated to seeking agreement by deliberation will sometimes be obliged to take a majority vote. He also allows that when democracy is regarded a matter of aggregating preferences by voting, the social choice problems are insurmountable. However, voting in the deliberative-democratic scheme takes place only *after* people have tried to reach agreement by giving each other reasons, which means that their preferences will have become transparent to one another and that some preferences will have changed as a result of deliberation (Miller 1993: 80–4).

Among the preferences that are filtered out in deliberation (provided it is undertaken according to the theory) are ones based on ignorance of relevant facts, including facts about others' preferences and purely self-regarding preferences. Miller thinks that elimination of such preferences goes a long way toward meeting the cyclical majority problem, which, in Arrow's formulation, assumes the 'unlimited domain' condition that votes may be taken over any preferences whatsoever. Cyclical majorities might still survive this initial cleansing when issues are linked such that voting in favour of one course of action will forestall taking others. Deliberation will reveal what the different priorities are regarding various possible such actions and allow participants to seek ways to decouple linkages in a series of votes in order to avoid circularity.

Similarly, regarding choice of voting methods, deliberation prior to a vote will indicate whether the issue at hand is most appropriately addressed by a series of majority votes (the Condorcet method), by a vote according to weighted preferences (a Borda count), or some other method. Miller recognizes that a strategic voter may try deliberately to link issues in a way that will lead to stalemate or to push a voting procedure to a desired outcome, but such self-serving efforts are just what open, reasoned deliberation is best at exposing. (In addition to Miller's argument, see the similar one by Mackie 1998).

The empty space

The empty space concern presents democratic theory with a dilemma: either popular sovereignty is regarded central to democracy in which case a mythical entity of 'the people' provides cover for demagogic tyranny, or democracy is reduced to a device for producing government officials, as the Schumpeterians would have it, thereby denuding it of the kind and degree of appeal requisite to engender popular democratic commitment and engagement. Habermas addresses this challenge in his view that deliberative democracy overcomes the exclusive alternative between republicanism and liberalism (1996: 29–30, 1998: 300–1). Essential for democracy is that reasoned deliberation generates and underwrites policies, and this allows for a more differentiated and complex view of democratic politics than either republicanism or liberalism permits. On the former view democracy is the exercise of sovereignty by the people, while for liberal democracy it is voting in accord with constitutionally prescribed procedures and constraints.

Habermas' more complex view seeks to avoid both these conceptions. An 'arena for the detection, identification, and interpretation of those problems that affect society as a whole' is set out in accord with constitutional principles, but this does not dictate the outcome of deliberations actually carried out. At the same time people organized into associations in civil society interact with formal procedures and institutions of the state, and 'communicative power,' which is neither rule by an undifferentiated people nor simply rule by elected officials, results from the interaction between these public and political spheres.

As noted, some deliberative democrats think Habermas gives too much prominence to formal state procedures, but this response to the empty space problem does not depend upon how important the state's role is taken to be. Generally, the deliberative democrat might be seen as replacing the idea of people's power with that of the ability of individuals to make decisions on the basis of deliberations they have undertaken as free and equal citizens seeking agreement, that is, with Habermas' communicative power. Exercise of communicative power reflects the fact that people have achieved a certain unity, at least around the values presupposed by deliberation, but it does not posit 'the people' as the undifferentiated entity that worried Tocqueville and Lefort. Of course, for this to be a viable solution, the deliberative democrat must avoid mystifying communicative power itself, as is charged by critics who think that the theory opens the door for some to allege in a paternalistic way that they speak for people as they would be were they properly deliberating.

Oppression

Nearly all deliberative democrats can trace the formation of their views to some version of left-wing counter establishment theoretical stances, such as the friendly (though not uncritical) stance toward Marxism of the early Frankfurt school and the critique of 'capitalist democracy' by Cohen in a popular book he coauthored with Joel Rogers (1983). Deliberative democrats are also known for support of social activism of the women's and other social movements, as in the cases of Benhabib, Gutmann, and Thompson. It is probably fair to say that in the minds of its major theorists deliberative democracy is mainly designed to justify antioppressive values and policies. Hence Cohen insists that substantive equality of resources is required for equal effective deliberative participation (1997b: 74) and 'conventional, historical justifications for exclusion from or inequalities of political rights' based on such things as race or gender are incompatible with public deliberation (1997a: 423).

Alternatively expressed, deliberative-democratic theory may be seen as a way to overcome the formalism of liberal democracy: by introducing the idea of deliberation and its conditions, substantive content for abstract democratic rights can be justified. A question that poses itself is whether deliberative democracy might not itself be too formal. 'Deliberation can occur,' Przeworski observes, 'only if someone pays for it' and this gives a deliberative edge to private corporations and to political parties capable of raising enough money (1998: 148, and see Stokes 1998). Some deliberative democrats wish to rule this obvious impediment out of the conditions for deliberation. So in *Between Facts and Norms*, Habermas notes the need for an 'unsubverted' sphere of political power and an informal public sphere 'that has emerged from the confines of class and thrown off the millennia-old shackles of social stratification' (1998: 308). However, as Scheuerman, citing other passages in the same book, argues (1999b: 161–8), Habermas might too severely qualify this assertion to escape the formalism charge. Also, not all deliberative democrats are as socialistic as Habermas regarding economic resources. For instance, Sunstein specifies that deliberative democrats believe 'in a norm of political (*not economic*) equality' (1997: 94, my emphasis).

The discussion of equality by Gutmann and Thompson illustrates a theoretical dimension of this question. They maintain that among the preconditions for deliberative democracy is that 'all citizens may secure the resources they need to live a decent life,' but that due to scarcity and absence of definitive information about where to allocate resources when hard decisions need to be made (they refer to decisions facing legislators in Arizona in the late 1980s about whether to fund expensive heart and liver transplants or to extend basic health care for the working poor) these decisions should be the outcome of public deliberation. At the same time, Gutmann and Thompson maintain that the opportunity precondition rules out strict libertarianism and that the requirement for deliberation rules out simply assuming that some level of scarcity is inevitable, for instance, such that it would be impossible to raise taxes in Arizona sufficient both to fund transplants and basic care (1996: 217–23).

The theoretical problem is occasioned by the deliberative-democratic view referred to earlier that putative conditions for deliberation and even principles of deliberation themselves should be subject to deliberation. Even if, as Gutmann and Thompson hold, a libertarian blanket opposition to taxation (considered a form of theft) could be ruled out as a viable deliberative option, severe restriction of taxation justified by the trickle-down principle could not be discounted from the start, and if its proponents carried the day, the basic opportunities principle would be rendered impotent. Also, if deliberation about deliberative principles is permissible, libertarian challenges should be sanctioned not only to claims about what is required for deliberation but (as libertarians in actual political arenas are wont to argue) to the claim that such requirements should be provided by the state.

Carol Gould (referring to Benhabib's defence of rights) maintains that the deliberative democrat is here confronted with another dilemma: if rights justified as conditions for deliberation are contestable the possibility of their abrogation must be admitted, but if they are not, then they must 'have their authority in something other than the discursive procedure' (1996: 178). One conceivable response would be to employ transcendental arguments to show that consistency requires anyone who engages in political reasoning to reject such things as libertarianism or the trickle-down theory, but this would push the method into matters of specific policy in a way resisted even by the arch transcendentalist, Kant. Another response is suggested by some left-wing theorists, such as Nancy Fraser and Iris Young, who, while critical of mainstream deliberative democrats, are sympathetic to central dimensions of the theory. This is to allow that anything is fair game for deliberation, but that effective deliberation should not be mainly confined to legislative or legal forums in which the wealthy, males, and those of dominant cultures and races are overrepresented, and that such forums should themselves be dramatically reformed (see Fraser 1989, 1997: ch. 3, Young 1990, 1993). Perhaps a reason that mainstream deliberative democrats do not vigorously pursue this line themselves is that they fear alienating pro-establishment political actors whom they hope to entice into value-transforming deliberation.

Fraser and Young launch another criticism, especially at Habermas, concerning the public sphere. From his earliest writings, he has argued for retrieval of a public sphere of uncoerced discussion that had been eroded in developed capitalism by apathy and the manipulation of public opinion by state and economic forces (1989 [1962]). Fraser maintains the public sphere on Habermas' interpretation is too weak in having only indirect effects on policy through influencing legislators, and that his assumption of the public sphere as a locus for reaching harmonious accord masks the fact that this sphere includes 'subaltern counterpublics' often organized into social movements dedicated to combating establishment forces within public as well as formal political spheres (1997: 81). Young pushes this criticism and extends it to deliberative democracy generally (so she prefers to speak of 'communicative democracy') by criticizing the 'norms of deliberation' that have evolved in spheres for public discussion because they are 'culturally specific and often operate as forms of power that silence or devalue the speech of some people' (1996: 123). She also resists the deliberative picture of the public sphere as a place for seeking common goods, since this has the effect of asking the less privileged 'to put aside the expression of their experience' in the interests of 'a common good whose definition is biased against them' (*ibid*:126).

In *Between Facts and Norms* (1998) Habermas makes reference to Fraser's views and, according to Scheuerman (1999b: 159), devotes not a small part of his analyses to trying to accommodate her concerns by acknowledging the role of oppositional social movements in the public sphere and by giving this sphere a more prominent role in the processes of democratic, discursive 'will formation.' Benhabib argues that 'communicative democracy' as advocated by Young is not at base different from deliberative democracy, since the standards of impartiality and fairness insisted on by deliberative democrats are those required to counter marginalization of subordinated groups in public spheres (Benhabib 1996: 82). Whether deliberative democrats can successfully accommodate the concerns of the sort expressed by Fraser and Young is a matter of ongoing dispute.

Fraser and Young share with mainstream deliberative democrats the view that *if* people could come to agree on common goods (in a way that protected substantive freedom and equality for all participants), this would be a good thing; hence there is a motive for Habermas and others to accommodate their worries. Such motive is, however, lacking in the case of the concern voiced by Chantal Mouffe, who argues against deliberative democracy that disputes over what are common goods are not just hard to resolve, but unresolvable and, moreover, *essential* to democratic politics (2000: 45–9). This is a critique from the point of view of radical pluralism, to which Chapter 10 is devoted.

Radical pluralism

Like the classic pluralists, radical pluralists such as Chantal Mouffe, Ernesto Laclau, Claude Lefort, and William Connolly concern themselves with conflict, and like the earlier power-political, interest group theorists they strive to turn conflict, seen by some as a problem for democracy, into one of its virtues. Not only is conflict an unavoidable fact of social and political life, but recognition and institutionalization of this fact within democratic culture, practices, and institutions is a necessary bulwark against autocracy. However, as will be seen, prescriptions by the radical pluralists diverge from those of the classic pluralists. This is due in large measure to the different ways the two theoretical camps conceive of power and of political identities.

For the classic pluralists (to review briefly), power is regarded in the first instance as possessed by groups who employ what they have of it to advance those interests that uniquely define them. The danger of mutually destructive conflict is headed off by ceding some of this power to a state charged with protecting the peace. These pluralists then depart from this otherwise Hobbesist scenario by rejecting the latter's authoritarian political recommendations in favour of democracy which is supposed both to regulate conflict and to prevent some groups from co-opting the power of the state. On the perspective of the radical pluralists this picture is profoundly *apolitical* in two senses: the state is seen as a recipient of power derived from prepolitical interest groups, and the interests that define these groups determine their political interactions rather than being themselves politically constructed.

Like their classic predecessors, the radical pluralists recommend some version of liberal democracy, rather than participatory or deliberative alternatives. However, their way of conceptualizing liberal democracy (at least on the version expounded by Mouffe) differs from typical treatments of it. In accord with its Madisonian roots, classic pluralism aims to contain conflict within formal, institutional arrangements, such as check and balance systems of government. That these are to function in a liberal-democratic framework is unquestioned. The pluralists, like other liberal democrats, recognize that within this framework there are different ways of conceiving the relation between liberalism and democracy. As discussed in Chapter 3, these range from mutual support, as in Mill's view, to liberal containment of democracy, as Riker or Hayek see it, and a main theoretical task is to identify the best or proper relationship within such a range. Mouffe, however, denies that there is any best or proper relationship between liberalism and democracy. Rather, the relation is itself always subject to contests, which take place not only or primarily among theorists, but within ongoing social and political conflicts themselves (2000: 2–5, ch. 1). In this respect conflict reaches into the very organizing structure where social contestations take place and is hence more thoroughgoing in this radical pluralist perspective than for the classic pluralists or for mainstream liberal democrats generally.

Democracy's empty space and conflicts

For radical pluralists, if there is anything problematic for democratic theory about conflict this is not its containment, but attempts to deny it. To see how this claim is arrived at it will be useful to return to the 'empty space' of democracy problem, as appropriated by Lefort and discussed in Chapter 2. Tocqueville perceived that democracy is unique since in it political power 'has been set free from the arbitrariness of personal rule' (such as of a king) which means it 'appears to belong to no one, except to the people in the abstract' which Tocqueville feared 'threatened to become unlimited, omnipotent, to acquire an ambition to take charge of every aspect of social life' (Lefort 1988: 15). Lefort does not think that democracy is therefore unavoidably oppressive, but because the space of political power is 'empty' it risks turning to tyranny when an individual, such as a populist demagogue or an autocratic political party, whether of the right as in Fascism, or the left, as in Bolshevism, 'occupies' the space by claiming to embody or speak for the 'People-As-One.'

Conflict within democratic politics involves competition among the various groupings in a society to turn state power to their own ends, and a principal challenge for democracies is to permit this while preventing any group from occupying and hence destroying the space that makes changing and confined deployment of state power possible. Human rights, such as those declared in the 1791 Proclamation of Human Rights in revolutionary France or the United Nations Declaration of Human Rights, are cited by Lefort as the most general examples of how democratic political space is simultaneously empty and contested: the abstractness of statements of these rights lends them to alternative interpretations over which there are ongoing contests.

Terms like 'right' are, to use the term appropriated by radical pluralists from Jacques Lacan, 'floating signifiers.' A right on some specific interpretation (an example that comes to mind is an entitlement to exclusive use of something as opposed to a claim on some resource) determines what is legitimate (for the time those favouring the interpretation carry the day), but democracy is retained as long as competing parties recognize 'the legitimacy of a debate as to what is legitimate and what is illegitimate' (Lefort 1988: 39, italics omitted). On this perspective the democratic state has the power to enforce rights, but this power is not viewed as a quantity of force previously attached to interest groups; rather inauguration of the democratic state creates a new and qualitatively different locus of political power, that of the empty space.

The emptying of the space of political power, Lefort emphasizes, is an historical event (specifically the French Revolution and subsequent transformations it inspired) which both comes from and in turn reinforces political cultures in which previously assumed dogmas that society has 'ultimate ends' and people are 'assigned to specific stations and functions' are called into question. Lefort thus regards democracy 'a double phenomenon' where political power is detached from specified persons and where 'the markers which once allowed people to situate themselves in relation to one another in a determinate manner have disappeared' (34). The contrasts Lefort has in mind are the feudal orders replaced by democratic revolutions from the eighteenth century and twentieth-century totalitarianisms which, in declaring themselves embodiments of the people and in claiming to further 'ultimate ends' of society (to serve the fatherland, to achieve full communist harmony of interests), strove to fix citizens' places in rigid social or political categories: friend or enemy of the national mission, proletarian or bourgeois. In modern democracy there are no goals of society – or rather, many such goals may be proposed but none by anyone who has succeeded (or fully succeeded) in being accepted as the incarnation of the people-as-one.

This means that there are contests over what specific aims a society should pursue and that, depending on the configurations of different aims in such contests, participants' identifications are formed and change. On the interpretation of Laclau and Mouffe, one way this happens is that people enter political arenas with particular interests to advance, and as alliances are formed and 'chains of equivalence' established among them in opposition to common foes, they come to identify with shared goals considered by them universal. This may simply be the goal of overcoming repression, as Laclau notes regarding the many different groups opposing the military regime in his native Argentina in the 1960s, or their later, populist identification with Peron and Peronism (Laclau 1997: 371–2). More ambitiously, he and Mouffe foresee the possibility, but by no means the necessity, of chains of equivalence among people around a common project of pluralist democracy itself. Among other things this would involve an identification with democratic and more specifically liberal-democratic values and institutions, thus displacing earlier political identities on the radical left, which set themselves in opposition to liberal democracy as essentially oppressive (Laclau and Mouffe 1985: ch. 4).

Some poststructuralist themes

If classic pluralist theory lends itself most conveniently to a Hobbesist inter-pretation in terms of presupposed philosophical tenets, radical pluralism explicitly draws upon key concepts of poststructuralist philosophers, such as Jean-François Lyotard, Michel Foucault, and Jacques Derrida. These thinkers, and radical pluralist theory itself, are sometimes also classified as 'post mod-ern,' and insofar as they reject Enlightenment ideas about a fixed human nature and universal, foundational moral norms, this is justified. Mouffe, however, resists such classification since she thinks that the postmodernists' focus on identities supposes its own kind of fixity or 'essentialism' and that they project an analogue of participatory or deliberative-democratic, conflict-free harmony achieved when people successfully affirm their identities (2000: 129–30, 1993: 7, 15). A brief review of some tenets of the theorists most often appealed to by radical pluralists (however they are classified) will help to explicate Lefort's concept of political power and identities as well as the specifically political-theoretical views to be summarized subsequently.

Metanarratives

Lyotard defines the postmodern attitude as 'incredulity toward metanarra-tives,' where by a metanarrative he means an effort to explain and justify the rules in accord with which a practice is conducted by assigning it a place or role within some 'grand narrative.' Though the practices Lyotard expli-citly refers to in his introduction of this concept are those of science and technology, the examples he gives of justifying metanarratives – 'the dialec-tics of the Spirit, the hermeneutics of meaning, the emancipation of the rational or working subject, or the creation of wealth' – lend themselves as well, and in some instances more obviously, to political practices (1984 [1979]: xxiii). Thus, Hegel explained and justified corporatist and constitu-tional monarchal politics by reference to their supposed roles in his philo-sophical story about a world spirit's coming to self-actualization, and Marx explained and justified working-class political organization as central to an historical process leading toward full human collective self-determination.

In the realm of science, metanarratives are typically built around para-digms (such as the Newtonian picture of the world) in which various sorts of phenomena are explained 'homologically' by reference to a single paradig-matic core (for instance, matter in motion obeying classical laws of physics). To homological accounts, Lyotard contrasts 'paralogical' ones where a variety of often incommensurate approaches are simultaneously taken to different subject matters not assumed to be parts of a unified whole, rather in the way that inventors pragmatically approach specific challenges without trying to unify all the challenges or derive their inventive ideas from universal scien-tific theories (ibid. ch. 13). The analogue of homology in ethical and political practices is seeking consensus about universal norms.

Such endeavours suppose 'the Enlightenment narrative, in which the hero of knowledge works toward a good ethico-political end – universal peace' (xxiii-iv). This passage alludes to Kant (who thought that history was evolving in just this way, 1988 [1784]), but Lyotard also has in mind Habermas. While Lyotard sees appeal to universal Enlightenment values as having the totalitarian potential, realized in Soviet communism, to justify political centralization and suppression of conflict and individuality, Habermas argues against postmodernism that Enlightenment values are essential bulwarks against politically dangerous nihilism of the sort that supported Nazism (Habermas: 1987). It might be noted that while Habermas can be located in the broad Kantian tradition and while Lyotard alludes to Kant's historical theory as an example of a modernist metanarrative, he also draws upon Kant for support of his own views, though referring mainly to Kant's aesthetics (Lyotard 1989, McKinlay 1998).

Democratic theorists like Lefort are attracted to Lyotard's critique since inscribing politics within metanarratives that describe a goal for democracy and assign political actors' roles with respect to it narrows democracy's 'space.' Lyotard's suspicion of these narratives and of privileged paradigms is often referred to as the rejection of 'foundationalism' in science, philosophy, or politics: foundational approaches aspire to step outside (or get under or above) a subject matter to identify first principles that unify and explain it in the manner of a metanarrative. Radical pluralists are also drawn to views of Lyotard that bear on the nonfixity of political identities. His more fine-grained criticism of Habermas pertains to the latter's notion summarized in Chapter 9 that linguistic communication carries within it the supposition of consensus over universal norms, such as mutual respect. Referring to Nietzsche and to Heraclitus, Lyotard argues that speech should be viewed on the model of a contest rather than of rational cooperation. He uses the term 'agon' or a 'joust' to describe this model: 'to speak is to fight, in the sense of playing, and speech acts fall within the domain of a general agonistics' (1984: 10).

Language games

Crucial in Lyotard's defence of this claim is reference to yet another philosopher often referred to by poststructuralists, namely Ludwig Wittgenstein. Attractive to them is Wittgenstein's idea that terms (therefore concepts) are meaningful just in virtue of how they are used in conjunction with other terms, similarly to the way that moves in a game have 'meaning' only in the context of the other moves in that game. Just as there is no mega- or metagame that explicates basic principles of rules for all games, so there is no single world structure or basic foundation to which reference can be made to give universal meaning to the terms by the use of which people get on with and make sense of their lives (Lyotard 1984: 9–11, Wittgenstein

1953). Speech thus conceived of is 'agonic' since different 'language games' carry with them their own criteria of legitimacy, and there are no overarching legitimating standards to which appeal can be made to settle disagreements among people whose worlds have different meanings (Lyotard 1988 [1983]: xi). This notion fits with Lefort's idea that democratic politics always involves contests, not just over such matters as who should enjoy what rights, but over how rights themselves are to be conceived.

Identifications

Lyotard's views on language and meaning join some related theses of Derrida and Foucault that are also important in the background of radical pluralism. In an intriguing argument that writing illustrates the unique powers of language better than does speaking, Derrida appropriates the theory of the linguist Ferdinand Saussure (whom he also criticizes for exclusive attention to speech) that language acquires its ability to signify only in virtue of the play of differences among signs. Derrida generalizes this to argue that the identity of anything – which, in agreement with Wittgenstein, he regards as linguistically or 'discursively' constructed – depends upon its differences from other things and hence is constituted by what is outside of it (Derrida 1978 [1967], 1998 [1967]).

For radical pluralist theory this means that because they depend upon changing and contingent relations to one another, identities are not fixed. They thus reject what they call 'essentialist' accounts which assign fixed roles to political subjects of the sort Lyotard saw being assigned them by meta-narratives. It also means that political identities involve exclusions, as Connolly puts it, or more dramatically, 'antagonisms,' in Laclau and Mouffe's formulation. Because for Connolly identities are crucially maintained and formed in contrast to alternative identities and because 'to establish an identity is to create social and conceptual space for it to be in ways that impinge on the spaces available to other possibilities,' the 'politics of identity' must always involve provision of space for some identifications to the exclusion of others. For instance, protecting family values (for those with patriarchal identities) militates against such things as affirmative action for women (Connolly 1991: 160).

Laclau and Mouffe focus on an unavoidable instability besetting identities and the contexts made up of differences in terms of which they are constructed. If such a context is closed, then the identities formed 'within' them are fixed, but if they are completely open then no identities could form at all. What makes identities possible, then, is that a 'context' (Laclau 1997: 367–8) or a 'society' (Laclau and Mouffe 1985: 125–7) is limited by its contrast to a context or society outside of it, and when the exterior contrasts become identity-threatening they cease to be mere differences and are 'antagonistic.' The situation is unstable since contexts cannot be wholly 'outside' one another if they are to have even negatively defining relations to one another, but nor can they be incorporated the one into the other if they are to retain their context-determining character; the result is that a society 'never manages fully to be a society' (ibid.: 127).

Political undertakings with respect to identities will always involve antagonisms, but they can be sorted according to whether identity-preserving antagonisms are retained or there are efforts to forge new identities by reference to alternative antagonisms. An example of the first tack given by Laclau and Mouffe is the millenarian politics of eighteenth-century England when the various identifications of rural peoples came to be integrated in virtue of a common antagonism to urban dwellers. Laclau and Mouffe describe such situations as ones where diverse identities have been 'sutured' or where 'chains of equivalence' have been established among them. By contrast, in the next century, the politics conducted by Disraeli succeeded in breaking equivalences that divided the people of England into those who are poor and those who are rich by establishing an equivalence among both rich and poor in terms of common English nationhood, now in opposition to the peoples of other nations (ibid.: 129–30).

Power and hegemony

A central theme in Foucault's writings bears on this conception of politics. Like other philosophers in the postmodern tradition, he rejected both the notion of an unconstructed 'sovereign Kantian subject' with a fixed nature and the related Enlightenment view that scientific and ethical truths are there to be discovered and then used in the cause of general human emancipation (1973 [1966]). In contrast to this Enlightenment thinking, Foucault advanced the provocative theses that 'people' (or, in keeping with his rejection of the notion of sovereign subjects, 'subject positions') are always enmeshed in relations of domination and subordination, that is in power relations, and that what passes for truth in science or philosophy is in the service of power (1972 [1969], 1980). Pertinent to radical pluralism is the way Foucault connects these two theses. Crudely put, this is that truth serves power by creating dominating/subordinated subject positions: the 'individual is not to be conceived as a sort of . . . inert material on which power comes to fasten [instead] it is one of the prime effects of power that certain gestures, certain discourses, certain desires, come to be identified and constituted as individuals' (1980: 98).

This is the conception of power that differentiates radical from classic pluralism, and it is central to the prominent role Laclau and Mouffe give to 'hegemony.' As employed by Mouffe and Laclau – who took this term over from Antonio Gramsci – hegemony does not mean the ability to impose one's will on others by force but rather to be able to forge a political will itself (1985: ch. 1 and passim). A common interpretation of hegemony distinguishes between a military sense of constraint by force and a political sense of forging consent. Neither side of this distinction captures the radical-pluralist use of the term, in which political hegemony centrally involves the exercise of power, but this is power in a Foucauldian sense of the construction of political identities. As Mouffe puts it: '[We] should conceptualize power not as an *external* relation taking place between two preconstituted identities, but rather as constituting the identities themselves' (1996: 247). When or to the extent that political actors (such as the millenarians or Disraeli in the earlier example) have succeeded in forging equivalent identities by reference to some antagonistic division, they are exercising hegemony.

The politics of radical pluralism

Two broad categories of political recommendations are advanced from these theoretical positions. The first systematic expression of the theory was by Laclau and Mouffe in their *Hegemony and Socialist Strategy* (1985). This book, as much of their earlier and subsequent work, was focused on two features of the political landscape on the political left: Marxist organization and political practices, which they criticized as flowing from a perspective in which the working class is the necessary agent of progressive social change, and the emergence of new social movements (around women's issues, environmentalism, antiracism, and so on), which they welcomed.

Reductionism

Marxist class reductionism on their view exhibited all the failings of essentialism and foundationalism correctly criticized by poststructuralist theory. To the extent that Marxism had been hegemonic (so to be a left radical was to be some variety of a Marxist), it precluded pluralism within the left and forced people either to denigrate forms of oppression or subordination not based on class or to try forcing them into limiting or entirely inappropriate molds of class struggle. Meanwhile, like any other form of political essentialism, class reductionism threatened to close off the empty space of democracy, as it succeeded in doing in the socialist world. This was not only antidemocratic in itself, but it set the left against democracy, thus leaving the terrain to the political centre and right. The alternative Laclau and Mouffe recommended was to abandon this or any other form of left essentialism, for instance, as in those streams of the women's movements that endorsed analogously reductionist views toward gender. Instead, they urged the many and varied components of the left to construct chains of equivalence among themselves around the common political project (and hence identity) of deepening and expanding existing liberal democracy, that is around the project they called 'radical and plural democracy' (Laclau and Mouffe 1985: 176, and see Mouffe 1993: 70–1).

Liberal democracy and capitalism

The second category of political recommendations follows from this one, but they are directed mainly at contemporary liberal-democratic political theorists. Laclau and Mouffe describe a 'liberal-conservative discourse' approaching hegemonic status in which neoliberal defence of a free market economy is articulated with 'the profoundly anti-egalitarian culture and social traditionalism of conservatism' (1985: 175–6). Against this they prescribe a counter-hegemonic effort undertaken within liberal-democratic theory and practice aiming to turn liberal democracy from this conservative direction. Concretely, this requires both defending liberal democracy from its critics on the left and on the right, while challenging and providing alternatives to the conservative interpretations of the floating signifiers of liberal democracy – freedom, equality, public and private, and so on.

Liberal democracy and Carl Schmitt

This effort is sometimes portrayed by Mouffe as the project to counter the theories of Carl Schmitt. She begins a book entitled *The Return of the Political* (1993) approvingly, referring to Schmitt's view that politics always and unavoidably involves antagonism. Politics arises whenever people see their identities not just as different from those of others but threatened by them: 'From that moment onwards, any type of we/them relation, be it religious, ethnic, national, economic or other, becomes the site of a political antagonism' (1993: 3). Schmitt himself saw liberal democracy as a doomed effort to deny antagonisms or cast them out of the realm of politics, which is then reduced mainly to futile parliamentary squabbling, and he prescribed instead the proud embrace of antagonism on the part of a homogeneously united people toward other peoples, expressed and decisively acted on by political leadership unburdened by liberal constraints. On Schmitt's view, avoiding such constraints was a virtue shared by Bolshevism and Fascism (1988 [1923]: 16, 29–30), and he, himself, embraced the latter.

Mouffe agrees with Schmitt that antagonisms cannot be expunged from politics, but she denies that liberal democracy must or should try to do this. Accordingly, she criticizes mainstream liberal-democratic theorists for their efforts to suppress political recognition of antagonistic conflict or to insulate politics from it. Such efforts are 'the real threat to democracy' because they lead to violence being unrecognized rather than acknowledged and politically confronted (1996: 248). Mouffe focuses especially on the approaches by liberal-democratic theorists (as reviewed in Chapter 3 above) to the problem of how public neutrality can be preserved in the face of value conflicts in the private realm. 'Political liberals,' such as Larmore or Rawls recognize persisting conflicts of the sort that are deeply implicated in people's identities, but they try to confine them to the private sphere, thus voiding the public realm of what is distinctive about politics. 'Value liberals' admit substantive values into politics, and some of them, such as Joseph Raz, even admit a measure of conflict over these values to be legitimate objects of political debate. But even for him, as for other value liberals, the ideal is consensus as a goal to be approximated (Mouffe 1993: 124–8, ch. 9, and see Connolly 1991: 160–1).

Mouffe's alternative is to promote 'agonistic pluralism' where antagonistic conflict is expected to be carried on but constrained and diffused by submission to liberal and democratic 'rules of the game' (1993: 4). This, she recognizes, requires that antagonistic political actors submit themselves to these rules, but rather than seeing this as achieved by their setting aside differences for the purposes of political interaction (the political-liberal notion) or acquiring consensual values that replace antagonistic ones (as value liberals would have it), she thinks what is required is to forge identifications on the part of conflicting parties with pluralist democracy itself, that is 'to establish the hegemony of democratic values and practices' (151). Success in this effort does not transform enemies into friends, but nor does it leave them the same antagonists, albeit ones accepting new constraints. The task, rather, is to provide conditions that will reconstruct the identities of those in conflict in such a way that they are not so threatened by one another that they get locked into antagonistic relations unconstrained by adherence to liberal and democratic values.

Alternative theories

An approach decisively rejected is that of Habermas and the deliberative democrats, who, drawing on the theory about a presupposed common ethical basis to human communication criticized by Lyotard, are seen as attempting to void conflict from politics (Mouffe 1993: 10, 2000: ch. 4). Mouffe has more sympathy for the civic republicans because they urge that identity-forming values about the good life or society should be seen as central to politics and they see involvement in political communities as a substantive virtue. She also approves of the anti-essentialism of civic republican communitarianism. However, she is also critical of civic-republican 'premodernism,' for failing to attempt integration of such things as pluralism and the defence of individual liberty into political identities (1993: 61–3).

Though sharing Richard Rorty's poststructuralist orientation, Mouffe is also critical of what she sees as his unnecessary parochialism. Rorty sides with Rawls in arguing for the priority of common, liberal-democratic political values which, as an antifoundationalist, he justifies on the communitarian ground that, imbued as he is with the values of his native US, these values are simply received as central to his 'moral identity' (Rorty: 1990). Rorty describes these inherited values as those of 'bourgeois liberalism' (Rorty: 1983). Mouffe's generic criticism is that, similarly to the civic republican communitarians, Rorty portrays the political culture of his own liberal democracy as monolithic and free of antagonistic conflict internal to itself.

In particular, by seeing capitalism and democracy as unproblematically conjoined, he fails to account for a persisting tension within liberal democracies between 'political liberalism' and 'economic liberalism' and thus ends up simply apologizing for American capitalism (Mouffe 1993: 10). Even if someone agreed with Rorty's politics (he describes himself as a social democrat who favours 'governmentally controlled capitalism plus welfare statism,' 1987: 565), this would be objectionable from a radical pluralist point of view. The reason for this is that his portrayal of liberal democracy is thought to blur political lines of difference within it thus impeding 'the constitution of distinctive political identities' and fostering democracy-impeding disaffection toward political engagement (Mouffe 1993: 5).

Reactions to radical pluralism

Laclau and Mouffe appeared on the scene of political theory by throwing a gauntlet to the traditional left, whose theorists were eager to pick it up and do battle with the new revisionists. The principal theoretical issues focused on were their critique of essentialism, which the critics thought denied radical pluralism the ability to identify the working class or any other social group as a reliable agent of progressive social change, and rejection of foundationalism, which critics regarded tantamount to embracing epistemological and moral relativism. A sample of these debates may be found in an exchange between Norman Geras (1987) and Laclau and Mouffe (1987).

A line of criticism of radical pluralism that comes to mind from the side of mainstream liberal-democratic theory is that by urging people to share common values favouring pluralism Mouffe's view does not differ from that of any liberal democrat, except that she forgoes an effort to justify embrace of these values by reference to philosophical foundational principles. Whether this claim is accurate depends upon how Mouffe's analysis of hegemony is viewed. If she thought that to be hegemonic, radical-pluralist commitments must displace or take priority over antagonistic stances and identities, the objection would be on target. An implicit rejoinder is in Mouffe's distinction between an 'enemy' and an 'adversary.' For radical pluralism to be hegemonic is not for it to replace or supersede adversarial identifications, but to interject into a political community the culture that an 'opponent should be considered not as an enemy to be destroyed, but as an adversary whose existence is legitimate and must be tolerated' (1993: 4, 2000: 13).

To pursue this line of response further would likely lead back to debates about the possibility of foundationalism, or the construction of a political theory on the basis of philosophical first principles. Mouffe does not argue that antifoundationalism must lead to radical pluralism: it might be used in service of Rorty's defence of mainstream US politics or even of the extreme rightist ones of Schmitt. By contrast, some who favour radical-pluralist political prescriptions wish to endorse them on foundational grounds. Fred

Dallmayr, for instance, looks to support radical pluralist political views with a version of Hegelianism (1989: ch. 6), and perhaps similar attempts could be made from within other philosophical perspectives more sympathetic to foundationalism than are Mouffe and Laclau.

I shall not take readers into the philosophical waters where debate over this topic would need to be pursued, as I wish to turn to a second aspect of the claim that Mouffe's position does not differ from that of core liberal-democratic theorists. In keeping with the notion referred to earlier that there cannot be a theoretically fixed way of relating liberalism to democracy, Mouffe's view about how alternative and conflictual values can coexist with pluralistic commitment to liberal democracy is not *pronounced* in the manner of standard liberal-democratic theoretical prescriptions: let there be neutrality in politics; or let people agree on common values to guide their political behaviour. Rather, proposals are urged as an ongoing project of cultural politics. Moreover, to mark another difference, this project is not to be carried out exclusively or even primarily in formal settings such as parliaments or courts, but it should be undertaken in 'as many social relations as possible' (Mouffe 1993: 151). In these ways the orientation of radical pluralism has something in common with the earlier-summarized pragmatic approach to democratic theory (see Chapter 8).

Radical pluralism and the problems

As in the case of some of the other theories surveyed, not all of the problems listed in Chapter 2 find explicit attempts at solution in radical pluralist writings. Connolly sees as a virtue of 'agonistic democracy' that it resists trying to force people into single collective molds and invites them to recognize the contingency of their identities. In this way, far from breeding a herd mentality (one way of interpreting the massification problem), democracy can facilitate radical questioning by people of their own identities and overcoming pettiness, complacency, and resentment in ways that even (a sanitized) Nietzsche might applaud (Connolly 1991: ch. 6). Mouffe shares with deliberative democrats the rejection of a view of democracy as just the aggregation of preferences (2000: 96), and to the extent that the 'irrationality' problem depends upon this view, radical pluralists might be seen as sharing this common reaction to it.

The empty space and conflict

One candidate for an orienting problem of radical-pluralist theory is the danger of democracy's empty space, and another is that of conflict. The first of these is approached, as has been noted, by insisting that the 'emptiness' of the space of democracy be maintained. Insofar as theory can help to do this it is by contesting participationist or other approaches that portray popular sovereignty as representing a common will or homogenous political identity. Connolly sees this orientation as also central for staving off destructive dimensions of conflict. A central thesis of his *Identity/Difference* (1991) is that democracy has the potential to allow for collective political action of people based on their group-derived identities while at the same time impeding destructive interactions resulting from a tendency for group identification to breed dogmatism and resentment. But democracy has this potential only if it is 'agonistic' by which Connolly means that it allows and invites the 'contestation of settled identities,' which in turn provides 'the best political medium through which to incorporate strife into interdependence and care into strife' (1991: 193).

Oppression

Mouffe's approach to the conflict problem is more direct than Connolly's and in form it is like that of the classic pluralists, namely to embrace conflict as an essential feature of democracy. A question raised by her stance is whether the embrace might be too tight. Not only conflict, but 'domination' and 'violence' are recognized by Mouffe as ineradicable aspects of 'the specificity of modern democracy' and hence things to be 'contested and limited' but not to be overcome (1996: 248). It is clear that Mouffe wants a radical-pluralist approach to democracy to combat such things as sexist and racist subordinations (*ibid.*: 247), and she includes a chapter in her *The Democratic Paradox* criticizing Anthony Giddens and other defenders of a Blairite 'third way' for giving aid and comfort to a procapitalist neoliberalism that she rejects (2000: ch. 5). Still, it might be argued that in seeing domination and violence as ineradicable, attitudes whereby they are fatalistically accepted are reinforced.

Mouffe's reaction to such a charge is clear. To recognize antagonisms is not to condone any form of them, and efforts to deny the always-present possibility even of strong and potentially destructive conflicts is to convert what can and should be a politics aimed at containing or even transforming such antagonisms to a futile politics of 'dialogue or moral preaching' (15). By contrast, when it is recognized that any 'hegemonic articulation of "the people"' creates a relation of inclusion and exclusion, it will also be recognized that such articulation is contingent and hence amenable to change (49). In particular, Mouffe thinks that this involves the effort referred to earlier to transform 'enemies,' between whom there are no shared liberal or democratic values to constrain their enmity, into 'adversaries,' who do share these commitments. Her way of putting this point is to urge that a politics of 'antagonism' be transformed into those of 'agonism' (101–5).

The tyranny of the majority

Similar comments apply to a radical-pluralist stance on the tyranny of the majority problem. Mouffe's reaction to this problem is that it does not admit either of theoretical or of final practical solution. Though proposed in general terms, recommendations by liberals to set fixed limits upon what a majority may do are in fact examples of specific moves in the unending conflict between liberalism and democracy. She grants that individual and majority rights should be secured against possible majority tyranny, but maintains that 'the opposite danger also exists,' when certain liberties (she probably has in mind economic market liberties) become 'naturalized' and have the effect of 'buttressing many relations of inequality' (2000: 150–1).

The 'tyranny of the majority' problem is thus generalized by Mouffe to the problem of how democratic equalities and liberal freedoms are to be related, and this is a matter of 'precarious and necessarily unstable' negoti-ation among contesting claims to freedoms and forms of equality (11). Except to note that such negotiations should take place in a multitude of forums where people politically (therefore, conflictually) interact, Mouffe does not spell out how this might be undertaken. Similarly, few indications are given about how transformations from antagonistic to agonistic politics might be achieved by Mouffe; nor does Connolly address the specifics of how, within agonistic democracy, dogmatic and resentfully hostile group identities can be combated. Whether these omissions are seen as a grave weakness in the theory or as an invitation to exercise imagination in pursuing such politics, the nature of which will depend upon specific circumstances, no doubt depends, again, upon how comfortable one is with pragmatic approaches to democratic politics.

Chapter 11

Applying democratic theories: globalization

While this introduction to democratic theories has been organized around problems, it could as well have been organized around 'problematics.' A problematic (often written in French as a *problematique* in English-language texts to highlight its technical character) is a core difficulty, the attempted overcoming of which focuses theoretical approaches to some subject. Half the meetings of the course which generated the lists of most and least democratic situations reported in Chapter 1, were devoted to subjects chosen by class members. Some of these were theoretical topics (rights theory, approaches to false consciousness, concepts of the self, ethics and democracy, and the like), but more frequently selected were real-world situations, policies, or movements: citizenship, multiculturalism, nationalism, religion, education, feminism, the media, democratic transformations, racism, and the environment. Each of these topics presented the class with one or more problematic.

For example, a problematic that focuses much debate about multiculturalism among democratic theorists is put by Bhikhu Parekh as 'how to create a political community that is both politically cohesive and stable and satisfies the legitimate aspirations of cultural minorities' (1999: 109, and see his 2000: ch. 7). Analogously to the 'fact/value/meaning' triangle seen to permeate approaches to democratic problems, is that statements of problematics almost always point in the general direction of favoured resolutions. So the guiding problematic of Nathan Glazer's *We are All Multiculturalists Now* 1997 [1977]) would more likely be put 'how can national unity be preserved in the face of strains put upon it by cultural diversity?' Parekh, a critic of liberal individualism, favours policies more supportive of the protection and preservation of minority cultures than does the individualist, Glazer. But debates on the topic are not adequately pictured by simple divisions. Will Kymlicka would endorse Parekh's way of formulating the problematic of muliculturalism, though he is a champion of liberal individualism, while Charles Taylor, writing from a position closer to Parekh's than to Kymlicka's would prefer a formulation in such terms as 'how can mutual respect and recognition among culturally divergent groups be achieved?' 1995, 2001).

A problematic motivating much theoretical work about democracy and the environment is: 'since political forums are made up of humans, how can other animals, much less forests or lakes, achieve democratic representation?' As in the case of statements of a multicultural problematic, this one would be resisted by those who question whether environmental challenges can be met democratically at all (Ophuls 1992). But aside from this sort of theorist (and, of course, one who doubts that there are significant environmental challenges for whom addressing this problematic or ways of formulating it are idle exercises), prodemocrats in the two major environmental 'camps' – biocentric or 'deep ecological' (Naess 1989) and anthrocentric (Bookchin 1990) – could agree that this is at least a core problematic. Such agreement is also possible for those who avoid lining up with either of these two camps (Paehlke 1989) or try pragmatically to displace the controversies among their adherents (Light and Katz 1996).

Some subjects may be approached through the lens of more than one problematic. An example is citizenship, which may initially be addressed by asking the question 'what is a (proper) citizen?' or the question 'who is (ought to be) a citizen?' The first problematic invites the theorist to decide whether citizenship is simply a matter of legal entitlements and responsibilities or carries with it moral and civic commitments and identifications as well. A point of entry into the topic approached from this angle is in the collection *Theorizing Citizenship* (Beiner 1995a). The other question is especially pertinent due to the increasing permeability of state borders and often forced migration, which makes the question of who merits rights of citizenship and under what conditions a pressing one. This problem and related ones are usefully addressed in ways that relate to democratic theory by Veit Bader (1997) and Joseph Carens (2000), among many other authors to whom they make reference. Obviously, reactions to the 'what is a citizen' and the 'who is a citizen' problematics will have implications for one another.

Globalization

The topic of citizenship shades into that of globalization, and the book will conclude by surveying some alternative approaches to this topic by a selection of contemporary democratic theorists. The aim of the survey is to provide a better feel for how democratic theories are applied to problematic situations than can be conveyed in capsule summaries. The treatment of this topic will also illustrate how the 'problematics' of globalization are differently conceived, and it will further indicate how social or political-scientific claims about what is possible, value judgments, and conceptions of how democracy ought to be conceived interact.

The 'problematic' addressed by (the late) Claude Ake is 'how can democracy be saved from globalization.' On his view globalization is 'rendering democracy irrelevant and in this it poses the most serious threat yet in the history of democracy' (1997: 285). Ake has in mind economic globalization where matters of state policy formerly amendable to democratic decision-making by citizens are either severely constrained by present-day global economic arrangements or dictated by extrastate economic agencies. An example of the constraints he has in mind are threats of capital flight to head off policies even with large majority support when they are regarded contrary to the interests of increasingly mobile manufacturing enterprises. An example of external dictation is the power of agencies such as the World Bank to extend or withhold economic aid or to lower or raise a country's credit rating depending on whether it follows dictated domestic policies, for instance, regarding taxation or social services.

Ake's conception of globalization as democracy-immune international economic practices and institutions is a pejorative one, as is another common concept pertaining to global culture. Globalization in a cultural and still pejorative sense refers to the homogenization of world cultures such that local, indigenous daily habits and forms of recreation are supplanted by the likes of Hollywood movies and US television, while popular values around the world are conforming to the consumerism typical of the wealthier, industrialized countries. Critics of globalization in this sense, such as Benjamin Barber – who calls the result 'McWorld' (1995) – see it as likewise imposed due to the domination of world entertainment markets and technology mainly by US-based film, television, and print media and to rulings by international bodies, like the World Trade Organization (WTO) prohibiting state support or protection of national culture on the grounds that this inhibits free trade (see Held and McGrew 2000: pt 3).

Ulrich Beck reserves the term 'globalism' to describe antidemocratic effects of a world capitalist market decried by Ake and Barber. To it he contrasts 'globality,' which he uses in a neutral sense simply to refer to the interconnectedness of countries (2000: 9–10). Similarly neutral is David Held's conception of globalization as a 'stretching and deepening of social relations' such that 'day-to-day activities are increasingly influenced by events happening on the other side of the globe' where 'the practices and decisions of local groups or communities can have significant global reverberations' (Held 1999: 92, and see Held *et al.* 1999: pt 1). In addition to the economy and culture, Held lists other domains within which this stretching and deepening take place, namely, the environment, law, defence, and he might have added communications technology. Though Held does not share Ake's or Barber's exclusive focus on negative dimensions of globalization, he identifies problems for democracy.

States and the globe

The problematic that Held and most other students of international relations concerned with democracy address is that citizens have channels for democratic action within states, but thanks to globalization there are increasing limitations on the actual sovereignty of states. This creates what he calls 'disjunctures' between global forces impinging upon citizens and the latters' ability to affect these forces. One disjuncture is between citizens and economic forces of the sort that concerned Ake. Another is that in many parts of the world the effective sovereignty of states is limited by their membership in overarching organizations such as the International Monetary Fund or the European Community and in military alliances like NATO. Held also lists as a weak but growing constraint on state sovereignty, international law such as regulations embodied in treaties or provision for individuals to appeal directly to the European Court of Human Rights (1991a: 212–22).

Held's disjunctures underscore mainly practical problems. One task (that taken on by Held) acknowledges global weakening of the autonomy of states and *applauds* the resulting potential for eroding confinement of democracy within state boundaries and aspirations to state sovereignty that sustains such confinement since these things impede a quest to democratize cross- and superstate domains. A contrasting task is to urge *strengthening* the sovereignty of (democratic) states by defending their internal political structures against external constraint and interference. We shall shortly return to these alternatives, but first a more deeply theoretical problem will be noted.

Democratic boundaries

As noted in Chapter 8, Robert Dahl observes (1982: 97–9) that since any democracy will exclude some people from participation in democratic procedures (for instance children and noncitizens) they will to this extent be deficient in democracy if the latter requires that those affected by a decision have a say in making it. To set democratic boundaries by popular vote supposes that the appropriate voters have already been selected, so extra-democratic criteria must be employed. Dahl thinks this problem is an unsolvable 'embarrassment of democracy, or would be were it not ignored' (1982: 97–9). In some cases, a criterion that presupposes an ethical theory, such as utilitarianism, will be employed, but ethical theories are contestable. Confinement of democratic decision-making within state boundaries is cited by Dahl as an especially arbitrary limitation, which he thinks simply rests on 'primordial attachments,' and yet, he maintains, nobody would or could reasonably advocate extending democratic inclusion to all of humanity, and he, himself, later argued that democracy is appropriate only within states (Dahl 1999).

Reflection on this theoretical problem highlights the practical democratic problems involved in confronting globalization. This is clearly the case for those who wish to preserve full state autonomy, as they need to justify the exclusion of those outside of a country who are affected by its actions from participation in the country's decisions. However, problems are also indicated for theorists in search of superstate forums. Unless they are prepared to endorse thoroughgoing world government, where and how are boundaries to be drawn? One orientation, labelled 'exogenous' by Susan Hurley (1999: 273–4), prescribes just making the best of whatever structures or institutions conducive to democratization are at hand, whether state contained, trans-state, or some combination. Robert Cox criticizes this approach maintaining that democracy-constraining political or economic circumstances in which people find themselves should not be simply taken as given, immune to human control, and that therefore assumptions about their inevitability should be subjected to critical scrutiny (1996: 87–91).

Hurley rejects the exogenous approach in favour of an 'endogenous' one according to which criteria of what democracy requires should be appealed to for identifying appropriate participants in democratic decision-making. She thus departs from Dahl's view that these criteria (if reasoned at all) must come from general ethical theories beyond considerations of democracy, but she is enabled to do this by invoking such 'distinctively democratic values' as 'self-determination, autonomy, respect for rights, equality, and contestability' (Hurley 1999: 274). Dahl would no doubt identify this as an appeal to debatable ethical theory.

Realism

Also pertinent to the subject at hand are theoretical disputes about international relations generally. This is not the place to survey the large number of political-scientific approaches to international relations, much less debates about how to conceive of the field itself (for instance, as surveyed by Smith 1995), but three groupings of approaches are worth noting, since democratic theorists concerned with globalization make reference to them. The dominant approach in North America from the 1940s until the collapse of the communist regimes was certainly the self-described 'realist' (and later neorealist) school associated with such names as Henry Morganthau (1985 [1948]) and Kenneth Waltz (1959), who, despite some differences of emphasis (Linklater 1995: 242–5), share the perspective that the globe is essentially made up of sovereign states related to one another in a condition of anarchy.

Realism exhibits affinities with classic pluralism. Just as countries for the pluralists are composed of groups using what power they have at their disposal to advance their unique and usually conflicting interests, so the world for the realist is composed of states, each primarily motivated to protect or achieve state security and advantage. A main difference is that whereas groups within a country are obliged to relate to one another under legal constraints, the absence of world government puts the relations among states outside of law; so force or the threat of its use is a prominent feature of state strategies.

Relevant to understanding and evaluating this approach is a distinction between 'sovereignty' and 'autonomy.' Taken in a narrow sense the sovereignty of a state is the monopoly it claims for itself, just in virtue of being constituted as a state, to have final authority over all public matters of both domestic and foreign political policy and conduct. As Charles Beitz notes this is a legal concept to be distinguished from 'autonomy,' which refers to 'the absence of significant external constraints on the actual conduct of a state's internal affairs' (1991: 241). In these terms, the realist approach assumes that the principal actors in the global arena are sovereign states primarily motivated to maintain their autonomy. As a country's room for control over its own economy or culture is narrowed by the activities of other countries or of transnational organizations, its autonomy may become so limited that sovereignty becomes merely formal. When globalization involves subjecting states to the legal authority of superstate bodies like the European Parliament, NATO, or tribunals of the WTO, even formal, juridic sovereignty is diminished.

One stream of thinking sees globalization as making realism irrelevant to the current world and in general highlights its time-bound nature. Held echoes several critics in noting that the system of sovereign states is a uniquely modern, European phenomenon, which can, moreover, be exactly dated, namely from 1648 and the Peace of Westphalia, when some major countries of Europe agreed to recognize one another's sovereignty to end (one phase of) the Thirty Years War (Held 1999: 87–8). Against any suggestion that this epoch marked the beginning of a permanently 'realist' world, theorists in this stream appeal to history to mark what they see as the transient and limited nature of state sovereignty. Thus, citing the neorealist Hedley Bull for support, Held foresees the possibility of a 'new Medievalism,' where, as in medieval Europe, sovereignty is shared among societies that interact in an ongoing way. Accepting common rules and not claiming exclusive jurisdiction over all matters of internal affairs (Bull 1995 [1977]: 254–66, Held 1991a: 223–4), Mary Kaldor sees a progression where feudalism was replaced by nation states, the autonomies of which were subsequently weakened by trade and military blocs which, she speculates, may in turn prefigure new, cosmopolitan forms of international association (Kaldor: 1995).

Some critiques of the realist picture of global relations developed from within realism. These started (arguably) with Kenneth Waltz's distinction among three 'levels of analysis' – human nature, the state, and relations among states, with a recommendation to focus attention on the relations (Walz 1959) – and gained influence with the theory of 'complex interdependence' by Robert Keohane and Joseph Nye (1972) among others according to which state autonomy is crucially affected by transnational political and economic structures. Some from this background (for instance Susan Strange 1988), insist that the most important of these structures are economic and accordingly argue that international relations are best studied by political economy. They are joined by Marxist-inspired and other radical theorists for whom specifically capitalist structures dominate international relations. This is the orientation of Cox and of Ake, who charges that 'globalization is driven by a vigorous, triumphant capitalism which is aggressively consolidating its global hegemony' (Ake 1997: 282). The import of theories of this sort depends upon whether the state is seen as a potential bulwark against globalizing capitalism or as first its pawn and now its victim. Analogous considerations pertain to radical critiques that view current globalization as part of the structured oppression of women (for example, Tickner 1992) or as environmentally destructive (Connelly and Smith 1999).

Orientations toward globalization and democracy

These approaches to international relations theories include (without perfectly matching) three general viewpoints on democracy and globalization, each posing itself a somewhat different problematic: those which see globalization, whatever democratic difficulties it engenders, as also offering exciting *opportunities* to transcend the confinement of democracy to the state; those for which globalization presents problematic *challenges to states* that need to be met by them in the interests of democracy; and viewpoints which focus on what are seen as grave *challenges to the people* posed by globalization.

Cosmopolitanism

The first and most optimistic of these orientations is reflected in democratic cosmopolitanism. Of the authors referred to above, Beck, in fact, defines the term 'globalization' (as opposed to the neutral term 'globality' and the pejorative one 'globalism') as a process which 'creates transnational solid links and spaces, revalues local cultures and promotes third cultures' (2000: 11–12). He joins Beitz, Held, Kaldor, and many other contemporary proponents of this orientation. Daniele Archibugi, collaborating with Held, locates a cosmopolitan model of democracy 'midway' between global federation and global confederation (Archibugi 1998). A federal system, where final sovereign authority over all important matters resides in a central body, as currently exists in the US and Switzerland and is globally prescribed by world federalists, he argues, fails to take account of the diversity among the world's nations, not just between those that favour democracy and those that do not, but also among prodemocratic nations, where democracy is conceptualized and pursued in different ways according to local traditions. A confederal model, as approximated in the UN, requires member states to cede a limited number of powers to a central authority while retaining power over all internal matters and some of foreign policy. Its problem is that, precisely because of globalization, this does not provide for much international coordination or regulation, and it does not at all address anti-democratic measures internal to member states.

The cosmopolitan model, according to Archibugi and Held, is most nearly exemplified in the European Union. Limitations of the sovereignty of member states in this model include enforceable transnational law governing a core of human rights and prohibiting harmful interference in the affairs of one state by another and direct central control of essentially global issues (Archibugi lists the environment, the survival of humanity, and future generations). In addition, cosmopolitan institutions should educate and encourage democratically deficient member states to change their ways, act as mediators and arbitrators in interstate disputes, and provide for institutions through which organizations of civil society can participate in decision-making over global matters. An example Archibugi could have in mind is the effort of nongovernmental organizations to gain voice and vote over designated matters before bodies like the UN or the EU.

State-based responses

Those who view globalization as a challenge to strengthen democracy within single states need not entirely reject cosmopolitan goals but could follow the approach of Norbeto Bobbio for whom democracy in transnational institutions and democracy in individual states are mutually dependent and reinforcing (Bobbio: 1995). Bobbio thus stands against those cosmopolitans who see the nation state as a major impediment to global democracy (Schmitter 1997, Galtung 2000), but his view is also in tension with theorists sceptical of cosmopolitan ventures.

One ground for such scepticism is expressed by Dahl for whom it is unrealistic to expect that trans-state institutions could be democratized. How, he asks (1999), could this be achieved in a world where the foreign policies of individual states are themselves outside the control even of the citizens of states whose policies they are? While Dahl doubts the *possibility* of cosmopolitan democracy, Kymlicka (disagreeing with Dahl about the amenability of foreign policy to citizen control) questions whether this is *necessary*. He argues that international institutions can potentially be held indirectly responsible by 'debating at the national level how we want our national governments to act in intergovernmental contexts' (1999: 123). Meanwhile Danilo Zolo calls into question the *desirability* of strong or pervasive cosmopolitan arrangements, especially those involving binding law. On his view anything beyond weak international regulations (essential if cosmopolitan government is to have any force) imposes common standards on countries with diverse political and legal cultures. Since international law is fashioned after Enlightenment, Western thinking, there is also often an ethnochauvinistic character to such imposition (2000).

Several theorists, all critics of what they see as pernicious economic, social, cultural, or environmental effects of globalization, look to activity from within nongovernmental, popular organizations such as trade unions and what Robert Walker (1988: 26–32) calls 'critical social movements' – of women, against poverty, for peace or environmental protection, in defence of human rights, and the like – for effective resistance. It is in this way that they fall into the category of those who see globalization as a challenge to 'the people.' Such groups sometimes gain seats on governmental delegations to meetings of international economic organizations like the World Trade Organization, and some NGOs have achieved observer status at the UN. To date these interventions have had little noticeable effect; although disruption of World Trade Organization meetings in Seattle in 1999 by a large and well-organized coalition at least drew widespread media attention to complaints that the Organization lacks democratic accountability and supports harmful practices.

People power

Theorists in this 'people power' camp diverge in their characterization of the nature of globalization. Richard Falk, for instance, describes the current world as one where 'globalization-from-above' has largely dismantled state sovereignty (1995, 2000), but Paul Hirst and Grahame Thompson, while sharing Falk's enthusiasm for the potentials of social movements, do not see in globalization a new diminution of state power; rather current use of global institutions functions according to them as covers for still largely state-based capitalist enterprises (1999, 2000). Among those concerned with the environment, especially as related to development, there are differences relevant to attitudes toward globalization between those (such as Paelkhe 1989) who endorse UN initiatives for 'sustainable development,' as formulated in the organization's commissioned report (the Bruntland Report) on the environment and development and those who criticize it for being excessively centralistic (Chatterjee and Finger 1994).

There is more convergence on the view that whatever the international import of their activities, the relevant social movements are in the main locally based and directed against actions (or inactions) of the states in which they are located (for example, Connelly and Smith 1999, Cox 1996: 308–9). Where they differ is in their projections for more than *ad hoc* coordination of locally based movements. Falk foresees the possibility of alliances of states and popular movements within them against globalism from above (2000: 176). Less ambitiously (and specifically addressing environmental concerns) Alain Lipietz recommends 'a modest internationalism' of NGOs bound by a principle of 'minimal universalism' (1995: ch. 7). The success of coalition building that makes use of internet communication evident in the Seattle demonstration has prompted some to see the use of this technology to build international social movements.

Democratic theories and globalization

The distinction among the three orientations and their challenges also serves as a convenient way to situate democratic theories with respect to globalization. For liberal-democratic theory globalization poses unique challenges to democracy within states. Some civic republican and deliberative-democratic themes fit with cosmopolitanism. Aspects of participatory democracy, radical pluralism, and democratic pragmatism can be drawn on by those who see globalization mainly as a 'challenge to the people.' Stances or potential stances of these theories will be identified after registering the exceptional situations of classic pluralism and catallaxy.

The affinity between realist theories of international relations and the descriptive side of classic pluralism has already been noted, but pluralist *prescriptions*, are hard to apply on a global scale. Check and balance systems of government, active promotion of global interest group overlap, and the like would require world political coordination beyond that favoured even by cosmopolitans. Moreover, those who do advocate global government, such as Johan Galtung (1980), project a world based on cooperation around common values rather than one marked by power politics among conflicting interests of the sort that motivates classic pluralist theory. Similar observations apply to catallaxy, since the political phenomena Downs, Buchanan, and Tullock wanted to analyze on an economic model are state bound: political parties, constitutions, voting citizens, legislators. Perhaps catallactic analysis could simply be transferred to global or regional governments, but this approach tends toward libertarianism. Consequently, its prescriptive dimensions are more in keeping with recommendations for *replacing* governments, state bound or trans-state alike, with economic markets, which is just what both cosmopolitan theorists like Held and champions of state sovereignty like Zolo fear.

Liberal democracy

As noted in Chapter 3, liberal-democratic theory also supposes the central role of states, since these are crucial for structured representation and the rule of law. However, most liberal-democratic theorists are more concerned with political values than with the sort of descriptive analyses emphasized in classic pluralism or catallaxy. With the exception of a minority of ethical relativist, communitarian theorists such as Richard Rorty (1983, 1990), these norms are typically projected as universal. Hence, in principle most liberal-democratic theorists could endorse trans-state and even global government provided it maintained constitutional protection of minority rights, representative democratic procedures, pluralism, and the like. Even the relativists, for whom the reason to endorse liberal-democratic values is only that they are 'ours,' could sanction enforcement of these values by regional governments as in a strengthened European Union as long as its member societies had similar political traditions.

Still, liberal democrats are loathe to abandon existing states as centres of sovereignty. As noted, some, like Kymlicka, question the practical feasibility of a cosmopolitan stance, but there are also more theoretical motivations, mainly having to do with pluralism. Though differing in their evaluations of the relative merits of the world's different political cultures, Zolo and Samuel Huntington (1996) share the view that efforts to extend sovereignty beyond existing states run afoul of the disparity of social and political values among them. By implication, Rawls shares this view when he argues that an 'overlapping consensus' required for a well-ordered liberal society differs from that required for nonliberal, yet still morally acceptable, ones (1999). For these reasons, liberal-democratic theorists are more prepared to recommend relaxing state sovereignty than dismantling it.

One challenge this orientation highlights for the liberal side of liberal-democratic theory is to identify principles in accord with which sovereignty may, legitimately, be relaxed. A related challenge addresses the question of when the sovereignty of a state is constrained by moral, if not legal obligations to those outside of it. (For pertinent discussions see Beitz 1979 and Pogge 1989). A challenge to the democratic side of liberal-democracy is the one raised by Dahl. Kymlicka, as noted above, maintains that global interactions may be indirectly subject to democratic control, since if the majority of citizens of a sovereign state were strongly enough opposed to the comportment of international institutions, they can elect state officials with mandates to shape them according to the citizens' wishes. The same point could be made regarding a public that wished its government to aid other countries for moral reasons. Dahl's sceptical view about the possibility of extending the 'boundaries' of democracy beyond sovereign states starts from his observation that foreign policy is already largely immune from effective public control in the liberal-democratic states (1999: 23–8). So the challenge here is to bring these aspects of governance under effective democratic control.

Civic republicanism

Civic-republican theorists typically concern themselves with democracy at local, national, and subnational levels, but one of their core theses is often appealed to in support of cosmopolitanism, namely the insistence that whatever divergent values they tolerate, democratic political associations require a core of shared norms regarding the good society. Martin Köhler applies this as well to the notion of a cosmopolitan world order which he optimistically thinks is now possible due to 'an emerging global civil society' bound together by common values including 'human rights, democratic participation, the rule of law, and the preservation of the world's ecological heritage' (1998: 232). Similarly, Bull thinks that his projected new medievalism requires a 'cosmopolitan culture' valuing, among other things, peace, justice, and environmental protection (1995: 284–5, 303–5), and Andrew Linklater sees the need for an 'expansion of moral community' beyond states (1990: 199). For Falk a 'global civil society' is made possible by the 'unifying ideology' of 'normative democracy,' which, in keeping with civic republicanism means not just political values such as accountability and transparency in government but also commitment to substantive goods like human rights and nonviolence (2000: 171–4).

Not all theorists share this view about a global civil society. The civic republican, Michael Sandel, is sceptical that transnational governments can inspire 'the identification and allegiance' required for a 'moral and civic culture' (1996: 339). Claims about the possibility and desirability of shared global norms are also targets of criticism by Zolo, who sees this as the imposition of specifically Western Enlightenment values on the rest of the world (1997, 2000). This charge is partly ceded by Falk, who speculates that though 'Eurocentric' in origin, the requisite norms may nonetheless become willingly embraced on a global level (1995: 243). The charge is also granted by Huntington. His view that a democratic world order based on shared values flies in the face of deep differences among the world's 'clashing' civilizations is appropriately cited by Zolo, without, however, endorsing Huntington's thesis that the predominantly Enlightenment and Christian values of the West are necessary preconditions for democracy for which other traditions are therefore unsuited. Debates over the appeal to global civic virtues, therefore, comprise both controversies over the extent to which this is realistic (which for different reasons Sandel and Huntington doubt) and over whether it is desirable (a claim denied by Zolo and defended by Falk).

Those writing about the prospects for a global civil society are not usually located within the civic republican camp, whose members mainly address the prospects for civic virtue within national or subnational communities. To the extent that civic republicanism contains a communitarian strain and that value-embodying communities are local, this is not surprising, but it need not mean that therefore civic republicanism is irrelevant to problems of globalization. An argument could be made that a necessary, if perhaps not a sufficient, condition for shared or at least complementary global values is the embrace of civic values within each of the globe's societies. This would be a civic-republican analogue of the claim that if every country in the world were a liberal democracy, there would be no war. The challenge for such a position is to find reasons for confidence that values conducive to global harmony can be found or nurtured within national or other local traditions.

Charles Taylor addresses this topic in an essay on global human rights (1999), and perhaps such a quest motivates a collection of essays edited by Michael Walzer and entitled *Toward a Global Civil Society*, most of which are concerned with local civil societies (1995).

Deliberative democracy

Similar considerations pertain to the deliberative-democratic theorists. Although their attention is largely focused on state and substate forums for public deliberation, they suggest views friendly to cosmopolitanism. Gutmann and Thompson allow for 'moral constituencies' cutting across borders (1996: 148–51). More explicit is Alan Gilbert, who concludes his book, *Must Global Politics Constrain Democracy?*, with a chapter invoking his earlier employment of deliberative-democratic theory (1999: ch. 5). Indeed, deliberative-democratic recommendations are especially well suited to transnational institutions like the European Parliament or UN sponsored forums such as its conferences on development and the environment, joint ventures by cross-national coalitions of nongovernmental organizations, and growing numbers of international tribunals and boards of inquiry. Partly *because* these forums have weak powers at best to enforce policies, they must be entered into with the primary purpose of promoting the sort of consensus-building discussion and debate encouraged by deliberative democrats at the heart of their theory.

Participatory democracy

Approaches that emphasize people power, at least as exercised by social movements may be seen as applying participatory-democratic principles, mainly defensive stances against globalization negatively interpreted. There are also more proactive suggestions, such as Kaldor's model for a new international order which centrally includes issue-based institutions whose sovereignty is derived from voluntary membership in them (1995: 88). Though Kaldor does not specify whether or how such institutions might include provision for direct democracy, the tone of her prescription is in keeping with participatory democracy and sometimes even of associational-democratic conceptions of self-government. In contrast to Kaldor, many, if not most, champions of participatory, social movement politics do not favour enlarging the scope of government. Some would agree with Ann Tickner who in the interests of a 'political economy from the bottom' advocates 'a state that is more self-reliant with respect to the international system' and hence 'more able to live within its own resource limits' (1992: 134–5).

Tickner's perspective locates participatory democracy along with liberal democracy as a perspective that mainly sees globalization as a challenge to be met within sovereign states. A case can be made, however, that this misses the primary motive of participationism, which is to promote direct involve-ment in the collective determination of their affairs by any people who share circumstances to which such involvement is appropriate. This is why social movement activists who promote environmental protection and combat practices like the creation of sweat shops in the developing world look to form alliances across national borders. What leads participatory democrats to focus on people power generally is that they are concerned with the prospects for popular involvement independently of questions of legal citi-zenship. The same thing applies to their concern with the impediments to this involvement, which may be global forces, but which may also be actions of a local state.

Radical pluralism

For the radical pluralists, it will be recalled, people unavoidably find them-selves in conflictual situations, partly in virtue of hegemonically forged identifications with some and in opposition to others. Frontiers dividing antagonistic groups are not confined to state boundaries, but may be smaller than states, as in local antagonisms, or larger than states, as in regional divi-sions, or they may be independent of territory altogether as in divides along religious, class, generational, or gender lines. In this respect radical plural-ists share the focus of participatory-democractic theorists on the situations of people in a variety of circumstances.

Where the radical pluralists differ from participationists is in seeking ways to encourage respect for democratic values within otherwise conflicting iden-tifications, thus converting antagonistic conflicts to 'agonic' ones (as this notion was summarized in Chapter 10), rather than trying in the manner of participationists to construct unity of action based on consensus. Also, while participationists would gladly accept the generic description of their problematic as addressing 'challenges to the people,' radical pluralists would not use the phrase 'the people' to avoid any Rousseauean connotations of a unified public. As to just how a radical-pluralist orientation might be applied to globalization, the related approaches of Robert Walker and Richard Ashley (1989) offer suggestions. Like the radical pluralists, their theories are shaped by poststructuralist philosophy, and Walker explicitly identifies himself with radical pluralism (1993: 157).

Walker quotes John Dunn in referring to democracy as 'the language in which all Nations are truly United, the public cant of the modern world,' which, however, Dunn sees as 'a dubious currency' that 'only a complete imbecile would be likely to take quite at face value' (Walker 1993: 141; Dunn 1979: 2). The puzzle Walker thinks Dunn has identified is that at least in the liberal-democratic countries a culture favouring globally universal democracy coexists with state-centred 'particularism' regarding the actual policies people think their states should pursue. Walker is clearly right on

this point, even regarding the strongest defenders of liberal-democratic principles, few of whom would unqualifiedly endorse open borders (Joseph Carens
is a rare exception, 1987) or mutual participation of citizens from different
countries in one another's elections.

Cosmopolitans in the traditions of Kant, for who humanity was evolving
toward a situation of morally regulated international peace (1998 [1785]), or
Hugo Grotius, an early advocate of international law (1949 [1625]), will
see this puzzle as a sign that moral consciousness has not yet matured or simply as a case of hypocrisy. Walker rejects these orientations for that of
Machiavelli, who (on Walker's radical-pluralist interpretation) held that the
political world is comprised of continuing projects to assert hegemonic civic
values in ongoing political contestations (Walker 1990: 172). From this vantage point, Walker sees the 'particularism' of democratic countries as a result
of successful campaigns for hegemony around common allegiance to a state
(much as Laclau and Mouffe interpreted Disraeli's success in suturing the
erstwhile antagonistic classes in England by construction of a common
national identification). The puzzle of how such particularism can coexist
with universal, internationalist values is explained when states, as Ashley
argues, propose themselves as key components in an 'international purpose,' for instance, to diffuse liberal democracy, capitalist markets, or Western
culture throughout the globe (1989).

A result of hegemonic campaigns on the part of the state is, as Walker
puts it, to perpetuate 'two abstract sovereignties of the modern world, the
state and the individual' thus leaving out of account the communities 'in
which people actually live, work, love and play together,' (1993: 152–3) as
these are regarded as outside of politics. Extrapolating from Walker's discussion, it should be added that the simple embrace of cosmopolitanism is not
an alternative for these communities either. One reason for this depends on
Ashley's charge that cosmopolitanism is implicated in its apparent opposite,
namely the effort of some states to strengthen their sovereignty by posing
as the bearer of cosmopolitan values. This charge is not unique to theorists
in the poststructuralist tradition. It is also suggested by Zolo's criticism of
cosmopolitanism, and it is central to Cox's application of a Gramscian theory
of hegemony to globalization (1996: ch. 7). Walker's alternative both to
loyalty to particular states and to embrace of general cosmopolitan values is
to seek 'novel forms of political practice' and in particular the political
activism of new social movements (1990: 181). William Connolly (in a
critique of sovereignty not unlike Ashley's) concurs, and sees movements
that cut across state boundaries as especially important to challenge state
sovereignty and to contribute to the 'nonterritorial democratization of global
issues' (1991: 218, italics omitted).

For none of these theorists does resisting statist hegemony entail rejection
of any political action within states, and it should be compatible with
defending those measures or kinds of state sovereignty that best serve

communities of people. Nor should recognizing the way cosmopolitan rhetoric can mask state hegemony dictate complete rejection of all aspects of cosmopolitanism. A case can be made that there is one way in which a radical-pluralist account (as constructed out of the theories of Walker and Ashley) may not be able to distance itself too far from cosmopolitanism. A reason for scepticism about simple embrace of cosmopolitan values that would apply to all countries, both big and small powers, is that the putative universalism of these values makes them subject to the same multiple interpretations and contestations as are universal liberal-democratic values. Just as radical pluralists do not abjure appeal to conceptions like 'right,' 'freedom,' 'equality,' and 'democracy,' but instead advocate waging hegemonic struggles to give them interpretations and hence construct identities consistent with agonic as opposed to destructively antagonistic conflict, so should this effort be prescribed with respect to global civic-republican values.

In keeping with their general suspicion of finality in politics, radical pluralists would probably deny that there is a final or unambiguously 'right' balance between sovereignty and cosmopolitanism. Rather, if radical-pluralist approaches to globalization are correctly classified in the 'problems for (the) people' category, what is important is that campaigns to infuse local identities with democratic values are to be encouraged in all the sites where people are affected by the interface between a state and its global settings. In this respect, as in some others, radical pluralism shares features of democratic pragmatism.

Pragmatism

Dahl's 'embarrassing' concern about the democratic arbitrariness of state boundaries is a special case of his dilemma of designating a democratic 'demos' discussed in Chapter 8. There it was suggested that the Deweyan approach to democratic theory contained resources for addressing this dilemma, and so democratic pragmatism ought to be able to meet the particular challenge as well. A short response to Dahl on this approach is that since democracy (being, in Dewey's phrase, 'the human condition') is of unlimited scope and thus appropriate whenever the activities of some people affect others in an ongoing way, there are are no boundaries, state-determined or otherwise, to it. An obvious counter is that if globalization means that people in one part of the world are affected by activities of people in the other parts, only world government including all people (children and adults) from all current states and regions would be democratic. Elements of a response to this counter were sketched in Chapter 8. Its key elements are that democracy (again contrary to the worries of Dahl) should be regarded a context-sensitive matter of degree and that it involves more than just participation in formal decision-making procedures.

Thinking of democracy as a matter of degree invites one to look for and promote conditions for making democratic progress, but this does not mean that global democratic institutions and practices suffice to secure maximum levels of democracy. A case can be made that global democracy requires local democracy in just the same way that, as Tocqueville observed in the case of the US, democracy in a state requires democracies in the regions and towns where citizens acquire democratic habits, skills, and dispositions. Also, while democracy at a 'macro' level may sometimes help to reinforce democratic activity at a corresponding 'micro' level, this may not always be the case. Were democracy nothing but adherence to formally prescribed procedures, this observation would still leave the difficulty of deciding when the procedures should be restricted to local associations of people and when expanded. To leave the decision to those already designated appropriate participants would militate against expansion of democracy's scope. It was notoriously difficult to persuade men to extend the franchise to women, just as it is now difficult to persuade citizens of a state to vote in favour of reducing their state's sovereignty. If, however, campaigns of the suffragettes or efforts by those coalitions of NGOs at the Rio conference and the Seattle demonstrations to garner general support for cross-border environmental protection are considered democratic activities, this problem may be more easy to address in practice than theory suggests.

Since less confrontational examples can be given, such as cross-border economic and cultural interactions that helped pave the way for the EU, the point is not that democratic boundary shifting must take place as a response to force. Rather, on the pragmatic perspective, questions about the proper boundaries of a democratic demos are not purely theoretical ones that must be answered *prior* to engaging in democratic politics; rather they arise as practical problems in the conduct of such politics itself. The central role of democratic theory in such activities is to identify institutional, economic, cultural, and moral impediments to broadening (or narrowing) democratic boundaries and to project consequences of alternative solutions to the problem of changing these boundaries in the same domains, as well as making recommendations.

Pragmatic democratic theorizing is thus implicated in rather than standing outside of ongoing problem-solving activities. To the extent, however, that one way of being implicated involves making recommendations, this raises questions about the basis on which to make them. To set oneself the goal simply of addressing whatever are generally thought to be the most pressing problems in some time and place opens one to Cox's challenge to the realists, when he insists that international relations theorists should subject putative goals themselves to critical examination. Similarly, to read the goals off the conventions of one's society, as Rorty is wont to do, is not only to embrace moral relativism and to assume that societies have single conventions, but also to suppose that they are self-contained as potentially democratic units, which is just what globalization calls into question. Two alternative directions suggest themselves by way of response. One is to adopt the 'endogenous' approach urged by Hurley and look to democratic criteria for making recommendations: those (formal or informal) 'boundaries' are to be observed which in the circumstances will both enhance local democracy and promote or at least not impede progress in democracy. The other direction is to allow that theorists can and should make recommendations on the basis of extrademocratic, moral value judgments.

A problem with the democratic progress alternative is that it supposes progress is possible and always desirable. Sometimes pragmatists write as if they believed in a sort of historical law of democratic progress, and this was a central tenet of the theory of social democracy advocated by Eduard Bernstein (1961 [1899]), but if this is so the progress must be of the two-steps forward, one-step back variety, with some rather large steps backwards. As to the desirability of always promoting democracy, the world has seen enough examples of democracy being shelved in the interests of supposed emergencies to warrant scepticism about claims that democracy must be curtailed. However, unless democracy is considered of intrinsic value (a claim questioned in Chapter 8) and, moreover, the *highest* value, the possibility must be allowed that sometimes it may be justifiably overridden, for example when following democratic procedures would, demonstrably and irreversibly, have terrible moral consequences. This invites taking the second direction for identifying goals, namely by appealing to moral standards. But if this means that democratic theory simply applies general ethical theory to democratic policy, not much is left of pragmatism. Also, an ethical theory-based approach is subject to Dahl's complaint that there is insufficient consensus over the foundations of ethics to make this a secure basis for policy recommendation.

If neither of these responses taken alone or unqualified is promising, perhaps they can be made acceptable if qualified and combined. Thus, the moral normative approach could be qualified by dissociating morality from ethical foundationalism and arguing with some current philosophers that objective value judgments do not require philosophical foundations (an example is Nielsen 1996). The democratic progress approach could be qualified to insist that democracy be the default position in political affairs, where this means that there is always a presumption in favour of defending or enhancing democracy and the burden of argument falls to those who claim it should be curtailed in specific circumstances.

Pursuit of this topic would lead onto philosophically problematic terrain (for both the pragmatist and the antipragmatist), but there is one aspect of democratic theory with respect to globalization where a pragmatic orientation is on strong ground. As noted earlier (see pp. 143–4), how democracy is secured, protected, or extended on this approach is a complex matter which offers both openings and impediments and where both confrontation of difficulties and ways of seizing opportunities are context sensitive, so any of several solutions or combinations of solutions might be apt depending on the ensemble of circumstances surrounding a specific democratically problematic situation.

An example of a context-sensitive orientation toward globalization is suggested by Michael Saward, who, in criticizing what he sees as Held's exclusive focus on cosmopolitanism, recommends locating a variety of 'democratic mechanisms' for responding to globalization. He locates such a mechanism within a conceptual space of four quadrants depending on whether the mechanisms depend upon permanent structures or are temporary measures and on whether they are undertaken by governments or by nongovernmental actors (2000: 39–44).

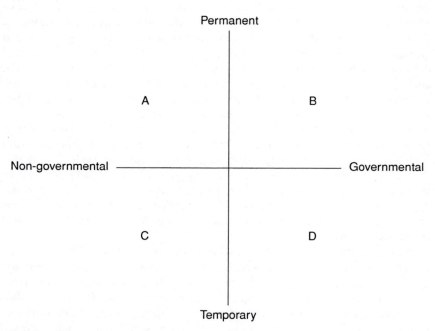

Figure 6

Saward criticizes the cosmopolitans for exclusive attention to quadrant 'B' thus failing to see the virtues in terms of democratic response to globalization of responses in the other quadrants. His main intent is to focus on the current opportunities offered within 'D,' which include cross-border referenda and reciprocal representation, where the legislative bodies of some countries would include seats for representatives from specified other countries (with a voice or even vote with respect to certain issues of shared concern). Also in this quadrant are such nonpermanent UN initiatives as the Rio, Cairo, and Bejing conferences (on, respectively, development and the environment, population, and women's rights), and he notes that activities of the NGOs active in and around these conferences can be located in 'A' or 'C' depending on whether they are *ad hoc* or standing. With a bit of reflection quite a large number of practices, institutions, and organizations can be located at points all over this chart, none of which, on the pragmatic viewpoint, can be presumed democratically superior to the others as a general approach to globalization.

A similar point can be made about how the various things that go under the name of globalization should be classified and appraised. Imagine an analogous chart with one axis ranging from opportunities to problems and the other from substates, through states to superstate collections of people. As such a chart is filled in with examples, it should become clear that globalization offers both challenges and opportunities to each of the states and various groupings of people within and outside of them.

In explicating some of the orientations toward globalization in more detail than others, I do not mean to imply that much more could not be said about all of them. But then, this is true of every subject addressed in this book: democracy would not be problematic if theories about it were simple either to describe or to evaluate.

Bibliography

The literature on democracy is so vast and growing so quickly that any attempt at completeness of references in the bibliography, as of topics and arguments covered in the book, would be futile. However, readers new to democratic theory will quickly find upon looking up some works referred to that each of them is a window to yet more material. These readers may also wish to consult one of the general collections of essays on democracy referred to in the bibliography, among them: Copp *et al.*, 1993, Duncan (1983), Green (1993), Hacker-Cordon and Shapiro (1999a and b), Hadenius (1997), and Held (1991b and 1993). Also worth consulting is the *Encyclopedia of Democracy*, Lipset (1995). Several collections of essays are on specific topics – deliberative democracy, civic republicanism, globalism, and so on. These are referred to in appropriate chapters of the book, as are many single-authored books that address specific themes. Some works listed in the bibliography aim to cover enough of the entire field to serve as introductory texts. In increasing order (roughly) of prior theoretical sophistication required of the reader (and leaving out earlier publications) these are: Dahl (1998), Arblaster (1994), Harrison (1993), Held (1996), Gould (1988), Dahl (1989), Beetham (1999), Christiano (1996), and Hyland (1995).

Aanund, Hylland and Elster, Jon (1986) (eds) *Foundations of Social Choice Theory*, Cambridge: Cambridge University Press.

Ackerman, Bruce (1980) *Social Justice and the Liberal State*, New Haven: Yale University Press.

Acton, Lord John E.E.D. (1955 [1862]) 'Nationality,' in *Essays on Freedom and Power*, Himmelfarb, Gertrude (ed.), Cleveland: Meridian Books, 141–70.

Adorno, Theodor and Horkheimer, Max (1972 [1947]) *Dialectic of Enlightenment*, New York: Herder and Herder.

Ake, Claude (1997) 'Dangerous liaisons: the interface of globalization and democracy,' in Hadenius, Alex (ed.) *Democracy's Victory and Crisis*, Cambridge: Cambridge University Press, 282–96.

Alfred, Taiaiake (1999) *Peace, Power, Righteousness: An Indigenous Manifesto*, Oxford: Oxford University Press.

Allen, Anita L. and Regan, Milton C. Jr. (eds) (1998) *Debating Democracy's Discontent: Essays on American Politics, Law, and Public Philosophy*, Oxford: Oxford University Press.

Allen, Theodore (1994) *The Invention of the White Race: Racial Oppression and Social Control*, Vol. 1, London: Verso.

Almond, Gabriel and Verba, Sidney (1965) *The Civic Culture*, Boston: Little, Brown.

Appiah, K. Anthony (1994) 'Identity, authenticity, survival: multicultural societies and social reproduction,' in Gutmann, Amy (ed.) *Multiculturalism*, Princeton: Princeton University Press, 149–63.

Arblaster, Anthony (1994) *Democracy* (2nd edn), Minneapolis: University of Minnesota Press.

Archibugi, Daniele (1998) 'Principles of cosmopolitan democracy,' in Archibugi, Daniele, Held, David, and Kohler, Martin (eds) *Re-imagining Political Community: Studies in Cosmopolitan Democracy*, Stanford: Stanford University Press, 198–228.

Arendt, Hannah (1977 [1963]) *On Revolution*, New York: Penguin Books.

Aristotle (1986 [c.320 BC]) *Aristotle's Politics*, translated with commentaries by Apostle, Hippocrates G., and Gerson, Lloyd, Grinnell, Iowa: The Peripatetic Press.

Arrow, Kenneth J. (1951) *Social Choice and Individual Values*, New York: John Wiley.

Ashley, Richard K. (1989) 'Imposing international purpose: notes on a problematic of governance,' in Czempiel, Ernst-Otto and Rosenau, James N. (eds) *Global Changes and Theoretical Challenges: Approaches to World Politics for the 1990's*, Lexington, MA: Lexington Books, 251–90.

Bachrach, Peter (1967) *The Theory of Democratic Elitism: A Critique*, Boston: Little, Brown.

Bachrach, Peter and Baratz, Morton S. (1969) 'Two faces of power,' in Connolly, William E. (ed.) *The Bias of Pluralism*, New York: Atherton Press, 51–61.

Bader, Veit (1997) *Citizenship and Exclusion*, London: Macmillan.

Balbus, Isaac (1971) 'Ruling-class elite theory vs. Marxian class analysis,' *Monthly Review* 23,1 (May): 36–46.

Barber, Benjamin (1984) *Strong Democracy: Participatory Politics for a New Age*, Berkeley: University of California Press.

—— (1995) *Jihad vs. McWorld: How Globalism and Tribalism are Reshaping the World*, New York: Ballantine Books.

Bardhan, Pranab K. and Roemer, John E. (eds) (1993) *Market Socialism: The Current Debate*, New York: Oxford University Press.

Barry, Brian (1969) 'The public interest,' in Connolly, William E. (ed.) *The Bias of Pluralism*, New York: Atherton Press, 159–77.

—— (1978) 'Comment' in Benn, Stanley (ed.) *Political Participation*, Canberra: Australian National University Press, 37–48.

—— (1991a) *Democracy, Power and Justice: Essays in Political Theory 1*, Oxford: Clarendon Press.

—— (1991b) *Liberty and Justice: Essays in Political Theory 2*, Oxford: Clarendon Press.

Bay, Christian (1965) 'Politics and pseudo-politics,' *American Political Science Review*, 59,1 (March): 39–51.

—— (1980) 'Rights: an exchange' (with Richard Flathman) *Political Theory*, 8,3 (August): 293–334.

Baynes, Kenneth (1996) 'Public reason and personal autonomy,' in Rasmussen, David M. (ed.) *The Handbook of Critical Theory*, Oxford: Blackwell Publishers, 243–54.

Beard, Charles Austin (1986 [1913]) *An Economic Interpretation of the Constitution of the United States*, New York: The Free Press.

Beck, Ulrich (2000) *What is Globalization?*, Cambridge: Polity Press.

Beetham, David (1993) 'Liberal democracy and the limits of democratization,' in Held, David (ed.) *Prospects for Democracy*, Stanford: Stanford University Press, 55–73.

—— (1999) *Democracy and Human Rights*, Cambridge: Polity Press.

Beiner, Ronald (1992) *What's the Matter with Liberalism?*, Berkeley: University of California Press.

—— (ed.) (1995a) *Theorizing Citizenship*, Albany: State University of New York Press.

—— (1995b) 'Why citizenship constitutes a theoretical problem in the last decade of the twentieth century,' in Beiner, Ronald (ed.) *Theorizing Citizenship*, Albany: State University of New York Press, 1–28.

Beitz, Charles R. (1979) *Political Theory and International Relations*, Princeton: Princeton University Press.

—— (1989) *Political Equality: An Essay in Democratic Theory*, Princeton: Princeton University Press.

—— (1991) 'Sovereignty and morality in international affairs,' in Held, David (ed.) *Political Theory Today*, Cambridge: Polity Press, 236–54.

Benello, George C. and Roussopoulos, Dimitrios (eds) (1972) *The Case for Participatory Democracy*, New York: Viking Compass.

Benhabib, Seyla (1996) 'Toward a deliberative model of democratic legitimacy,' in Benhabib, Seyla (ed.) *Democracy and Difference: Contesting the Boundaries of the Political*, Princeton: Princeton University Press, 67–94.

Bentley, Arthur (1967 [1908]) *The Process of Government*, Cambridge, MA: Belknap Press of Harvard University Press.

Berelson, Bernard R., Lazarsfeld, Paul F., and McPhee, William N. (1954) *Voting*, Chicago: University of Chicago Press.

Berle, Adolf (1959) *Power Without Property: A New Development in American Political Economy*, New York: Harcourt Brace.

Berlin, Isaiah (1969 [1958]) *Four Concepts of Liberty*, Oxford: Oxford University Press.

Bernstein, Eduard (1961 [1899]) *Evolutionary Socialism*, New York: Schocken Books.

Bernstein, Richard (1971) *Praxis and Action*, Philadelphia: University of Pennsylvania Press.

Bobbio, Norberto (1987 [1976]) *Which Socialism?: Marxism, Socialism, and Democracy*, Cambridge: Polity Press.

—— (1995) 'Democracy and the international system,' in Archibugi, Daniele and Held, David (eds) *Cosmopolitan Democracy: An Agenda for a New World Order*, Cambridge: Polity Press, 17–41.

Bohman, James (1996) 'Critical Theory and Democracy,' in Rasmussen, David M. (ed.) *The Handbook of Critical Theory*, Oxford: Blackwell Publishers, 190–215.

Bohman, James and Rehg, William (1997) 'Introduction' in Bohman, James and Rehg, William (eds) *Deliberative Democracy: Essays on Reason and Politics*, Cambridge, MA: The MIT Press, ix–xxx.

Bookchin, Murray (1990) *The Philosophy of Social Ecology*, Montreal: Black Rose Books.

Bowles, Samuel and Gintis, Herbert (1986) *Democracy and Capitalism: Property, Community, and the Contradictions of Modern Social Thought*, New York: Basic Books.

—— (1993) 'Post-Walrasian political economy,' in Bowles, Samuel and Gintis, Herbert (eds) *Markets and Democracy: Participation, Accountability, and Efficiency*, Cambridge: Cambridge University Press, 1–10.

Buchanan, James M. (1975) *The Limits of Liberty: Between Anarchy and Leviathan*, Chicago: University of Chicago Press.

—— (1986) *Liberty, Market and State: Political Economy in the 1980s*, Brighton: Harvester Press.

Buchanan, James M. and Tullock, Gordon (1962) *The Calculus of Consent: Logical Foundations of Constitutional Democracy*, Ann Arbor: The University of Michigan Press.

Budge, Ian (1993) 'Direct democracy: setting appropriate terms of debate,' in Held, David (ed.) *Prospects for Democracy: North, South, East, West*, Cambridge: Cambridge University Press, 136–55.

Bull, Hedley (1995 [1977]) *The Anarchical Society: A Study of Order in World Politics* (2nd edn), New York: Columbia University Press.

Burnheim, John (1985) *Is Democracy Possible?*, Cambridge: Polity Press.

Calhoun, John C. (1953 [1850]) *A Disquisition on Government*, New York: Liberal Arts Press.

Callinicos, Alex (1993) 'Socialism and democracy,' in Held, David (ed.) *Prospects for Democracy*, Stanford: Stanford University Press, 200–12.

Carens, Joseph H. (1987) 'Aliens and citizens: the case for open borders,' *Review of Politics* 49,2 (Spring): 251–73.

—— (1989) 'Membership and morality: admission to citizenship in liberal democracy,' in Brubacker, William Rogers (ed.) *Immigration and the Politics of Citizenship in Europe and North America*, Lanham, MD: German Marshall Fund and University Press of America, 31–49.

—— (2000) *Culture, Citizenship, and Community: A Contextual Exploration of Justice as Evenhandedness*, Oxford: Oxford University Press.

Chatterjee, Pratap and Finger, Matthian (1994) *The Earth Brokers*, London: Routledge.

Christiano, Thomas (1996) *The Rule of the Many: Fundamental Issues in Democratic Theory*, Boulder: Westview Press.

Cohen, Carl (1971) *Democracy*, New York: The Free Press.

Cohen, G.A. (1995) *Self-Ownership, Freedom, and Equality*, Cambridge: Cambridge University Press.

Cohen, Joshua (1995a) 'Secondary associations and democratic governance,' in Cohen, Joshua and Rogers, Joel (eds) *Associations and Democracy*, London: Verso, 7–98.

—— (1995b) 'Solidarity, democracy, association,' in Cohen, Joshua and Rogers, Joel (eds) *Associations and Democracy*, London: Verso, 236–67.

—— (1997a) 'Procedure and substance in deliberative democracy,' in Bohman, James and Rehg, William (eds) *Deliberative Democracy: Essays on Reason and Politics*, Cambridge, MA: The MIT Press, 407–37.

—— (1997b) 'Deliberation and democratic legitimacy,' in Bohman, James and Rehg, William (eds) *Deliberative Democracy: Essays on Reason and Politics*, Cambridge, MA: The MIT Press, 67–91. This often-cited essay was first published in Hamlin, A. and Pettit, Philip (eds) (1989) *The Good Polity*, Oxford: Blackwell Publishers, 17–34.

Cohen, Joshua and Rogers, Joel (1983) *On Democracy*, Harmondsworth, England: Penguin Books.

—— (1995) 'Secondary associations and democratic governance,' in Wright, Erik Olin (ed.) *Associations and Democracy*, London: Verso, 7–98.

Cole, G.D.H. (1980 [1920]) *Guild Socialism Re-Stated*, New Brunswick, NJ: Transaction Books.

Coleman, James S. (1990) *Foundations of Social Theory*, Cambridge, MA: Harvard University Press.

Coleman, Jules and Ferejohn John (1986) 'Democracy and social choice,' *Ethics* 97, 1 (October): 6–25.

Collins, Joseph and Lear, John (1995) *Chile's Free Market Miracle: A Second Look*, Oakland: Food First.

Connelly, James and Smith, Graham (1999) *Politics and the Environment: From Theory to Practice*, London: Routledge.

Connolly, William E. (1969) 'The challenge to pluralist theory,' in Connolly, William E. (ed.) *The Bias of Pluralism*, New York: Atherton Press, 3–34.

—— (1991) *Identity/Difference: Democratic Negotiations of Political Paradox*, Ithaca: Cornell University Press.

—— (1993a [1988]) *Political Theory and Modernity*, Ithaca: Cornell University Press.

—— (1993b) *The Terms of Political Discourse*, Princeton: Princeton University Press.

Constant, Benjamin (1988 [1819]) 'Speech given at the Athénée Royal in Paris,' in Fontana, Biancamaria (ed.) *Constant: Political Writings*, New York: Cambridge University Press, 309–28.

Copp, David, Hampton, Jean, and Roemer, John E. (1993) *The Idea of Democracy*, Cambridge: Cambridge University Press.

Cox, Robert W. (1996) *Approaches to World Order*, Cambridge: Cambridge University Press.

Crozier, Michel J., Huntington, Samuel P., and Watanuki, Joji (1975) *The Crisis of Democracy: Report on the Governability of Democracies to the Trilateral Commission*, New York: New York University Press.

Cunningham, Frank (1987) *Democratic Theory and Socialism*, Cambridge: Cambridge University Press.

—— (1994) *The Real World of Democracy Revisited and Other Essays on Democracy and Socialism*, Atlantic Highlands, NJ: Humanities Press.

—— (1995) 'Socialism,' entry in Lipset, Seymour Martin (ed.) *The Encyclopedia of Democracy*, Vol. IV, Washington, DC: Congressional Quarterly Books, 1147–53.

—— (1997a) 'Critical notice of Russell Hardin, *one for all*,' *Canadian Journal of Philosophy* 27,4 (December): 571–94.

—— (1997b) 'On relating justice and democracy: a strategy and a hypothesis,' in Bontekoe, Ron and Stepaniants, Marietta (eds) *Justice and Democracy: Cross-Cultural Perspectives*, Honolulu: University of Hawai'i Press, 77–91.

—— (2000) 'Positive action and democracy,' in Appelt, Erna and Jarosch, Monika (eds) *Combatting Racial Discrimination: Affirmative Action as a Model for Europe*, Oxford: Berg, 41–59.

—— (2001) 'Whose socialism?, Which democracy?,' in Howard, Michael (ed.) *Socialism*, Amherst, NY: Humanity Books.

Dahl, Robert A. (1956) *A Preface to Democratic Theory*, Chicago: University of Chicago Press.

—— (1961) *Who Governs?: Democracy and Power in an American City*, New Haven: Yale University Press.

—— (1967) *Pluralist Democracy in the United States*, Chicago: Rand McNally.

—— (1970a) *After the Revolution*, New Haven: Yale University Press.

—— (1970b [1963]) *Modern Political Analysis* (2nd edn), Englewood Cliffs, NJ: Prentice Hall.

—— (1982) *Dilemmas of Pluralist Democracy: Autonomy vs. Control*, New Haven: Yale University Press.

—— (1985) *A Preface to Economic Democracy*, Berkeley: University of California Press.

—— (1989) *Democracy and Its Critics*, New Haven: Yale University Press.

—— (1998) *On Democracy*, New Haven: Yale University Press.

—— (1999) 'Can international organizations be democratic? A skeptic's view,' in Hacker-Cordon, Casiano and Shapiro, Ian (eds) *Democracy's Edges*, Cambridge: Cambridge University Press, 17–40.

Dallmayr, Fred (1989) *Margins of Political Discourse*, Albany: State University of New York Press.

Daniels, Norman (1975) 'Equal liberty and unequal worth of liberty,' in Daniels, Norman (ed.) *Reading Rawls: Critical Studies of A Theory of Justice*, Oxford: Blackwell, 253–81.

Dasgupta, Partha and Maskin, Eric (1999) 'Democracy and other goods,' in Hacker-Cordon, Casiano and Shapiro, Ian (eds) *Democracy's Value*, Cambridge: Cambridge University Press, 69–90.

Davis, Michael (1974) 'Avoiding the voter's paradox democratically,' *Theory and Decision* 5,3 (October): 295–311.

Derrida, Jacques (1978 [1967]) *Writing and Difference*, Chicago: University of Chicago Press.

—— (1998 [1967]) *Of Grammatology*, Baltimore: Johns Hopkins Press.

Dewey, John (1927) *The Public and Its Problems*, Denver: Alan Swallow.

Dewey, John and Tufts, James H. (1908) *Ethics*, New York: Henry Holt and Company.

—— (1985 [1932]) *Ethics* (2nd edn), in *John Dewey: The Later Works, Vol. VII*, Carbondale, IL: Southern Illinois University Press.

Domhoff, G. William (1967) *Who Rules America*, Englewood Cliffs, NJ: Princeton University Press.

—— (1970) *The Higher Circles: The Governing Class in America*, New York: Random House.

Downs, Anthony (1957) *An Economic Theory of Democracy*, New York: Harper and Row.

Drèze, Jean and Sen, Amartya (1989) *Hunger and Public Action*, Oxford: Oxford University Press.

Duncan, Graeme (ed.) (1983) *Democratic Theory and Practice*, Cambridge: Cambridge University Press.

Dunn, John (1979) *Western Political Theory in the Face of the Future*, Cambridge: Cambridge University Press.

—— (1999) 'Democracy and development?' in Hacker-Cordon, Casiano and Shapiro, Ian (eds) *Democracy's Value*, Cambridge: Cambridge University Press, 132–40.

Durkheim, Emile (1957 [1950]) *Professional Ethics and Civil Morals*, London: Routledge and Kegan Paul.

Dworkin, Peter (1981) 'Chile's brave new world of Reaganomics,' *Fortune*, November 2, 136–44.

Dworkin, Ronald (1977) *Taking Rights Seriously*, London: Duckworth.

—— (1981) 'What is equality? Part 2: equality of resources,' *Philosophy and Public Affairs* 10,4 (Fall): 283–345.

—— (1983) 'In defense of equality,' *Social Philosophy and Policy* 1,1 (Autumn): 24–40.

Eagleton, Terry (1991) *Ideology: An Introduction*, London: Verso.

Eisenstein, Zillah (1981) *The Radical Future of Liberal Feminism*, New York: Longman.

Elshtain, Jean Bethke (1993) *Democracy on Trial*, Concord, ON: Anansi.

Elster, Jon (ed.) (1986a) *Rational Choice*, Oxford: Blackwell.

—— (1986b) 'Introduction' in Elster, Jon (ed.) *Rational Choice*, Oxford: Blackwell, 1–33.

—— (1986c) 'The Market and the forum: three varieties of political theory,' in Hylland, Aanund and Elster, Jon (eds) *Foundations of Social Choice Theory*, Cambridge: Cambridge University Press, 103–32.

—— (1998a) 'Introduction,' in Elster Jon (ed.) in *Deliberative Democracy*, Cambridge: Cambridge University Press, 1–18.

—— (1998b) 'Deliberation and constitution making' in Elster, Jon (ed.) *Deliberative Democracy*, Cambridge: Cambridge University Press, 97–122.

Ely, John Hart (1980) *Democracy and Distrust*, Cambridge, MA: Harvard University Press.

Estlund, David (1997) 'Beyond fairness and deliberation: the epistemic dimension of democratic authority,' in Bohman, James and Rehg, William (eds) *Deliberative Democracy: Essays on Reason and Politics*, Cambridge, Mass.: The MIT Press, 173–204.

Eze, Emmanuel Chukwudi (ed.) (1997) *Race and the Enlightenment: A Reader*, Cambridge, MA: Blackwell.

Falk, Richard (1995) *On Humane Governance: Toward A New Global Politics*, Cambridge: Polity Press.

—— (2000) 'Global civil society and the democratic project,' in Holden, Barry (ed.) *Global Democracy: Key Debates*, London: Routledge, 162–78.

Fazio, Hugo and Riesco, Manuel (1997) 'The Chilean pension fund association,' *New Left Review*, 223 (May/June): 90–100.

Fearon, James D. (1998) 'Deliberation as discussion,' in Elster, Jon (ed.) *Deliberative Democracy*, Cambridge: Cambridge University Press, 44–68.

Figgis, John Neville (1914) *Churches in the Modern State*, London: Longmans.

Flathman, Richard E. (1980) 'Rights: an exchange' (with Christian Bay) *Political Theory*, 8,3 (August): 293–334.

Foucault, Michel (1972 [1969]) *Archeology of Knowledge*, New York: Harper and Row.

—— (1973 [1966]) *The Order of Things*, New York: Vintage Books.

—— (1980) *Power/Knowledge: Selected Interviews and Other Writings 1972–1977*, New York: Pantheon Books.

Fraser, Nancy (1989) *Unruly Practices: Power, Discourse and Gender in Contemporary Social Theory*, Minneapolis: University of Minnesota Press.

—— (1997) *Justice Interruptus: Critical Reflections on the 'Postsocialist' Condition*, London: Routledge. The essay cited, 'Rethinking the public sphere,' is reprinted in Calhoun, Craig (ed.) (1993) *Habermas and the Public Sphere*, Cambridge, Mass.: The MIT Press, 109–42.

Friedman, Milton (1962) *Capitalism and Freedom*, Chicago: University of Chicago Press.

Frye, Marilyn (1983) 'Oppression,' in *The Politics of Reality: Essays in Feminist Theory*, Trumansburg, NY: Crossing.

Fukuyama, Francis (1992) *The End of History and the Last Man*, New York: The Free Press.

—— (1994) 'Comments on nationalism and democracy,' in Diamond, Larry and Plattner, Marc (eds) *Nationalism, Ethnic Conflict, and Democracy*, Baltimore: The Johns Hopkins University Press, 23–8.

Gagnon, V.P. Jr (1994) 'Serbia's road to war,' in Diamond, Larry and Plattner, Marc F. (eds) *Nationalism, Ethnic Conflict, and Democracy*, Baltimore: The Johns Hopkins University Press, 117–31.

Gallie, W.B. (1955/6) 'Essentially contested concepts' *Proceedings of the Aristotelian Society*, Vol. 56, London: Harrison and Sons, 167–98.

Galston, William (1991) *Liberal Purposes: Goods, Virtue and Diversity in the Liberal State*, New York: Cambridge University Press.

Galtung, Johan (1980) *The Two Worlds: A Transitional Perspective*, New York: The Free Press.

—— (2000) 'Alternative models for global democracy,' in Holden, Barry (ed.) *Global Democracy: Key Debates*, London: Routledge, 143–61.

Gambetta, Diego (1998) ' "Claro!": an essay on discursive machismo,' in Elster, Jon (ed.) *Deliberative Democracy*, Cambridge: Cambridge University Press, 19–43.

Gaus, Gerald F. (1997) 'Reason, justification, and consensus: why democracy can't have it all,' in Bohman, James and Rehg, William (eds) *Deliberative Democracy: Essays on Reason and Politics*, Cambridge, MA: The MIT Press, 205–42.

Geras, Norman (1987) 'A Critique of Laclau and Mouffe' *New Left Review* 163, May/June, 40–82. This and a subsequent article in the same journal, 'Ex-Marxism without substance: being a real reply to Laclau and Mouffe,' no. 169, May/June, 1988, 34–61, were reproduced by Geras in (1990) *Discourse of Extremity*, London: Verso.

Gilbert, Alan (1999) *Must Global Politics Constrain Democracy?: Great-Power Realism, Democratic Peace, and Democratic Internationalism*, Princeton: Princeton University Press.

Girard, René (1979) *Violence and the Sacred*, Baltimore: The Johns Hopkins University Press.

Glazer, Nathan (1975) *Affirmative Discrimination: Ethnic Inequality and Public Policy*, New York: Basic Books.

—— (1997) *We Are All Multiculturalists Now*, Cambridge, MA: Harvard University Press.

Goldberg, David Theo (1993) *Racist Culture: Philosophy and the Politics of Meaning*, Oxford: Blackwell.

—— (ed.) (2000) *Social Identities* (Special issue devoted to democracy and racism) 6,4 (December).

Goldstick, Daniel (1973) 'An alleged paradox in the theory of democracy,' *Philosophy and Public Affairs*, 2,2 (Winter): 181–9.

Gould, Carol C. (1988) *Rethinking Democracy: Freedom and Social Cooperation in Politics, Economy, and Society*, Cambridge: Cambridge University Press.

—— (1996) 'Diversity and democracy: representing differences,' in Benhabib, Seyla (ed.) *Democracy and Difference: Contesting the Boundaries of the Political*, Princeton: Princeton University Press, 171–86.

Graham, Keith (1982) 'Democracy and the autonomous moral agent,' in Graham, Keith (ed.) *Contemporary Political Philosophy: Radical Studies*, Cambridge: Cambridge University Press, 113–37.

Green, Donald P. and Shapiro, Ian (1994) *Pathologies of Rational Choice Theory: A Critique of Applications in Political Science*, New Haven: Yale University Press.

Green, Philip (1985) *Retrieving Democracy: In Search of Civic Equality*, Totowa, NJ: Rowman and Allanheld.

—— (ed.) (1993) *Democracy*, Atlantic Highlands, NJ: Humanities Press.

—— (1998) *Equality and Democracy*, New York: The New Press.

Grotius, Hugo (1949 [1625]) *The Law of War and Peace*, translated by Loomis, Louise R., Roslyn, NY: published for the Classics Club by W.J. Black.

Gutmann, Amy (1980) *Liberal Equality*, Cambridge: Cambridge University Press.

Gutmann, Amy and Thompson, Dennis (1996) *Democracy and Disagreement*, Cambridge, MA: Belknap Press of the Harvard University Press.

—— (1999) 'Democratic Disagreement,' in Macedo, Stephen (ed.) *Deliberative Politics: Essays on Democracy and Disagreement*, New York: Oxford University Press, 243–79.

Habermas, Jürgen (1973 [1963]) *Theory and Practice*, Boston: Beacon Press.

—— (1975) *Legitimation Crisis*, Boston: Beacon Press.

—— (1979) *Communication and the Evolution of Society*, Boston: Beacon Press.

—— (1984) *The Theory of Communicative Action: Volume 1, Reason and the Rationalization of Society*, Boston: Beacon Press.

—— (1987) *Philosophical Discourse of Modernity*, Cambridge, MA: The MIT Press.

—— (1989 [1962]) *The Structural Transformation of the Public Sphere: An Inquiry into a Category of Bourgeois Society*, Cambridge, MA: The MIT Press.

—— (1990) *Moral Consciousness and Communicative Action*, Cambridge: MA: The MIT Press.

—— (1996) 'Three normative models of democracy' in Benhabib, Seyla (ed.) *Democracy and Difference: Contesting the Boundaries of the Political*, Princeton: Princeton University Press, 21–30.

—— (1998) *Between Facts and Norms: Contributions to a Discourse Theory of Law and Democracy*, Cambridge, MA: The MIT Press.

Hacker-Cordon, Casiano and Shapiro, Ian (eds) (1999a) *Democracy's Edges*, Cambridge: Cambridge University Press.

—— (eds)(1999b) *Democracy's Value*, Cambridge: Cambridge University Press.

Hadenius, Alex (ed.) (1997) *Democracy's Victory and Crisis*, Cambridge: Cambridge University Press.

Hale, Myron Q. (1969) 'The cosmology of Arthur F. Bentley,' in Connolly, William E. (ed.) *The Bias of Pluralism*, New York: Atherton Press, 35–50.

Hampton, Jean (1989) 'Should political philosophy be done without metaphysics?,' *Ethics* 99,4 (July): 791–814.

Hanson, Russell L. (1985) *The Democratic Imagination in America: Conversations with Our Past*, Princeton: Princeton University Press.

Hardin, Russell (1982) *Collective Action*, Baltimore: The Johns Hopkins University Press.

—— (1993) 'Public choice versus democracy,' in Copp, David, Hampton, Jean, and Roemer, John E. (eds) *The Idea of Democracy*, Cambridge: Cambridge University Press, 157–72.

—— (1995) *One for All: The Logic of Group Conflict*, Princeton: Princeton University Press.

Harrison, Ross (1993) *Democracy*, London: Routledge.

Hartz, Louis (1955) *The Liberal Tradition in America: An Interpretation of American Political Thought Since the Revolution*, New York: Harcourt Brace.

Hauptmann, Emily (1996) *Putting Choice Before Democracy: A Critique of Rational Choice Theory*, Albany: State University of New York Press.

Hayek, Friedrich A. (1944) *The Road to Serfdom*, Chicago: University of Chicago Press.

—— (1960) *The Constitution of Liberty*, Chicago: University of Chicago Press.

—— (1976) *Law, Legislation and Liberty, Volume 2: The Mirage of Social Justice*, Chicago: University of Chicago Press.

—— (1979) *Law, Legislation and Liberty, Volume 3: The Political Order of a Free People*, Chicago: University of Chicago Press.

Hegel, G.W.F. (1942 [1821]) *Hegel's Philosophy of Right*, Oxford: The Clarendon Press.

—— (1949 [1807]) *The Phenomenology of Mind*, London: George Allen and Unwin.

Held, David (1991a) 'Democracy, the nation-state and the global system,' in Held, David (ed.) *Political Theory Today*, Cambridge: Polity Press, 196–235.

—— (ed.) (1991b) *Political Theory Today*, Cambridge: Polity Press.

—— (ed.) (1993) *Prospects for Democracy*, Stanford: Stanford University Press.

—— (1996) *Models of Democracy* (2nd edn), Stanford: Stanford University Press.

—— (1999) 'The transformation of political community: rethinking democracy in the context of globalization,' in Hacker-Cordon, Casiano and Shapiro, Ian (eds) *Democracy's Edges*, Cambridge: Cambridge University Press, 84–111.

Held, David and McGrew, Anthony (eds) (2000) *The Global Transformation Reader*, Cambridge: Polity Press.

Held, David, McGrew, Anthony, Goldblatt, David, and Perraton, Johnathan (1999) *Global Transformations: Politics, Economics and Culture*, Stanford: Stanford University Press.

Hirst, Paul (1989) *The Pluralist Theory of the State: Selected Writings of G.D.H. Cole, J.N. Figgis, and H.J. Laski*, London: Routledge.

—— (1993) 'Associational democracy,' in Held, David (ed.) *Prospects for Democracy*, Stanford: Stanford University Press.

—— (1994) *Associative Democracy: New Forms of Economic and Social Governance*, Cambridge: Polity Press.

—— (1995) 'Can secondary associations enhance democratic governance?' in Cohen, Joshua and Rogers, Joel (eds) *Associations and Democracy*, London: Verso, 101–13.

Hirst, Paul and Thompson, Grahame (1999) *Globalization in Question* (2nd edn), Cambridge: Polity Press.

—— (2000) 'Global myths and national policies,' in Holden, Barry (ed.) *Global Democracy: Key Debates*, London: Routledge, 47–59.

Hobbes, Thomas (1968 [1651]) *Leviathan*, Harmondsworth, England: Penguin Books.

Hoffman, John (1983) *Marxism, Revolution, and Democracy*, Amsterdam: Gruner.

Holmes, Stephen (1993) 'Tocqueville and democracy,' in Copp, David, Hampton, Jean, and Roemer, John E. (eds) *The Idea of Democracy*, Cambridge: Cambridge University Press, 23–63.

Horkheimer, Max (1974 [1967] *Critique of Instrumental Reason*, New York: The Seabury Press.

Horowitz, Donald L. (1985) *Ethnic Groups in Conflict*, Berkeley: University of California Press.

Howard, Michael W. (2000) *Self-Management and the Crisis of Socialism: The Rose in the Fist of the Present*, Lanham, MD: Rowman and Littlefield.

Howse, Robert (1998) 'The Supreme Court ruling, a lesson in democracy,' *Cité Libre* 26,4 (October/November): 42–6.

Hume, David (1978 [1740]) *A Treatise of Human Nature*, Oxford: The Clarendon Press.

Huntington, Samuel P. (1991) *The Third Wave: Democratization in the Late Twentieth Century*, Norman: University of Oklahoma Press.

—— (1996) *The Clash of Civilizations and the Remaking of World Order*, New York: Simon and Schuster.

Hurley, Susan L. (1999) 'Rationality, democracy, and leaky boundaries: verticle vs horizontal modularity,' in Hacker-Cordon, Casiano and Shapiro, Ian (eds) *Democracy's Edges*, Cambridge: Cambridge University Press, 273–93.

Hyland, James (1995) *Democratic Theory: The Philosophical Foundations*, Manchester: Manchester University Press.

Isaac, Jeffrey C. (1998) *Democracy in Dark Times*, Ithaca: Cornell University Press.

Jaggar, Alison (1988) *Feminist Politics and Human Nature*, Totowa, NJ: Roman and Littlefield.

Jefferson, Thomas (1975 [1816]) 'Government by the people, letter to Samuel Kercheval, July 12, 1816,' in *The Portable Jefferson*, New York: The Viking Press, 552–61.

Johnson, James (1998) 'Arguing for Deliberation: Some Skeptical considerations,' in Elster, Jon (ed.) *Deliberative Democracy*, Cambridge: Cambridge University Press, 161–84.

Kaldor, Mary (1995) 'European institutions, nation-states and nationalism,' in Archibulgi, Daniele and Held, David (eds) *Cosmopolitan Democracy: An Agenda for a New World Order*, Cambridge: Polity Press, 68–95.

Kant, Immanuel (1965 [1797]) *The Metaphysical Elements of Justice* (pt. 1 of *The Metaphyscs of Morals*), Indianapolis: Bobbs-Merrill.

—— (1988 [1784]) 'The idea of a universal world history from a cosmopolitan point of view,' in Beck, Lewis White (ed.) *Kant Selections*, New York: Bobbs-Merrill.

—— (1998 [1785]) *Groundwork of the Metaphysics of Morals*, Cambridge: Cambridge University Press.

Kaplan, Robert D. (1994) *Balkan Ghosts: A Journey Through History*, New York: Vintage Books.

Kateb, George (1975) 'Comments on David Braybrooke's "The meaning of participation and the demands for it,"' in Chapman, John W. and Pennock, J. Roland (eds) *Participation in Politics (Nomos XVI)*, New York: Lieber-Atherton, 89–97.

Kaufman, Arnold S. (1969 [1960]) 'Human nature and participatory democracy' and a more sober 'Participatory democracy: ten years later,' both in Connolly, William E. (ed.) *The Bias of Pluralism*, New York: Atherton Press, 174–200, 201–12.

Keim, Donald W. (1975) 'Participation in democratic theories,' in Chapman, John W. and Pennock, J. Roland (eds) *Participation in Politics (Nomos XVI)*, New York: Lieber-Atherton, 1–38.

Keohane, Robert and Nye, Joseph (eds) (1972) *Transnational Relations and World Politics*, Cambridge, MA: Harvard University Press.

Kernohan, Andrew (1998) *Liberalism, Equality, and Cultural Oppression*, Cambridge: Cambridge University Press.

Key, V.O. (1958) *Politics, Parties, and Pressure Groups*, New York: Crowell.

Köhler, Martin (1998) 'From the national to the cosmopolitan Public Sphere,' in Archibugi, Daniele, Held, David, and Köhler, Martin (eds) *Re-imagining Political Community: Studies in Cosmopolitan Democracy*, Stanford: Stanford University Press, 231–51.

Kramnick, Isaac (1987) Editor's Introduction to *The Federalist Papers*, London: Penguin, 11–82.

Krouse, Richard W. (1983) ' "Classical" images of democracy in America: Madison and Tocqueville,' in Duncan, Graeme (ed.) *Democratic Theory and Practice*, Cambridge: Cambridge University Press, 58–78.

Kukathas, Chandran (1992a) 'Are there any cultural rights?,' *Political Theory* 20,1 (February): 105–39.

—— (1992b) 'Cultural rights again: a rejoinder to Kymlicka,' *Political Theory* 20,4 (November): 674–80.

Kymlicka, Will (1989) *Liberalism, Community and Culture*, Oxford: Clarendon Press.

—— (1990) *Contemporary Political Philosophy: An Introduction*, Oxford: Clarendon Press.

—— (1995) *Multicultural Citizenship*, Oxford: Clarendon Press.

—— (1998) 'Liberal egalitarianism and civic republicanism: friends or enemies?,' in Allen, Anita L. and Regan, Milton C. Jr. (eds) *Debating Democracy's Discontent: Essays on American Politics, Law, and Public Philosophy*, Oxford: Oxford University Press, 131–48.

—— (1999) 'Citizenship in an era of globalization: commentary on Held,' in Hacker-Cordon, Casiano and Shapiro, Ian (eds) *Democracy's Edges*, Cambridge: Camridge University Press, 112–26.

Laclau, Ernesto (1995) 'Universalism, particularism and the question of identity,' in Rajchman, John (ed.) *The Identity in Question*, New York: Routledge, 93–108.

—— (1997) 'Subject of politics, politics of the subject,' in Bontekoe, Ron and Stepaniants, Marietta (eds) *Justice and Democracy: Cross-Cultural Perspectives*, Honolulu: University of Hawai'i Press, 363–79.

Laclau, Ernesto and Mouffe, Chantal (1985) *Hegemony and Socialist Strategy: Toward a Radical Democratic Politics*, London: Verso.

—— (1987) 'Post-Marxism without apologies,' *New Left Review* 166 (November/ December): 79–106, reproduced in Laclau, Ernesto *New Reflections on the Revolution of Our Times*, London: Verso, ch. 4.

Larmore, Charles E. (1987) *Patterns of Moral Complexity*, Cambridge: Cambridge University Press.

Laski, Harold J. (1921) *The Foundations of Sovereignty and Other Essays*, London: Allen and Unwin.

Lasswell, Harold D. (1948) *Power and Personality*, New York: Norton.

Lasswell, Harold D. and Kaplan, Abraham (1950) *Power and Society: A Framework for Political Inquiry*, New Haven: Yale University Press.

Lefort, Claude (1988) *Democracy and Political Theory*, Cambridge: Polity Press.

Lenin, V.I. (1965 [1918]) *The Proletarian Revolution and the Renegade Kautsky* in *V.I. Lenin Collected Works*, Vol. 28, Moscow: Progress Publishers, 226–325.

Levine, Andrew (1981) *Liberal Democracy: A Critic of Its Theory*, New York: Columbia University Press.

—— (1984) *Arguing for Socialism: Theoretical Considerations*, Boston: Routledge and Kegan Paul.

—— (1987) *The End of the State*, London: Verso.

—— (1993) *The General Will: Rousseau, Marx, and Communism*, Cambridge: Cambridge University Press.

—— (1995) 'Democratic corporatism and/versus socialism,' in Cohen, Joshua and Rogers, Joel (eds) *Associations and Democracy*, London: Verso, 157–66.

Light, Andrew and Katz, Eric (eds) (1996) *Environmental Pragmatism*, London: Routledge.

Lijphart, Arend (1968) *The Politics of Accommodation: Pluralism and Democracy in the Netherlands*, Berkeley: University of California Press.

—— (1977) *Democracy in Plural Societies: A Comparative Exploration*, New Haven: Yale University Press.

—— (1984) *Democracies: Patterns of Majoritarian and Consensus Government in Twenty-One Countries*, New Haven: Yale University Press.

Linklater, Andrew (1990) *Men and Citizens in the Theory of International Relations*, London: Macmillan.

—— (1995) 'Neo-realism in Theory and Practice,' in Booth, Ken and Smith, Steve, (eds) *International Relations Theory Today*, University Park, PA: The Pennsylvania University Press, 241–62.

Lipietz, Alain (1995) *Green Hopes: The Future of Political Ecology*, Cambridge: Polity Press.

Lipset, Seymour Martin (1960) *Political Man*, Garden City, NY: Doubleday.

—— (1994) 'The social requisites of democracy revisited,' *American Sociological Review* 59(1) February, 1–22.

—— (ed.) (1995) *The Encyclopedia of Democracy*, Washington, DC: Congressional Quarterly Books.

Locke, John (1963 [1690]) *Two Treatises of Government*, Cambridge: Cambridge University Press.

Lukes, Steven (1973) *Individualism*, New York: Harper and Row.

—— (1974) *Power: A Radical View*, London: Macmillan.

Lyotard, François (1984 [1979]) *The Postmodern Condition: A Report on Knowledge*, Minneapolis: University of Minnesota Press.

—— (1988 [1983]) *The Differend*, Minneapolis: University of Minnesota Press.

—— (1989) 'The Sublime and the Avant-Garde,' in Benjamin, Andrew (ed.) *The Lyotard Reader*, Oxford: Basil Blackwell, 196–211.

Machiavelli, Niccolo (1979 [1527], posthumous) *The Prince*, in *The Portable Machiavelli*, New York: Viking Penguin.

MacIntyre, Alisdair (1981) *After Virtue: A Study in Moral Theory*, South Bend, IN: University of Notre Dame Press.

MacIver, R.M. (1950) 'Interest,' in *Encyclopedia of the Social Sciences*, Vol. 8, New York: Macmillan, 147.

Mackie, Gerry (1998) 'All men are liars: is democracy meaningless?' in Elster, Jon (ed.) *Deliberative Democracy*, Cambridge: Cambridge University Press, 69–96.

McKinlay, Patrick F. (1998) 'Lyotard's Kantian account of the sublime and democratic discourse,' in Langsdorf, Lenore and Watson, Stephen H. (eds) *Reinterpreting the Political: Continental Philosophy and Political Theory*, Albany: The State University of New York Press, 107–24.

McLean, Iain (1990) *Democracy and New Technology*, Cambridge: Polity Press.

Macpherson, Crawford Brough (1965) *The Real World of Democracy*, Concord, ON: Anasi.

—— (1973) *Democratic Theory: Essays in Retrieval*, Oxford: Clarendon Press.

—— (1977) *The Life and Times of Liberal Democracy*, Oxford: Oxford University Press.

McRae, Kenneth (ed.) (1974) *Consociational Democracy: Political Accommodation in Segmented Societies*, Toronto: McClelland and Stewart.

Madison, James, Hamilton, Alexander, and Jay, John (1987 [1788]) *The Federalist Papers*, London: Penguin Books.

Mandeville, Bernard de (1970 [1723]) *The Fable of the Bees*, London: Pelican.

Manin, Bernard (1987) 'On legitimacy and political deliberation,' *Political Theory* 15,3 (August): 338–68.

Manin, Bernard, Przeworski, Adam, and Stokes, Susan C. (1999) 'Introduction,' in Manin, Bernard, Przeworski, Adam, and Stokes, Susan C. *Democracy, Accountability, and Representation*, Cambridge: Cambridge University Press, 1–26.

Mansbridge, Jane J. (1983) *Beyond Adversary Democracy*, Chicago: University of Chicago Press.

—— (1995) 'Does participation make better citizens?' *The Good Society* 5,2 (Spring 1995): 1–7.

Marcuse, Herbert (1964) *One Dimensional Man*, Boston: Beacon Press.

Margolis, Michael (1979) *Viable Democracy*, Harmondsworth, England: Penguin Books.

Marx, Karl (1975a [1843]) 'On the Jewish question,' *Karl Marx, Frederick Engles Collected Works*, Vol. 3, New York: International Publishers, 146–74.

—— (1975b [1843]) 'Contribution to the critique of Hegel's philosophy of law,' *Karl Marx, Frederick Engels Collected Works*, Vol. 3, New York: International Publishers, 3–129.

Mason, Michael (1999) *Environmental Democracy*, London: Earthscan.

Mathews, John (1989) *Age of Democracy: The Political Economy of Post-Fordism*, New York: Oxford University Press.

May, Kenneth O. (1952) 'A set of independent, necessary and sufficient conditions for simple majority decision,' *Econometrica* 20,4 (October): 680–4.

Mill, John Stuart (1969 [1874], posthumous) 'Nature,' in *Essays on Ethics, Religion and Society, Collected Works of John Stuart Mill*, vol. 10, Toronto: University of Toronto Press, 373–402.

—— (1971 [1869]) *On the Subjugation of Women*, Greenwich, CT: Fawcett.

—— (1973 [1843]) *On the Logic of the Moral Sciences*, in *A System of Logic: Ratiocinative and Inductive, Collected Works of John Stuart Mill*, vol. 6, Toronto: University of Toronto Press, bk. 4.

—— (1976 [1835/40] 'M. de Tocqueville on democracy in America,' in Williams, Geraint L. (ed.) *John Stuart Mill on Politics and Society*, Brighton: Harvester Press, 186–247.

—— (1991a [1861]) *Considerations on Representative Government* in *John Stuart Mill On Liberty and Other Essays*, Oxford: Oxford University Press.

—— (1991b [1859]) *On Liberty* in *John Stuart Mill On Liberty and Other Essays*, Oxford: Oxford University Press.

Miller, David (1983) 'The competitive model of democracy,' in Duncan, Graeme (ed.) *Democratic Theory and Practice*, Cambridge: Cambridge University Press, 133–55.

—— (1993) 'Deliberative democracy and social choice,' in Held, David (ed.) *Prospects for Democracy: North, South, East, West*, Stanford: University of Stanford Press, 74–111.

—— (2000) *Citizenship and National Identity*, Cambridge: Polity Press.

Mills, C. Wright (1956) *The Power Elite*, London: Oxford University Press.

Mills, Charles (1997) *The Racial Contract*, Ithaca: Cornell University Press.

Misak, Cheryl (2000) *Truth, Politics, Morality: Pragmatism and Deliberation*, London: Routledge.

Morganthau, Henry (1985 [1948]) *Politics Among Nations: The Struggle for Power and Peace* (6th edn), New York: Knopf.

Mouffe, Chantal (1993) *The Return of the Political*, London: Verso.

—— (1996) 'Democracy, power, and the "political",' in Benhabib, Seyla (ed.) *Democracy and Difference: Contesting the Boundaries of the Political*, Princeton: Princeton University Press, 245–56.

—— (2000) *The Democratic Paradox*, London: Verso.

Mueller, Dennis (1979) *Public Choice*, Cambridge: Cambridge University Press.

—— (1997) 'Public choice in perspective,' in Mueller, Dennis (ed.) *Perspectives on Public Choice: A Handbook*, Cambridge: Cambridge University Press, 1–17.

Naess, Arne (1989) *Ecology, Community, and Lifestyle*, Cambridge, Cambridge University Press.

Naess, Arne, Christophersen, Jens A., and Kvalo, Kjell (1956) *Democracy, Ideology and Objectivity*, Oxford: Basil Blackwell.

Nagel, Thomas (1989) 'Moral conflict and political legitimacy,' *Philosophy and Public Affairs* 18,3 (Summer): 259–96.

Nelson, William (1980) *On Justifying Democracy*, London: Routledge and Kegan Paul.

Nielsen, Kai (1985) *Equality and Liberty: A Defence of Radical Egalitarianism*, Totawa, NJ: Roman and Allanheld.

—— (1996) *Naturalism Without Foundations*, Amherst: Prometheus Books.

Nozick, Robert (1974) *Anarchy, State, and Utopia*, New York: Basic Books.

Okin, Susan Moller (1989) *Justice, Gender and the Family*, New York: Basic Books.
—— (1998) 'Gender, the public and the private,' in Phillips, Anne (ed.) *Feminism and Politics*, Oxford: Oxford University Press, 116–41.
Ollman, Bertell (ed.) (1998) *Market Socialism: The Debate Among Socialists*, New York: Routledge.
Olson, Mancur (1971) *The Logic of Collective Action: Public Goods and the Theory of Groups* (2nd edn), Cambridge, MA: Harvard University Press.
Ophuls, William (1992) *Ecology and the Politics of Scarcity Revisited: The Unraveling of the American Dream* (2nd edn), New York: W.H. Freeman.
Oppenheim, Felix (1971) 'Democracy: characteristics included and excluded,' *The Monist* 55,1 (January): 29–50.
Ordeshook, Peter (1992) *A Political Theory Primer*, London: Routledge.
Paehlke, Robert C. (1989) *Environmentalism and the Future of Progressive Politics*, New Haven: Yale University Press.
Parekh, Bhikhu (1999) 'Balancing unity and diversity in multicultural societies,' in Avon, Dan and de-Shalit, Avner (eds) *Liberalism and Its Practice*, London: Routledge, 106–26.
—— (2000) *Rethinking Multiculturalism: Cultural Diversity and Political Theory*, London: MacMillan.
Pateman, Carole (1970) *Participation and Democratic Theory*, Cambridge: Cambridge University Press.
—— (1985) *The Problem of Political Obligation: A Critique of Liberal Theory*, Berkeley: The University of California Press.
—— (1987) 'Feminist critiques of the public/private dichotomy,' in Phillips, Anne (ed.) *Feminism and Equality*, New York: New York University Press, 103–26.
—— (1988) *The Sexual Contract*, Stanford: Stanford University Press.
Peffer, Rodney G. (1990) *Marxism, Morality and Social Justice*, Princeton: Princeton University Press.
Pennock, J. Roland (1979) *Democratic Political Theory*, Princeton: Princeton University Press.
Pettit, Philip (1997) *Republicanism: A Theory of Freedom and Government*, New York: Oxford University Press.
—— (1998) 'Reworking Sandel's republicanism,' in Allen, Anita L. and Regan, Milton C. Jr. (eds) *Debating Democracy's Discontent: Essays on American Politics, Law, and Public Philosophy*, Oxford: Oxford University Press, 30–59.
—— (1999) 'Republican freedom and contestatory democratization,' in Hacker-Cordon, Casiano and Shapiro, Ian (eds) *Democracy's Value*, Cambridge: Cambridge University Press, 163–90.
Phillips, Anne (1991) *Engendering Democracy*, University Park, PA: Pennsylvania University Press.
—— (1993) *Democracy and Difference*, University Park, PA: Pennsylvania University Press.
—— (1995) *The Politics of Presence*, Oxford: Clarendon Press.
Pitkin, Hanna Fenichel (1967) *The Concept of Representation*, Berkeley: University of California Press.
Pogge, Thomas (1989) *Realizing Rawls*, Ithaca: Cornell University Press.
Polsby, Nelson (1963) *Community Power and Political Theory*, New Haven: Yale University Press.

Popper, Karl (1962) *The Open Society and Its Enemies*, London: Routledge and Kegan Paul.

Pranger, Robert (1968) *The Eclipse of Citizenship*, New York: Holt, Rinehart and Winston.

Proudhon, Pierre-Joseph (1979 [1863]) *The Principle of Federation*, Toronto: University of Toronto Press.

—— (1994 [1863–4]) *What is Property?*, Cambridge: Cambridge University Press.

Przeworski, Adam (1998) 'Deliberation and ideological domination,' in Elster, Jon (ed.) *Deliberative Democracy*, Cambridge: Cambridge University Press, 140–60.

—— (1999) 'Minimalist conception of democracy: a defense,' in Hacker-Cordon, Casiano and Shapiro, Ian (eds) *Democracy's Value*, Cambridge: Cambridge University Press, 23–55.

Putnam, Robert (1993) *Making Democracy Work: Civic Traditions in Modern Italy*, Princeton: Princeton University Press.

Rasmussen, David M. (1990) *Reading Habermas*, Oxford: Basil Blackwell.

Rawls, John (1971) *A Theory of Justice*, Cambridge, MA: Harvard University Press.

—— (1996) *Political Liberalism*, New York: Columbia University Press.

—— (1999) *The Law of Peoples*, Cambridge, MA: Harvard University Press.

Raz, Joseph (1986) *The Morality of Freedom*, Oxford: Oxford University Press.

Rehg, William (1996) 'Habermas's discourse theory of law and democracy,' in Rasmussen, David M. (ed.) *The Handbook of Critical Theory*, Oxford: Blackwell Publishers, 166–89.

Resnick, Philip (1984) *Parliament vs. People: An Essay on Democracy and Canadian Political Culture*, Vancouver: New Star Books.

Riker, William H. (1982) *Liberalism Against Populism: A Confrontation Between the Theory of Democracy and the Theory of Social Choice*, San Francisco, W.H. Freeman & Company.

Riley, Johnathan (1988) *Liberal Utilitarianism: Social Choice Theory and J.S. Mill's Philosophy*, Cambridge: Cambridge University Press.

Roemer, John E.(1994) *A Future for Socialism*, Cambridge, MA: Harvard University Press.

—— (1988) *Free to Lose: An Introduction to Marxist Economic Philosophy*, Cambridge, MA: Harvard University Press.

Rorty, Richard (1983) 'Postmodern bourgeois liberalism,' *The Journal of Philosophy*, 80 (October): 583–9.

—— (1987) 'Thugs and theorists: a reply to Bernstein,' *Political Theory* 15,4 (November): 564–80.

—— (1990) 'The priority of democracy to philosophy,' in Malachowski, Alan (ed.) *Reading Rorty*, Cambridge, MA: Blackwell.

Rose, Arnold M. (1967) *The Power Structure: Political Process in American Society*, Oxford: Oxford University Press.

—— (1970) *The Higher Circles: The Governing Class in America*, New York: Random House.

Rousseau, Jean-Jacques (1950a [1762]) *The Social Contract* in *The Social Contract and Discourses*, New York: E.P. Dutton, The Everyman Library.

—— (1950b [1755]) *A Discourse on the Origins of Inequality* in *The Social Contract and Discourses*, New York: E.P. Dutton, The Everyman Library.

—— (1979 [1762]) *Emile or On Education*, New York: Basic Books.

Sandel, Michael (1982) *Liberalism and the Limits of Justice*, Cambridge: Cambridge University Press.

—— (1996) *Democracy's Discontent: America in Search of a Public Philosophy*, Cambridge, MA: Harvard University Press.

—— (1998) 'Reply to critics,' in Allen, Anita L. and Regan, Milton C. Jr (eds) *Debating Democracy's Discontent: Essays on American Politics, Law, and Public Philosophy*, Oxford: Oxford University Press, 319–35.

Sartori, Giovanni (1987) *The Theory of Democracy Revisited*, Catham, NJ: Catham Publishers.

Saward, Michael (2000) 'A critique of Held,' in Holden, Barry (ed.) *Global Democracy: Key Debates*, London: Routledge, 32–46.

Schafer, Arthur (1974) 'Citizen participation, democratic elitism, and participatory democracy,' in Thompson, Dixon (ed.) *The Allocative Conflicts in Water Management*, Winnipeg: University of Manitoba Press, 487–508.

Schattschneider, E.E. (1960) *The Semisovereign People: A Realist's View of Democracy in America*, New York: Holt, Rinehart and Winston.

Scheuerman, William E. (1999a) *Carl Schmitt: The End of Law*, Oxford: Roman and Littlefield.

—— (1999b) 'Between radicalism and resignation: democratic theory in Habermas's *Between Facts and Norms*,' in Dews, Peter (ed.) *Habermas: A Critical Reader*, Oxford: Blackwell Publishers, 153–77.

Schmitt, Carl (1988 [1923]) *The Crisis of Parliamentary Democracy*, Cambridge, MA: The MIT Press.

Schmitter, Philippe C. (1995) 'The irony of modern democracy and the viability of efforts to reform in practice,' in Cohen, Joshua and Rogers, Joel (eds), *Associations and Democracy*, London: Verso, 167–87.

—— (1997) 'Exploring the problematic triumph of liberal democracy and concluding with a modest proposal for improving its international impact,' in Hadenius, Alex (ed.) *Democracy's Victory and Crisis*, Cambridge: Cambridge University Press, 297–307.

Schumpeter, Joseph (1962 [1942]) *Capitalism, Socialism and Democracy*, New York: Harper and Row.

Schweickart, David (1996) *Against Capitalism*, Boulder: Westview Press.

Sen, Amartya K. (1970) 'The impossibility of a paretian liberal,' *Journal of Political Economy*, 78, 1 (January/February): 152–7.

Shanley, Mary Lyndon (1998) 'Unencumbered individuals and embedded selves: reasons to resist dichotomous thinking in family law,' in Allen, Anita and Regan, Milton C. Jr. (eds) *Debating Democracy's Discontent: Essays on American Politics, Law, and Public Philosophy*, Oxford: Oxford University Press, 229–47.

Shapiro, Ian (1999a) *Democratic Justice*, New Haven: Yale University Press.

—— (1999b) 'Enough of deliberation: politics is about interests and power,' in Macedo, Stephen (ed.) *Deliberative Politics: Essays on Democracy and Disagreement*, New York, Oxford University Press, 28–38.

Singer, Peter (1974) *Democracy and Disobedience*, Oxford: Oxford University Press.

Skinner, Quentin (1978) *The Foundations of Modern Political Thought*, 2 vols., Cambridge: Cambridge University Press.

—— (1985), 'The paradoxes of political liberty,' in *The Tanner Lectures on Human Values*, Cambridge: Cambridge University Press, 227–50.

—— (1992) 'On justice, the common good and the priority of liberty,' in Mouffe, Chantal (ed.) *Dimensions of Radical Democracy: Pluralism, Citizenship, Community*, London: Verso, 211–24.

Smith, Adam (1937 [1776]) *The Wealth of Nations*, New York: Modern Library.

Smith, Rogers (1997) *Civic Ideals: Conflicting Visions of Citizenship in US History*, New Haven: Yale University Press.

Smith, Steve (1995) 'The self-images of a discipline: a genealogy of international relations theory,' in Booth, Ken and Smith, Steve, (eds) *International Relations Theory Today*, University Park, PA: The Pennsylvania University Press, 1–37.

Stokes, Susan C. (1998) 'Pathologies of deliberation,' in Elster, Jon (ed.) *Deliberative Democracy*, Cambridge: Cambridge University Press, 123–39.

Strange, Susan (1988) *States and Markets: An Introduction to International Political Economy*, London: Pinter.

—— (1995) 'Political economy and international relations' in Booth, Ken and Smith, Steve, (eds) *International Relations Theory Today*, University Park, PA: The Pennsylvania University Press, 154–74.

Strom, Gerald S. (1990) *The Logic of Lawmaking: A Spatial Theory Approach*, Baltimore: The Johns Hopkins University Press.

Sullivan, John L., Pierson, James, and Marcus, George E. (1982) *Political Tolerance and American Democracy*, Chicago: University of Chicago Press.

Sunstein, Cass R. (1997) 'Deliberation, democracy and disagreement,' in Bontekoe, Ron and Stepaniants, Marietta (eds) *Justice and Democracy: Cross-Cultural Perspectives*, Honolulu: University of Hawai'i Press, 93–117.

—— (1998) 'Constitutions and democracy' in Elster, Jon and Slagstad, Rune (eds) *National Self-Determination and Secession*, Oxford: Oxford University Press, 327–56.

Sylvester, Christine (1994) *Feminist Theory and International Relations in a Postmodern Era*, Cambridge: Cambridge University Press.

Talmon, J.L. (1970) *The Rise of Totalitarian Democracy*, New York: W.W. Norton.

Tamir, Yael (1993) *Liberal Nationalism*, Princeton: Princeton University Press.

Taylor, Charles (1979) 'What's wrong with negative liberty,' in Tyan, Alan (ed.) *The Idea of Freedom: Essays in Honour of Isaiah Berlin*, Oxford: Oxford University Press, 175–93.

—— (1989a) 'Cross-purposes: the liberal-communitarian debate,' in Rosenblum, Nancy L. (ed.) *Liberalism and the Moral Life*, Cambridge, MA: Harvard University Press, 159–82.

—— (1989b) *The Sources of the Self: The Making of the Modern Identity*, Cambridge, Mass.: Harvard University Press.

—— (1993) *Reconciling the Solitudes: Essays on Canadian Federalism and Nationalism*, Montreal: McGill-Queen's University Press.

—— (1994) 'The politics of recognition,' in Gutmann, Amy (ed.) *Multiculturalism*, Princeton: Princeton University Press, 25–73.

—— (1999) 'Conditions of an unforced consensus on human rights,' in Bauer, Joanne R. and Bell, Daniel A. (eds) *The East Asian Challenge for Human Rights*, Cambridge: Cambridge University Press, 124–44.

Taylor, Michael (1982) *Community, Anarchy and Liberty*, Cambridge: Cambridge University Press.

Teodori, Massimo (ed.) (1969) *The New Left: A Documentary History*, Indianapolis: Bobbs-Merrill.

Thucydides (1972 [c.404 BC]) *History of the Peloponnesian War*, introduction by M.I. Finley, New York: Penguin Books.

Tickner, J. Ann (1992) *Gender in International Relations: Feminist Perspectives in Achieving Global Security*, New York: Columbia University Press.

Tocqueville, Alexis de (1969 [1835–40]) *Democracy in America*, New York: Harper and Row (Doubleday Anchor Books publication).

Tollison, Robert D. (1982) 'Rent seeking: a survey,' *Kyklos* 35, 4: 575–602.

—— (1997) 'Rent seeking,' in Mueller, Dennis (ed.) *Perspectives on Public Choice: A Handbook*, Cambridge: Cambridge University Press, 506–25.

Truman, David B. (1951) *The Governmental Process*, New York: Knopf.

Tullock, Gordon (1970) *Private Wants, Public Means*, New York: Basic Books.

—— (1980 [1967]) 'The welfare costs of tariffs, monopolies, and theft,' in Buchanan, James M., Tollison, Robert D., and Tullock, Gordon (eds) *Toward a Theory of the Rent-Seeking Society*, College Station, TX: Texas A & M University Press, 39–50.

Tully, James (1995) *Strange Multiplicity: Constitutionalism in an Age of Diversity*, Cambridge: Cambridge University Press.

Udehn, Lars (1996) *The Limits of Public Choice: A Sociological Critique of the Economic Theory of Politics*, London: Routledge.

Unger, Roberto Mangabeira (1976) *Knowledge and Politics*, New York: The Free Press.

Van Parijs, Phillipe (1999) 'Contestatory democracy vesus real freedom for all,' in Hacker-Cordon, Casiano and Shapiro, Ian (eds) *Democracy's Value*, Cambridge: Cambridge University Press, 191–8.

Verba, Sidney and Nie, Norman N. (1972) *Participation in America: Political Democracy and Social Equality*, New York: Harper and Row.

Wagner, Richard E. (1987) 'Parchment, guns, and the maintenance of constitutional contract,' in Rowley, Charles K. (ed.) *Democracy and Public Choice: Essays in Honor of Gordon Tullock*, Oxford: Blackwell, 105–21.

Waldron, Jeremy (1998) 'Virtue *en masse*,' in Allen, Anita L. and Regan, Milton C. Jr (eds) *Debating Democracy's Discontent: Essays on American Politics, Law, and Public Philosophy*, Oxford: Oxford University Press, 32–9.

Walker, R.B.J. (1988) *One World, Many Worlds: Struggles for a Just World Peace*, Boulder: Lynne Rienner.

—— (1990) 'Sovereignty, identity, community: reflections on the horizons of contemporary political practice,' in Walker, R.B.J. and Mendlovitz, Saul H. (eds) *Contending Sovereignties: Redefining Political Community*, Boulder: Lynne Rienner, 159–85.

—— (1993) *Inside/Outside: International Relations as Political Theory*, Cambridge: Cambridge University Press.

Waltz, Kenneth (1959) *Man, the State and War: A Theoretical Analysis*, New York: Columbia University Press.

Walzer, Michael (1983) 'Philosophy and democracy,' in Nelson, John S. (ed.) *What Should Philosophy Be Now?*, Albany: State University of New York Press, 75–99.

—— (1988) *The Company of Critics: Social Criticism and Political Commitments in the 20th Century*, New York: Basic Books.

—— (1990) 'The communitarian critique of liberalism,' *Political Theory* 18,1 (February): 6–23.

—— (1994) *Thick and Thin: Moral Argument at Home and Abroad*, Notre Dame: University of Notre Dame Press.

—— (ed.)(1995) *Toward a Global Civil Society*, Providence: Berghahn Books.

Ware, Robert (1996) 'Nations and social complexity,' in Couture, Jocelyne, Nielson, Kai, and Seymour, Michel, (eds) *Rethinking Nationalism*, Calgary: University of Calgary Press, 133–57.

West, Cornell (1989) *The American Evasion of Philosophy: A Geneology of Pragmatism*, Madison: University of Wisconsin Press.

Williams, Melissa S. (1998) *Voice, Trust and Memory: Marginalized Groups and the Failings of Liberal Representation*, Princeton: Princeton University Press.

Wittgenstein, Ludwig (1953) *Philosophical Investigations*, New York: Macmillan.

Wolff, Robert Paul (1976) *In Defense of Anarchism* (2nd edn), New York: Harper and Row.

Wood, Ellen Meiksins (1981) 'Liberal democracy and capitalist hegemony,' *The Socialist Register 1981*, 169–89.

Wolheim, Richard (1964) 'A paradox in the theory of democracy,' in Laslett, Peter and Runciman, W.G. (eds) *Philosophy, Politics and Society II*, Oxford: Basil Blackwell, 71–87.

Wright, Frank (1987) *Northern Ireland: A Comparative Analysis*, Dublin: Gill and Macmillan.

Young, H. Peyton (1997) 'Group choice and individual judgments,' in Mueller, Dennis (ed.) *Perspectives on Public Choice: A Handbook*, Cambridge: Cambridge University Press, 181–200.

Young, Iris Marion (1990) *Justice and the Politics of Difference*, Princeton: Princeton University Press.

—— (1993) 'Justice and communicative democracy,' in Gottlieb, Roger S. (ed.) *Radical Philosophy: Tradition, Counter-Tradition, Politics*, Philadelphia: Temple University Press, 23–42.

—— (1995) 'Social groups in associative democracy,' in Cohen, Joshua and Rogers, Joel (eds) *Associations and Democracy*, London: Verso, 207–13.

—— (1996) 'Communication and the other: beyond deliberative democracy,' in Benhabib, Seyla (ed.) *Democracy and Difference: Contesting the Boundaries of the Political*, Princeton: Princeton University Press, 120–35.

—— (1999) 'State, civil society, and social justice,' in Hacker-Cordon, Casiano and Shapiro, Ian (eds) *Democracy's Value*, Cambridge: Cambridge University Press, 141–62.

—— (2000) *Inclusion and Democracy*, Oxford: Oxford University Press.

Zimmerman, Joseph F. (1986) *Participatory Democracy: Populism Revived*, New York: Praeger.

Zolo, Danilo (1997) *Cosmopolis: Prospects for World Government*, Cambridge: Cambridge University Press.

—— (2000) 'The lords of peace: from the Holy Alliance to the new international criminal tribunals,' in Holden, Barry (ed.) *Global Democracy: Key Debates*, London: Routledge, 73–86.

Subject index

Name index